Cutting through the Worry Knot!

How to Reduce and Control Your Anxiety Level:

Using a whole body-brain-mind approach

And without using drugs, alcohol or escapism!

By Jim Byrne and Renata Taylor-Byrne

The Institute for E-CENT Publications: 2020

"Worry does not empty tomorrow of its sorrow. It empties today of its strength"

Corrie Ten-Boom

~~~

Dedication

This book is dedicated to the generations of thinkers, writers, theorists, researchers and others who have investigated the nature of anxiety and worry; and tracked it back to its roots in lifestyle factors and philosophies of life.

~~~

Disclaimer

This book is intended for *educational* purposes only, and does not purport to be *medical* advice. Bear in mind that each individual body is probably pretty unique, because of its unique nutritional journey through life. We are changed by the foods we eat, and some experts would say we 'are what we eat'. However, we also know that physical exercise changes the biochemistry of the body-brain, which changes moods and emotions, as well as promoting better cardio-vascular health, and oxygenation of the whole system. And sleep and relaxation are shown to be linked to anxiety in numerous research studies.

Despite the caveats and reservations above, there is undoubtedly a lot of very useful *educational* material in this book, based on recent, sound, scientific research, which could be helpful in guiding you towards your own answers to your questions about anxiety, worry and/or panicky feelings, and the connections to lifestyle choices and personal attitudes.

Foreword

By Dr Jim Byrne

Preamble

Many people live lives which are tied up in knots of worry, anxiety, fear, apprehension and dread. They can hardly remember what it was like to feel relaxed, happy and at ease. This book will teach you how to cut through these kinds of emotional knots, from various angles, *one at a time*, to produce a state of greatly improved relaxation and ease.

This book will show you *how to tackle* **one thing at a time**; one aspect of your anxiety problem(s) at a time; so you do not become overloaded or overwhelmed.

~~~

We have all heard of a 'Gordian knot', which is a very difficult or intractable problem. Many of our problems consist of getting ourselves tied up in knots, trying to avoid the unavoidable difficulties of life. We also tend to tie ourselves in knots trying to avoid the necessity to take responsibility for our own lives. And we weave some knotty, tangled webs when we fail to be scrupulously honest with ourselves. (But, of course, our early childhood, which is normally something of a nightmare, tends to throw us into a tangle of knots, which are not of our own making!)

And all of this tangling and knotting goes on as we sleepwalk through our lives. The important thing is to wake up, and to address the knots in our emotions, and to begin to untangle them, *one by one*.

Most people would agree that anxiety is *a state of feeling fear, fright, alarm, or intense worry*[1]. It is *an **intense** emotion*, which pains us in a way which is comparable to a physical pain. It is not easy to ignore or brush off. It can tighten our breathing, and make us tremble and become clammy. We often feel we are out of control, and in great danger.

Anxiety is not a disease; not a mental illness. Anxiety – *at its best* - is part of our normal, innate, mental signalling system which tells us what is happening to us, and what to do about it. That is to say, it is part of our emotional wiring. Our emotional intelligence. (For an official definition of anxiety, please see this endnote)[2]. But – *at its worst* – anxiety, in the body-brain-mind of an individual human being, often proves to be *a complex knot of non-conscious self-mismanagement!*

Trying to get rid of anxiety with drugs is like hanging two overcoats and a duvet over your burglar alarm bell when it goes off. The burglar alarm is designed to give you helpful information, which you can then use to guide your action. *Should you check to see if a burglar has got into your house? Or call the police? Or realize that you've mismanaged your alarm system, producing a false alarm, and that you should therefore switch it off?*

Getting rid of the alarm signal, by dampening it down, defeats the whole object of having it in the first place!

Once you understand anxiety correctly, it becomes as useful as a burglar alarm; and you can learn how to manage it correctly. (It's just the exaggerated knotting of strands of anxiety, worry and stress that you need to cut through!)

When you buy a burglar alarm, it comes with a little Instruction Book about how to set it; calibrate it; monitor it; reset it; and switch it on and off.

You should have got just such an Instruction Book about your anxiety alarm, from your parents, when you were very young – and some people did. But if your alarm goes off at all times of day and night, in unhelpful ways, then I guess you were one of the unlucky ones who did not get your Instruction Book. This current book contains your Instruction Book, plus lots of other backup information, which will help to make you the master of your anxiety, instead of its quaking slave.

Don't let your burglar alarm make your life a misery. Learn how to use it properly! (Learn how to cut the *inappropriately alarming connections* that do not serve you well).

~~~

Just when we thought the state of the economy was *the biggest threat* to our survival, along came the coronavirus (or Covid-19) pandemic. So now, many people are extremely anxious about the possibility of serious illness or death; if not of themselves, then at least of some close relative who is weak or vulnerable.

And some elements of the mass media love to whip up this kind of fear.

But even as the virus spreads, it is perfectly possible for any of us to become more anxious about the loss of income, or our small business, or an online presentation we have to do, next week, to an important customer; or a letter we have to write to our bank, to sort out an overdraft to cope with the loss of income due to the lock-down. And some of us may pick up a whisper that our job is on the line, and then Covid-19 disappears into the shadows, as this new anxiety emerges.

That's how we are about threats and dangers. Our body-brain-mind automatically focusses attention upon an apparent threat or danger, and our alarm bell begin to ring, loud and shrill, causing us to quake and quiver. And it is not just humans that are wired up like this. All animals are wired up by nature (with nerves and hormones) to feel anxiety, which causes us to flee (or freeze) when we sense the arrival of a predator, or some other threat or danger which we sense we cannot defeat. (If we sense that we can defeat the threat, we are more likely to respond with anger!)

However, we cannot flee from Coronavirus; or from the challenge of making a presentation in work or business, or in college, etc.; or from the insecurity of the 'free market' economic system which was introduced by Thatcher and Reagan. But we can learn to manage these and others threats and dangers, if we know how our nervous system works.

So what can you do when faced with a gut-wrenching fear of some threat or danger? How can you cope?

Firstly, if you wait until a threat or danger manifests itself, you have no choice but to respond with your habitual level of anxiety. You are a creature of habit, and whatever you did before, you will do it again, and again; until you take action to change how you are wired up (in your central nervous system, which means in your body-brain-mind).

Secondly, you need to understand:

- How to manage your *lifestyle* in order to develop a central nervous system which is calm, relaxed, and not overly-sensitive to low-level threats and dangers;

- How to manage your *philosophy of life* (or your set of values, attitudes and beliefs) so that you have realistic expectations of life; and a self-soothing attitude when dealing with adversities, like threats and dangers.

And, **thirdly**, you need to:

- Understand which aspect of your anti-anxiety programme you need to prioritize – because you can only work on *one aspect at a time* (which means one chapter of this book at a time);

- Understand how to change bad, anxiety-inducing lifestyle habits into good habits (as described in Appendix F, below);

- Then make a commitment to change the most important thing that needs changing: (sleep; relaxation; exercise; diet; or philosophy of life);

- And take action by reading the relevant chapter of this book, and implementing your learning.

~~~

In Chapter 1, I will present a small amount of essential theoretical background on *current ways of understanding anxiety*; and I'll go into more detail about how to reduce and control it.

I will also introduce you to a quick and easy summary of some of the *key actions* you can take to begin, immediately, in small, manageable steps, to reduce and control your stress and anxiety level. By the end of Chapter 1 you will be very well equipped to begin the process of getting your anxiety under conscious control.

Dr Jim Byrne, Doctor of Counselling
Hebden Bridge, April 2020

~~~

Contents

Chapter 1: Current, popular ways of understanding anxiety

This book is uniquely placed to help you to master your anxiety level, and to keep it at reasonable levels in most situations that you will ever encounter.

Why is this the case?

Because this book is *a post-CBT perspective* on anxiety. The dominant theory of anxiety in the world today is that created by Albert Ellis and Aaron Tim Beck, which claims that anxiety can best be understood using their 'simple ABC model'.

But what are the A's, B's and C's referred to in this model?

'A' is an 'Activating Event'. *Something* happens. (In the case of anxiety, this has to be some kind of *threat* or *danger*). For example: You are told you probably have a particular health problem, which threatens your happiness, and possibly your life.

'B' is your 'Belief System' (or Automatic Thoughts). When you become aware that you probably are seriously ill, this is assumed to trigger a Belief, or Thought, or Schema[1] in your brain, which either causes you to over-react, or to react-reasonably, at an emotional/behavioural level.

'C' is the (emotional/behavioural) Consequence of your Belief System (or Automatic Thoughts). And the assumed consequence of triggering a Belief/Thought about a threat or danger - which causes an over-reaction - is some degree of *anxiety* or *panic*. And the assumed consequence of triggering a Belief/Thought about a threat or danger – which causes a reasonable-reaction - is mild to strong concern; but no anxiety.

---

[1] A *schema* is a 'packet of information' about a particular kind of event or object. For example, you will have a schema for how to relate to the process of *entering a restaurant for a meal,* which will differ from your *schema* for getting a quick snack from a *café*.

That's basically what the ABC model of CBT/REBT[2] claims to be the process of generating anxiety in a person.

The first major problem with this simple *ABC theory* is that *it cannot be validated scientifically*. (See Bond and Dryden, 1996[3]; and Byrne, 2019a[4]).

The second major problem with this model is that it ignores the body, as if a human being was just a mind on legs. But, as I will show below, the body plays *a central role* in the generation and registration of the emotion of anxiety (and all other feeling states).

And the third major problem with the ABC's of CBT is that a major study by the Swedish government has demonstrated that CBT does not work, in the sense that it does not deliver what it claims to deliver. (See Byrne, 2018)[5]. (It is convenient for US insurance companies to opt for CBT, because it is *cheaper* than the main alternatives. And the UK government has followed in the wake of the US approach).

Furthermore, it is worth mentioning in passing that there is evidence that the combined strategy of *CBT and drugs for anxiety* is also not working. (Byrne, 2018b).

***

The 'Human Givens' model

A better model for describing your anxious responses to situations of threat or danger is the one developed by Griffin and Tyrrell (2003)[6]; which is called the APET model:

The APET model has the following four elements:

'A' (as before) is an 'Activating Event'. *Something* happens. For example: You are told you probably have a particular health problem, which threatens your happiness, and possibly your life.

---

[2] CBT = Cognitive Behavioural Therapy; and REBT = Rational Emotive Behaviour Therapy.

'P' is a 'Pattern Match'. Your brain is designed to find patterns in nature, to help to guide your understanding of 'what is happening?' and 'how must I respond (in order to survive)?' So, let us assume your doctor presents you with diagnosis of the illness you now have, and your brain quickly searches through its memory banks for an earlier occasion or occasions when you received similar or comparable news (or you witnessed somebody close to you in a similar or comparable situation). You automatic/ non-conscious brain-mind quickly finds apparently relevant results, which reveals the way you (or somebody close to you) responded at that time, or during those times. You now have a 'pattern match': "When X-like things happen, I normally respond (or must respond) with Y-like feelings/behaviours".

'E' is an Emotional Response. Your brain now tells your body how your whole body-brain-mind should respond to the news of this illness. For example: *"Respond like last time* – which means, become anxious (to a reasonable or over-reacting degree)".

'T' is a subsequent-Thought. Once your body begins to crank up the anxious feelings that go with the arousal of your heart and lungs and guts, enough time will have elapsed *for a **thought** to emerge,* such as: "Wow! I'm feeling really bad about this terrible news! I hope there's a cure for my illness!"

In this model, the (habitual) feelings come first, and the (habitual) thoughts come later.

The role of habits, and innate emotions

Humans are *creatures of habit!*

We do not go around *thinking* about how to respond to situations as they arise!

If we were wired up like that, *we would not have survived*, because there are and always have been a lot of very fast predators out there, in our long history, which would have gobbled us up if we'd *stopped for one second* to consider our options.

We *automatically* *become anxious* in those situations in which we are in the habit of getting anxious feelings. And this helped us to survive by making us run for cover when faced with threats and dangers.

In Appendix G, I make this point:

The perspectives of *evolutionary psychology* and *affective neuroscience* are excellent sources of explanation of human emotions. According to Panksepp and Biven (2012) our evolutionary adaptations (as mammals) laid down certain subcortical structures in the limbic areas of the brain. These neurological structures underpin seven emotional systems (including fear, which is socialized into anxiety):

Fear: This system is about how the brain responds to the threat of physical danger and death. (I am wired up by nature [natural selection] to fear threats and dangers, because my ancestors who survived long enough to reproduce were kept alive by their fear of predators; and they passed that fear down the line, biochemically. This is my innate 'flight response'. I 'want' to survive, because I am programmed by nature to 'want' to survive! [Again, of course, I can learn to fear things that are not real threats or dangers]).

~~~

Humans, like all other animals, are born with an innate set of feelings or emotions, which are often referred to as 'affects'.

But unlike most other animals, who are **hard wired** for a lifetime of set responses (with a few minor deviations being possible) – humans are born with a set of **Basic Emotions** – including *fear* - which are then refined into **Culturally Shaped Emotions** by our family of origin; our schooling; and other socialization experiences. And those emotions are wired into our brains and our hearts/lungs/guts, and our major muscles.

So, *your* **way of being anxious** (in terms of contexts, intensities, etc.) will be *more like that of your family of origin*, or as you were *shaped* by them; and *my* **way of being anxious** (in terms of what frightens me, and how much) will be *more like the pattern shown in my family of origin*, or as I was *shaped* by them.

And, whatever emotional wiring was originally shaped (or knotted!) in your body-brain-mind, in your family of origin, *can be reshaped* (with some difficulty) in therapy, today. You can learn to be less easily triggered into feeling anxious; although it would be suicidal to try to get rid of your anxiety completely (since it helps to keep you alive, by promoting reasonable levels of caution, wariness and reticence in your speech and actions). What you need to learn is how to feel *appropriately anxious* when it is *helpful* to feel appropriately anxious; and to feel *totally relaxed* when it's *possible* to feel totally relaxed.

Building a better understanding of anxiety

The simple ABC model of human disturbance is too simplistic to be able to account for innate affects - and how feelings are stored and registered in the human body - because the ABC model *does not contain a* **body**! It only contains *a* **belief** *system*.

The APET model is a step up, in that it acknowledges innate emotions, and emotional-habits, which precede thinking; but it, like the simple ABC model, *also ignores the* **body**.

So, in the period 2007-2015, I went back to the beginning of psychological theorizing about human emotions, and I re-thought and re-built a number of theories of human emotion. (See Byrne, 2019, which was originally published in 2016)[7]. One strand of that work involved going back to the model which preceded the simple ABC model. That was the simple Stimulus-Organism-Response model (or SOR model). This is how that model was conceptualized, by the neo-behaviourists and behaviour therapists:

'S' is a Stimulus (or Activating Event, as before): Something happens which is witnessed by an *Organism* – in our case, an *animal*, and specifically a *human* animal. (Let's say, for illustration purposes, that 'S' is a huge dark shadow, accompanied by a loud noise, and a strong, obnoxious smell!)

'O' is the Organism (or animal: [in our case, a human animal]), which registers the *Stimulus* in its body-brain-mind. And:

'R' is the Response (in our case, an emotional-behaviour response of anxiety-panic, defecation, surge of adrenaline, and instant jumping and running rapidly away from the shadow). (Stimulus-Response: No choice!)

That's how anxiety works in practice. It's an instantaneous, habit based, survival-oriented form of fleeing from *apparent threat or danger*. And the whole body-brain-mind is involved.

And, because the whole body-brain-mind is involved, it matters whether the organism has had a good night's sleep; has strong well-exercised muscles; is well fed (with glucose) for running and jumping (and/or fighting!); and is in a state of good physical and mental health.

For these reasons, we expanded the simple SOR model into a Holistic-SOR model – (see Byrne, 2019; and the illustration below).

This model takes account of the individual's relationships in their family of origin as much as their current relationships; plus their routine diet, exercise, sleep and relaxation patterns.

Plus a range of current stressors, from various sources, including the state of the economy, their housing situation, and so on.

Plus their philosophy of life.

All of those elements are relevant to how well any individual will cope with an extreme, anxiety-inducing problem situation: like *an **apparent** threat or danger*.

The Holistic Stimulus-Organism-Response Model (H-SOR)		
Column 1	Column 2	Column 3
S = Stimulus	O = Organism	R = Response
When something significant happens, which is apprehended by the organism's (or person's) nervous system, the organism is activated or aroused (positively or negatively)	The organism responds, well or badly. The incoming stimulus may activate or interact with: (1) Innate needs and tendencies; (2) Family history and attachment style; (3) Recent personal history; (4) Emotive-cognitive schemas (as guides to action); (5) Narratives, stories, frames and other storied elements (which may be hyper-activating, hypo-activating, or affect regulating); (6) Character and temperament; (7) Need satisfaction; goals and values; (8) Diet and supplementation, medication, exercise regime, sleep and relaxation histories; (9) Ongoing environmental stressors, state of current relationship(s), and satisfaction with life stages, etc., etc.	The organism outputs a response, in the form of visible behaviour and inferable emotional reactions, like anger, anxiety, depression, embarrassment, etc.

This model takes account of the individual's relationships in their family of origin as much as their current relationships; plus their routine diet, exercise, sleep and relaxation patterns.

Plus a range of current stressors, from various sources, including the state of the economy, their housing situation, and so on.

Plus their philosophy of life.

All of those elements are relevant to how well any individual will cope with an extreme, anxiety-inducing problem situation: like *an **apparent** threat or danger*.

However, there is a further problem for humans, which does not exist for non-human animals. And it is this: Most of the problems that stress us cannot be solved by jumping nervously, and running away as quickly as we can go!

Instead, we have to develop a *range of strategies* which involve being able to manage our own body, brain, mind; and to problem-solve in areas of difficulty that arise in our social environment. We have to learn:

- When and how to fight: (and the importance of *fighting fair*; and fighting *assertively* rather than aggressively; how to be self-protective; etc.);

- When and how to flee: (or when and how to withdraw; and how to keep a safe distance in relationships [using *boundaries*, rather than barriers]; and how to be appropriately intimate; etc.);

- When and how to freeze; (As we say in Yorkshire: "When in doubt, do *nowt!*" [Meaning 'do *nothing'*]. And: "The right kind of inaction is far better than the wrong kind of action". Etc.); and:

- When and how to hide! (A poker player knows how to keep their information private. A chameleon can cross any territory without being spotted. A good Buddhist knows how to judge the appropriacy of a potential statement; when to speak; and when to remain silent!)

- When and how to think/feel. (You cannot be fully human unless you know how to perceive-feel-think systematically. You cannot get to the bottom of your feelings of anxiety, unless you learn how to track back, [preferably in writing, in a journal] using questions like these: *What happened? Who said or did what? Why did that make me anxious? What would have made me feel less anxious in that situation? What do I need to do to avoid this happening again in the future?*) See Appendix E, below, on journal writing.

How to reduce your anxiety

Which brings us to how this book can help you. I assume you would not be reading this text unless your anxiety level is uncomfortably high, and needs moderating. So how can this book help? What will you gain from reading it?

Because this book is based on a whole body-brain-mind-environment approach to understanding and managing your anxiety level, it will benefit you in the following ways:

You will learn how to:

- recognize when you are feeling anxious, and to track back to *the source* of the anxiety;

- train yourself to *calm* your body-brain-mind;

- persuade yourself to eat those foods that *reduce* anxiety, and avoid those foods that *fuel* anxiety;

- teach yourself to manage your sleep and relaxation needs, so as to maximize your emotional intelligence; avoid tension and unnecessary or unhelpful stress;

- persuade yourself to avoid sedentary lifestyle, and to take adequate amounts of the right kind and frequency of physical exercise, so as to burn off stress hormones, to calm your body and mind; and to:

- train yourself to think-feel appropriately about stressful situations, in such a way as to *minimize* the activation of your stress response; and to maintain a calm, relaxed, and anxiety-free mental-physical state.

~~~

Chapter 2 will introduce you to a quick and easy summary of some of the key actions you can take to begin, immediately, in small, manageable steps, to reduce and control your stress level.

Chapter 3 presents nine different ways of looking at a problematical stimulus (or noxious activating event) so as to keep your body-mind calm and clear and ready to problem-solve. If you study this chapter, over and over again, you will develop an anxiety-free philosophy of life!

Chapter 4 presents a brief introduction to the best system of physical relaxation ever devised on a scientific basis. This system can effectively close down your anxious feelings, and flood your body with relaxing and soothing hormones.

Chapter 5 contains my Stress and Anxiety Diet, which will teach you the foods to avoid and the best foods to keep yourself anxiety-free.

Chapter 6 explores the ways in which our management of our sleep patterns impacts our ability to reduce and control our anxiety levels, for better or worse.

Chapter 7 contains some of our research results on the benefits of particular forms of physical exercise, for stress and anxiety reduction.

After the conclusion, which is Chapter 8, there are then several helpful appendices, as follows:

Appendix A introduces you to a particular approach to breathing – called 'belly breathing', or diaphragmatic breathing – which can switch off the stress and anxiety response.

Appendix B presents additional information about nutrition and its effects upon our emotional states.

Appendix C describes how to meditate, which is another way of reducing feelings of anxiety by calming the body-mind.

Appendix D presents three strategies for managing anxiety, by managing your philosophy of life.

Appendix E contains a few journal writing strategies for anxiety reduction.

Appendix F teaches you how to reliably change any habit you want to change (as you will almost certainly need to change some of your lifestyle habits).

And Appendix G goes more deeply into how to understand and manage your emotions, including anxiety.

If you study this book in the manner recommended below, then you will insulate yourself against the kinds of unnecessary, intense anxiety and panic which very many people experience as they go about their difficult, challenging lives.

How to prioritize your first action

I now want to help you to decide which chapter you should read first, unless you opt to read the book from cover to cover.

Consider the question of your sleep pattern. People who do not get enough sleep are twice as likely to suffer from anxiety problems as people who get enough sleep. Do you get eight hours of uninterrupted sleep each night, for seven nights each week? If so, then sleep is not going to be part of your problem. If you get less than eight hours sleep each night, every night, then you should begin at Chapter 6, and work at fixing your sleep.

If your sleep pattern is okay, or you have now fixed it, then we need to consider the question of exercise. Sedentary lifestyle is a risk factor for anxiety and panic conditions. Do you do at least one hour of physical exercise every day, *apart from* the physical activity you do for your work or housework? If not, then lack of physical exercise may be feeding your feelings of anxiety. Please turn to Chapter 7 to find out about the importance of physical exercise for managing your feelings of anxiety; and also for guidance on the best kinds of exercise to do.

Once you are sure your sleep and exercise regimes are okay, if you are still feeling excessive or troublesome anxiety, you should look at the problem of physical tension. Although sleep is highly restorative, very tense individuals can hold on to their tension throughout the night, and carry it into the following day, where it feeds inappropriate anxiety responses to minor difficulties. The solution to this problem is to study and practice Progressive Muscle Relaxation, which is introduced in Chapter 4. And see also Appendix A, on anti-anxiety breathing exercises.

If you are confident that your feelings of anxiety are not being driven by inadequate sleep, lack of physical exercise, or chronic tension or anxious breathing, then the next area to investigate is your diet and nutrition, including liquids and solids, foods and supplements. Please see Chapter 5.

If you make any necessary changes to your diet, and you still feel excessive levels of anxiety, or feel anxious inappropriately, then you should look at your philosophy of life. This is *a set of beliefs and attitudes towards life*, which, together with your lifestyle factors discussed above, automatically trigger appropriate or inappropriate emotional responses to apparent threats and dangers. For example, *if you believe you are weak and defenceless*, you will feel *a lot more social anxiety* than individuals who believe they have an average or above average level of strength and capacity to defend themselves against attack. To work at improving your philosophy of life, please turn to Chapter 3.

I hope you enjoy this program for improving your lifestyle and philosophy of life, and reducing your feelings of excessive or inappropriate anxiety or panic.

Dr Jim Byrne, Doctor of Counselling
Hebden Bridge, April 2020

~~~

Chapter 2: What is anxiety, and how can we quickly and easily control it?

Copyright © Jim Byrne, April 2020

Initial introduction to anxiety

People normally become (appropriately or inappropriately) anxious about future threats and dangers.

Anxiety is a normal, innate response, designed by biological evolution to ensure our survival. However, the system can malfunction if a person fails to maintain their physical and emotional health and wellbeing; or if they come from a family in which anxiety was *modelled* (or *displayed*) for them (by fearful parents); or if it was *induced in them* by stressful parenting or teaching strategies.

As explored briefly in Chapter 1, above, anxiety is a whole body-brain-mind-environment phenomenon. You can make yourself anxious by sitting around allowing stress hormones to build up in your body; or by focusing on negative possibilities. (And when I say 'focusing', I am not talking about the CBT/REBT idea of 'thinking'. I am talking about a process of cogitation is which involves interrelated perceiving/ feeling/ thinking, which are all of a piece!)

As discussed above, you can reduce your feelings of anxiety by getting the right kind and amount of sleep; doing the right kind of physical exercise and relaxation activities; avoiding the wrong kinds of foods and drinks, and consuming the right kinds of foods and drinks; and so on.

Of course, your philosophy of life, or general belief system, is also important. But, as argued in Chapter 1, beliefs are not the only factor to take into account, because anxiety is a whole body-brain-mind phenomenon.

But if we were to look at philosophy of life, then the CBT/REBT belief about philosophy of life could be expressed like this: 'A person is highly likely to make themselves anxious if they hold this kind of belief: "I must be able to prevent (some particularly nasty thing) happening (to me, my partner, or my children, etc.) in the future".

On the face of it, this is a *highly likely response,* by many people, to the threat of corona-virus (Covid-19).

Or even this: "I dread the idea of (some particularly nasty thing) happening (to me, my partner, or my children, etc.) in the future".

Or even this: "I want to always be safe, and I would hate it if I proved to be unsafe!"

Or: "I must be able to control the future, in general, so it works out well for me and my loved ones!"

Of course, it has to be said that the Buddha argued that the source of human emotional disturbance was *Desire.* That is to say, desiring something which is not available; such as desiring that there be no such thing as coronavirus (or some other deadly disease, like cancer); or that it not affect my country or town of residence; or that it not affect me or my nearest and dearest.

So the mere fact of *desiring safety* is a source of potential anxiety. And it also seems to be the case that the anxiety arises before any 'declarative position' can be identified (as suggested by the APET model, from the Human Givens; and also from the Holistic SOR model, from E-CENT; both of which were discussed above).

This **attitude** (of *desiring* safety, and being *aversive to* threats and dangers) may be assumed to come from at least three places:

1. Anxious feelings are innate in all of us. This helps to keep us alert to dangers, and alive for longer. It seems we are designed to desire pleasure and to feel aversion towards pain of any kind, physical, psychological or symbolic.

2. Some individuals may be born with a higher than average anxiety level. This could apply to you if – for example - your mother was highly stressed while you (as a child) were in her womb.

3. We learn how to manage our emotions from observing and interacting with our parents when we are babies and infants – and the most important influence is normally our mother. (Father also plays a role, normally a little later than mother, so she puts in the 'affect regulating' foundations – or our biochemical brain 'wiring' for 'emotion management'). If we have an anxious mother, we will almost certainly copy her anxious responses to threatening stimuli and future possibilities.

Some of the factors that determine the intensity of our response to threats and dangers today include the following:

1. We automatically respond, (today), to anticipated threats or dangers (in the future), on the basis of...

- how we were wired up by the *interactive experiences* of our early socialization (with mother, father, etc.)...

- and how that experience *interrelated* with our innate emotional wiring...

- and what went on in our mother's womb when we were resident there.

Or as stated earlier: we are creatures of habit, and our emotional patterns are habit-based.

2. Our anxiety level can be reduced by physical exercise, and/or relaxation exercise, and/or nourishing sleep, any and all of which can switch off the stress response.

> - At least 30 minutes of continuous exercise each day. (See Chapter 7);

> - At least eight hours of restful sleep - in a darkened room, with no TV, no blue light: e.g. from mobile screen, tablet, laptop, etc. (See chapter 5);

- About 10 minutes of progressive muscle relaxation (See Chapter 4, below)

3. Our anxiety level can be increased by drinking too many caffeinated drinks (e.g. more than two cups of coffee, or three cups of tea, or a couple of cola drinks) each day. Or by drinking sugary drinks, or more than one unit of alcohol every other day. Some people are so sensitive to caffeine that they should avoid it altogether in order to keep their anxiety level low. (That means no tea, no caffeine, and no cola ['soda'] drinks). (See Chapter 5, below).

4. People who eat junk food – containing too much salt, sugar and/or trans-fats - are likely to be more prone to anxiety problems than people who are on something like the Mediterranean diet, or the Nordic diet. (Chapter 5).

5. People who get less than eight hours sleep per night - or who are in conflictual relationships; who are in financial difficulty; or who are subject to too many pressures at once; or who have inadequate coping resources - are more likely to have ongoing problems with anxiety. (Chapter 6).

6. People who have 'uncontrolled monkey mind'[8] (or a strong 'inner critic' voice in their head) will most often become 'worry warts'. While people who tame their minds, with something like meditation, and a mind-calming philosophy of life (like the Nine Windows Model described in Chapter 3, below), will handle threats and dangers more calmly.

How to understand and manage your anxiety

Here is a more general statement about anxiety, and how to manage it, from Byrne (2019) - *Holistic Counselling in Practice*:

The E-CENT theory of anxiety says that we are born with an innate sense of fear: (Darwin, 1872/1965; and Panksepp, 1998). Babies begin to display a pronounced sense of fear from about the age of six or seven months. This sense of fear is of something that is present – like loud noise; a furry animal; something that looks like a snake; etc. In time, we learn to *feel anxious*, which is to say, *fearful about things that are **not** present*, but which we 'think-feel' (consciously and/or non-consciously) might represent threats and dangers just a little while in the future.

People feel different intensities of anxiety, depending upon the seriousness of the threat or danger that they are anticipating, and how that degree of seriousness interacts with their felt sense of 'coping capability'.

The less serious the inferred threat is assumed to be, and the more coping capability we sense that we have, then the lower our intensity of anxiety is likely to be. (Our coping capability seems to be a combination of physical solidity or confidence; emotional stability and optimism; and security of attachment. And these capabilities are fed by healthy diet, regular physical exercise, relaxation/meditation, good relationships and social connections, adequate sleep, and so on).

On the other hand, the more serious the inferred threat is assumed to be, and the less coping capability we sense that we have, then the higher our intensity of anxiety is likely to be.

REBT theorists distinguish between anxiety (which is intense) and concern (which is much less intense); and some others theorists distinguish between anxiety (which is helpful) and panic (which is unhelpful)[9].

In E-CENT counselling we do not go along with those kinds of distinctions.

We see our clients as having a range of anxious-feeling potential, from very low to very high; and we normally work with clients whose anxiety level is high or very high, and our aim is to help them to reduce it until it is low, or very low. But they will never get rid of it; nor should they try to do so, as we **need** each of our basic emotions. *What needs to be reformed is **how** those basic emotions became socialized!* We each need to *re-learn* how to *emote*, as we become adults, so that we behave *appropriately* with those people with whom we work, rest and play.

~~~

Managing panic attacks

We also work with clients whose anxiety gets out of control, and becomes panic – which we conceptualize as *anxiety about anxiety about anxiety* – spiralling out of control. And we teach panicky clients the following guidelines:

(1) Accept your panic as your own (non-conscious, habitual) creation. Embrace it rather than trying to push it away. You *cannot* push your *own agitated lungs and guts away*! If you were being attacked by a big dog, you could push it away with a stick or a broom, but you cannot push your own agitated heart, lungs and guts away with anything. So accept them the way they are, and they will slowly calm down again.

(2) Recognize that panic passes in a matter of a couple of minutes, so 'play a waiting game'. And:

(3a) If you are in a public building, like a supermarket, shop or office: Take yourself outside and lean against a wall; focus on your breathing, and make your outbreath longer than your inbreath. Use diaphragmatic or 'belly breathing'. (See Appendix A, below). You can guess at that, or you can count your outbreath to the count of eleven, and your inbreath to the count of seven.

Or, if that's too complex, *breathe **out** for a much **longer** period that you breathe in*. Try to empty your lungs completely. Then let go and the inbreath will take care of itself.

(3b) Get into the habit of sitting quietly with one hand on your belly. Deepen your breathing so that your hand moves significantly each time you take an in-breath. Think of this as 'belly breathing', or 'breathing into my hand'. (Again, see Appendix A).

Try to do at least ten minutes of belly breathing each day. And always use belly breathing when you feel your anxiety level rising. Use belly breathing to outlast any sense of rising panic. (The panic will not last as long as the belly breathing, if you work at it!)

(4) If you are at home when the panic strikes, you have a choice. You can do the exercise described in (3a and 3b) above, or you can do this: Lie flat on a bed, or on a carpeted floor, on your belly and face; with your arms relaxed by your sides. If you are using the floor, use a towel, if necessary, to protect yourself from dust, etc.; and relax. Turn your head sideways. Let go of your breathing, and watch to see if your belly moves as your breath goes in and out. Do this for ten to twenty minutes. Feel your belly expanding against the bed or floor.

Practical strategies for managing anxiety

Here is some advice for managing anxiety in general:

1. Make sure you get enough sleep. (See Appendix B. below).

2. Arise in a timely manner to get on top of the challenges of the day.

3(a). Never skip breakfast, as that lowers your blood sugar, and pushes up stress levels in your body. Eat a hearty breakfast of either complex carbohydrates, or protein, but it is perhaps best not to mix them (for most purposes: according to Dr Hay[10]; although Patrick Holford[11] advises mixing them!) If you have agitated guts, which promote frequent defecation, then do mix protein and starch for breakfast, in order to make your digestive system more sluggish, and move in the direction of mild constipation. You can have eggs on toast; beans on toast; root and leafy vegetable salad. And so on.

3(b). Avoid caffeine drinks and sugary drinks. (One mug of real coffee each day is a good upper-limit guideline) Avoid junk foods because they are high in sugar and bad fats (trans-fats).

4. Make sure you have a mid-morning snack – e.g. a piece of fruit, or some nuts and seeds (assuming you are not allergic to fructose and/or nuts.)

5. Do not skip lunch or evening meals. Eat a healthy, balanced diet. (The Mediterranean diet is widely recommended. As is the Nordic diet. If you're a vegetarian, make sure you supplement with iron, zinc and get

extra protein. Regardless of whether you are a vegetarian or an omnivore, make sure you take the 'stress busting' vitamin combination: a good multivitamin tablet; a strong B-complex tablet; a 400 iu natural source vitamin E capsule; and at least 1,000 mg of vitamin C each day, and preferably 1,000 mg with each meal. You should also take a strong Magnesium citrate supplement. And eat a couple of Brazil nuts per day, for the selenium content, which helps with anxiety).

6. Meditate after breakfast (which just means doing ten minutes or so of belly breathing, while letting your thoughts die down); and then do about thirty minutes of physical exercise at the start of each day (even if this just means brisk walking; or jogging on the spot in your living room).

If it helps, you could start off doing ten minutes of each (meditation and exercise), and then gradually increase the time over the first couple of years, until you reach thirty minutes of each, every day – or at least five or six days per week). These two processes tend to calm your central nervous system, making it less reactive. (For help establishing these kinds of habits, please see Appendix F, below).

7a. Whenever you feel tense, take a mental break, and take five deep, slow, relaxing breaths. If that does not relax you, then stand up and walk around, counting to twenty silently in your mind. (Sitting around for too long can increase your anxiety level. Sedentary lifestyle is bad for both physical health and emotional wellbeing. So, take frequent breaks and walk around)[12].

7b. And if none of that helps, then sit quietly and do ten minutes or so of belly breathing – as in Appendix A, below - while telling yourself: "All will be well; and all will be well; and all manner of things will be well. And this too will pass. And this too will pass. And all will be well!"

7c. Learn a good system of physical relaxation, such as Jacobson's Progressive Muscle Relaxation, which we teach in Chapter 4, below.

8. Set a few (say 3 to 6) *realistic* goals for the day, and try to achieve them. Do not aim for perfection. Only try to control what seems likely to be controllable, and leave the rest. Accept the things you cannot change. (See Chapter 3 for coaching on this philosophy of life).

9. Watch comedy shows on TV or DVDs, when you get home, instead of bad News, or stressful Current Affairs. Have a hobby. Read something enjoyable before bedtime.

9b. Understand the link between Blue Light and the sleep-linked hormone, Melatonin. Blue light in the home comes from fluorescent lights and LED's, TV screens, and from mobile phones, laptops, PCs, and so on. Switch off all lights in your bedroom at bedtime. Do not have a TV or computer in the bedroom. Switch off your mobile phone (if you have one) at tea-time, and leave it off until **after breakfast** in the morning. We need our bodies to build up melatonin in order to fall asleep and stay asleep for our 8 or more hours. But blue light disrupts the production of melatonin. Melatonin is a sleep hormone in our bodies that helps to regulate our circadian rhythms. Our eyes have receptors that contain a photopigment called melanopsin that is sensitive to blue light. These cells give information to our body that regulates our sense of whether it's day or night. Blue light has been shown by researchers to actually boost attention and mood during the day, but chronic exposure to blue light at night can give messages to our brain to reduce melatonin secretion, which tells us to wake up and be more alert - potentially disrupting our circadian rhythm.

10. Work at developing good, supportive relationships, at home and at work, and in your community.

11. Keep a journal, and write about your anxiety symptoms. What are the triggers? (What do you worry about?) Which aspects of those triggers are controllable? What could you do to problem-solve in that area of your life? Set goals to change those changeable aspects of your life that cause you anxiety. And accept the rest! (See Appendix E for guidance on journal writing).

12. Identify a good counsellor or psychotherapist to whom you can talk about your anxiety problems, with a view to changing what can be changed, and learning to accept what is beyond your control. If you leaned to be anxious from your mother when you were very young, you might need to work with an Attachment Therapist, so you can be re-parented, and thus to build a better set of Affect Regulation responses to threats and dangers (which are managed from the right, orbitofrontal cortex of your brain).

13. Additional dietary advice might include the following:

- You might need to supplement your vitamin intake from food with:

  o a good multi-vitamin and mineral tablet;

  o plus B-Complex;

  o at least one gram of vitamin C per day;

  o plus omega-3 fatty acid capsules (or strong cod liver oil; or Krill oil capsules);

  o and perhaps kava kava.

  o (If you are a vegetarian, you will need to pay particular attention to how you are going to get enough omega-3 fatty acids, since the stronger sources are animal-based – especially salmon, sardines and other oily fish).

- Drink lots of water, by taking a sip every 15 minutes or so throughout the day; and limit alcohol consumption to one unit every other day, or less. (For example, you could have a glass of red wine with your evening meal on Monday, Wednesday, Friday and Sunday. But bear in mind: there is no longer any such thing as a 'safe limit' for alcohol consumption!)

- Drink herbal tea instead of caffeinated drinks, especially if you have difficulty reducing your anxiety by other means. And drink lots of camomile tea; and eat anxiety-reducing foods like lettuce, bananas, turkey, and Brazil nuts.

Anxiety management: The impact of diet and nutrition

It has been proven empirically that dietary changes can reduce the experience of anxiety: as demonstrated in Taylor-Byrne and Byrne (2017)[13].

Firstly, 2011 was the first year in which there was a double-blind trial establishing that there was a link between omega-3 fatty acids and a reduction in anxiety. This connection has been confirmed by many hundreds of anecdotal accounts by clients (to their professional practitioners) in which those clients have attested to the benefits in anxiety reduction, which they personally gained from omega-3 fatty acids.

~~~

Secondly, both magnesium and GABA (gamma-amino-butyric acid) are very valuable for the body-brain-mind in terms of reducing tension, anxiety and hyper-arousal. The recommended foods are as follows: dark green leafy vegetables, (like spinach and kale); nuts (walnuts and almonds); and seeds; fruit (e.g. bananas); and oats; and extracts of Reishi (described as the power mushroom).

~~~

Thirdly, the management of our blood sugar levels can stop the following vicious circle happening:

(1) A person (ill informed) eats white bread, or white pasta, white rice, chocolates and drinks fizzy drinks;

(2) As a direct consequence of this ill-advised activity, this person experiences a rapid rise in blood sugar.

(3) Soon afterwards, this is followed by a big drop in blood sugar levels, as the person's body releases insulin to cope with the sudden influx of sugar. And then,

(4) *Because* of the sudden drop in blood sugar, the hormone, adrenalin, is released into the bloodstream. This results in experiencing a racing heart and rapid breathing, and negative *perfinking* (or perceiving-feeling-thinking) processes, which create the symptoms of anxiety.

(The vicious circle, of course, is this: When some people feel anxious, they reach for 'comfort foods', which boost their blood sugar levels – and the whole cycle begins all over again!)

The recommended solution is to alter the combination of foods that you eat, so the release of energy, from the digestion of the food, is slowed down. Also it is recommended that people avoid refined carbohydrates, and simple sugars. Eating vegetables, oily fish and reducing meat consumption; plus eating nuts and seeds; would mean that the blood-sugar roller-coaster effect would be avoided. (This is called 'eating slow-burning fuels').

~~~

Fourthly, there is growing evidence that the state of our guts, including our gut bacteria, is very important in managing the experience of anxiety. This view is expressed by Dr David Perlmutter (2015). He cites many research studies which establish several facts:

(1) When we eat foods containing gluten, this affects the junctions between cells in the intestines, called the 'tight junctions'. This makes them leaky, and this enables toxins that come from within the bacteria in the intestines to enter the bloodstream. As a consequence they bring about a massive inflammatory response in the body-brain.

(2) Perlmutter (2015) also considers that there are physical vulnerabilities which can precipitate high levels of inflammation in the body, such as antibiotic use, manner of birth, and the balance of bacteria in the gut.

(3) Dietary changes therefore are necessary to heal the gut, such as:

(a) Giving up gluten-containing foods (like: wheat; rye; [non-organic] oats; and barley – and any foods containing those grains); and:

(b) Consuming oral probiotic supplements, and vitamin supplements. (Specific probiotics [e.g. *lactobacillus* and *bifidobacterium*] reduce anxiety and return the intestines to full health and proper functioning.)

(4) But he also considers lifestyle changes such as sufficient sleep and aerobic exercise as necessary to complete the process.

There is also research supporting the conclusion that the consumption of caffeine, sugar, artificial sweeteners and alcohol actually *create* anxiety in the human body. Two relevant examples to mention are the consumption of caffeine and sugar. High levels of caffeine in coffee bring about a sudden increase in tension and anxiety, and sugar causes a drop in our blood sugar as the body tries to cope, and this results in feelings of anxiety and weakness in the body.

For further information, please see Taylor-Byrne and Byrne (2017), for specific dietary guidance and advice. (But also remember to 'find out for yourself'; perhaps by consulting a nutritional therapist or alternative or lifestyle medical practitioner). Also, see Chapter 5 and Appendix B, below.

Anxiety management: How anxiety can be reduced by exercise:

If we do not exercise, we are asking for trouble, for our body-minds. This is because, as human animals, we have evolved to handle threats and dangers *by taking physical action*. If we don't take physical action when presented by a threat, we will experience anxiety and a build-up of stress hormones in our body-mind.

We need to process the stressors in our daily lives and remove the stress hormones from our body-mind by taking physical action. Exercise is a form of managed stress exerted on the body-brain-mind, which actually *reduces* stress hormones and the feeling of anxiety.

Joshua Broman-Fulks proved this in 2004 with students suffering from anxiety. (See Broman-Fulks and Storey, 2008)[14]. Two weeks of exercise reduced their anxiety levels, and made the students less sensitive to anxiety.

If our bodies are tense, the brain-mind registers this and starts to go on red alert.

But if we exercise, this action reduces the tension in our muscles – and if our bodies are relaxed the brain-mind does not worry.

So exercise stops the anxiety 'feedback loop', whereby we become anxious about being anxious, which then activates the brain into starting the 'fight or flight' response.

Exercise works by making chemical alterations in our bodies. As our muscles move, fat molecules are broken down to provide energy for this extra demand on the body.

This then releases fatty acids into the bloodstream, and tryptophan and serotonin - (which some theorists call the *'feel-good' hormone*) - increase, and (it is thought by some), serotonin calms us down and also increases our feelings of safety.

For further information please see Chapter 7, below; and Byrne (2018).

~~~

Finally, try to 'reframe' – or rethink – the problem that is causing your anxiety.

One way to do that is to use Window No.1 from the Nine Windows Model:

Window No.1: What can you control?

Imagine you are looking out through a window which has this wise slogan written around the window frame: *"In life, some things are within our control, and some things are beyond our control."*

Outside the window, you can see a current 'big worry', such as this: "What if I lose control, and run amok?! That would be so shaming!" "What if my health fails, or I catch a deadly disease, and I die young?! That would be so tragic!" "What if I am in an accident, and am seriously injured?! That would be most unfortunate!"

If you are older, you might worry about family problems, such as this: "My children may become ill, and die young".

All of these statements are true. Accidents may happen. People may make the wrong choices, and have unhappy lives. But it is **wrong** to assume that, just because I can identify **a feeling** that something **might** happen, than this **proves** that this is likely to happen! It proves nothing of the kind. Your feelings are just your feelings, and they are not predictors of the future. Your anxious feelings tell us more about *your past* than your future.

But this much **is** true: Something **might** go wrong in your life in the future.

So now, about this, what can YOU control (today), and what is beyond your control?

Let us think about that for a moment.

Epictetus, who made some moderately stoical statements (which are helpful), and some extreme stoical statements (which are unhelpful), said the following, which was perhaps his greatest contribution to reasonable mind-management:

"Freedom and happiness consist of understanding one principle: There are certain things you can control and certain things you can't. It is only after you learn to distinguish between what you *can* and *cannot control* and to act upon that distinction, that inner harmony and outer effectiveness become possible".

In other words, you cannot get rid of anxiety about future threats, which are beyond your control, if you are insisting that you must be able to control them.

The more you try to control the uncontrollable, the more upset you will become. This is roughly what the Buddhists mean when they say: "One hairsbreadth difference between what you've got and what you want, and heaven and earth are set apart".

The solution is to accept the things you cannot change, and only try to change the things you can.

Try this:

Take an A4 pad, and draw a line down the middle of the page, and create a matrix like the following image:

Column 1: What I can control (most likely)	Column 2: What is (clearly) beyond my control
1.	1.
2.	2.
3.	3.
4.	4.
5.	5.
Etc.	Etc.

Then, in column one, begin to write down those things which you *want* to be able to control in the future (about which you are concerned, anxious, or worrying), and which seem at least *potentially controllable.*

Then ask yourself this, and write down both the questions and your answers:

Q1: With regard to these items, in column 1, which I definitely *want* to control, in the future, what actions can I take **today** to *try* to control them?

Answers: Answers which occur to you should be written down, preferably on a list of Action Items, which you strongly intend to implement.

Q2: With regard to the actions that I intend to take, what *conditions* apply, (such as "I can control doing X, **IF** I can first achieve Y".)

Answers: Write down any answers that occur to you, and set out to take action to "achieve Y", or several "Y's". (Such as: "I can control catching Covid-19, provided I engage in social distancing, and wash my hands regularly, and avoid touching public surfaces which might contain the virus". And, "I can control my financial situation, provided I reduce my expenditure to keep it in line with my reduced income".)

~~~

Next:

Q3: Which items clearly belong in Column 2 (because you certainly, or *almost* certainly, cannot control them right now)?

Answers: Write down any answers that occur to you, and write the items in question in Column 2. (For example: "I cannot control the existence of viruses and bacteria. I cannot control government policy regarding lock-down [during the Covid-19 pandemic]. Etc.)

~~~

Then:

Q4: With regard to those items that you felt compelled to put in Column 2, what *conditions* could apply, such as: "I cannot control doing P, **UNLESS** I First figure out how to do Q".

Answers: If you come up with any 'unless' clauses, write them down in a second action list; and consider whether you should try to test some of those 'unless' clauses. (For example: "I cannot control government policy, unless national petitions are started, to influence the government, and I both sign those petitions, pass them on for my friends and colleagues to sign).

Try following this process for any worry or concern that comes up, and write frequently in your Morning Pages[3] (or your diary, or journal) about these concerns, until you reach the point where you know which bits are (potentially) within your control (IF...), and which bits seem to be (largely)

---

[3] 'Morning Pages' is a writing therapy process, recommended by Julia Cameron (1992), the author of 'The Artist's Way'. (See Appendix E, below). It involves writing three pages of stream of consciousness every morning, to get any mental clutter out of your mind, to calm your emotions, and to improve your self-management and creative thinking.

beyond your control (UNLESS...). (See Appendix E for guidance on writing therapy and journal writing).

~~~

Next, in Chapter 3 below, we have presented nine different ways to reframe any threat or danger that worries or concerns you; including revisiting Window No.1 from above.

~~~

Chapter 3: Nine ways to re-frame threats and dangers to reduce their impact

A powerful way to improve your philosophy of life

By Dr Jim Byrne

Copyright (c) Jim Byrne, March 2020

Preamble

As emphasized above, anxiety, like all other human emotions, is both innate and socially shaped, and enacted in a stimulus-response pattern, as a habitual response to particular stimuli.

I have mentioned various factors which contribute to the easing or worsening of symptoms of anxiety, from diet, exercise and sleep, to relaxation and philosophy of life.

In this chapter, I want to introduce my Nine Windows Model, which is designed to help you to change your philosophy of life from one that makes problems of anxiety worse, to one that makes problems of anxiety better.

Case illustration

Let me begin by presenting a case illustration, based on my own experience of suffering from a specific problem of anxiety.

When I was in my mid-forties, I had a job as Deputy Chief Executive of an educational charity in the City of Bradford, West Yorkshire. I had a nice office, and a feeling of being in the driving seat of my life, from dawn to dusk.

Then, around six or seven o'clock every evening, Monday to Friday, I would take the train from Bradford to Hebden Bridge, walk up the hill to my home, turn the corner of the road which led almost immediately to my own road, and then my guts would tighten, my temperature would drop, and my body would begin to shiver. In an instant, I went from being my confident work role, to being *a frightened little boy!*

I was about to enter the road on which I lived, which was patrolled, at unpredictable times, and certainly on most evenings, by a huge Alsatian dog, called Sonny. For me he might as well have been called *The Hound of Death.*

I was terrified of him. I felt powerless around him. He was quite aggressive, barking noisily, and pursuing anybody who entered or crossed the road. I had a deep apprehension that he would pounce on me and rip my jugular vein out of my neck before anybody could help me.

I found this nightly ordeal very stressful. I was anxious; panicky; terrified. Eventually I got up the courage to share my ordeal with my wife, who had done some training as a Gestalt therapist. She suggested that I should adopt a particular attitude – which I would have to train myself to adopt – which would be this: Every time I suspected that I might run into Sonny, I was to tell myself, over and over again:

"I'm the kind of person who will probably always be somewhat afraid of dogs".

"I'm the kind of person who will probably always be somewhat afraid of dogs".

"I'm the kind of person who will probably always be somewhat afraid of dogs".

This is an example of changing – or working at changing - an aspect of my philosophy of life.

However, to me, at that time, it did not seem like much of a solution, since I thought/felt the solution should be something like this: "Here's a gun with a silencer. Just point it at Sonny next time he comes near you, without letting anybody see what you are doing, and just pull the trigger".

That is to say, I wanted an 'action solution' which would change the 'Activating Event', or Stimulus (namely, Sonny). It did not occur to me that it would be easier and more socially acceptable to change my attitude towards Sonny, and my 'relationship' to him. That is to say, by changing my 'attitude', or *my 'philosophy' of coexisting with dogs* in a world in which dogs were going to be a regular, consistent feature of my environment.

But I trusted my wife, Renata, who is the wisest person I have ever met. So, from the very next night, as I walked up the hill, I began to recite my mantra, or affirmation, silently in my frightened mind (which, remember, is really a body-mind):

"I'm the kind of person who will probably always be somewhat afraid of dogs".

"I'm the kind of person who will probably always be somewhat afraid of dogs".

"I'm the kind of person who will probably always be somewhat afraid of dogs".

Over and over and over again.

And as I entered my own road, that night, and for month after month after month, I slowed by pace to a crawl, and recited the same affirmation, silently in my mind, all the way up the road, past the cars between which I sensed Sonny was hiding.

As I got to the point where he was waiting for me, I would slow my pace to very, very slow, lest I startled him, and provoked him into attacking me.

~~~

I continued to be afraid of Sonny, weeks and weeks after beginning this process. But I did also have a sense that I had *some control*. This mantra was *something I could control* in this otherwise uncontrollable situation.

And my fear level did fall, perhaps some weeks into the process; and I also noticed something else. I was not just *afraid* of Sonny. I was also *extremely angry* at him for showing me how weak I was. For showing how shallow my Deputy Chief Executive role was. Inside, and at root, I was just a little frightened kid; just as I had been for my ten years in school. (See Byrne, 2020/In press)[15].

~~~

Years went by, and I moved home, and set up as a self-employed counsellor. One day I realized: "I haven't seen a dog for years! Everywhere I used to go, dogs would come out of the woodwork and attack me. Where have they all gone?"

In fact, I realized that dogs had so totally fallen out of my world that, if somebody had knocked at my front door and said, "I'll give you a million pounds (GBP) if you can find a dog in the next two hours", I would not have been able to find one.

~~~

Some more years went by, and I found myself smiling at dogs in the street. Smiling! At those things that used to terrify me.

I had become *desensitized*. (But not totally. Once in a while, when I am in strange territory, off the beaten track, the old fear returns, at a reduced level. *"I'm the kind of person who will probably always be somewhat afraid of dogs"*; but it's no longer a big deal!)

Analysis of how I lost my anxiety about dogs

One way of understanding what happened to reduce and then largely eliminate my fear of dogs is this:

I subjected myself to a process of 'gradual desensitization'. I allowed myself to experience Sonny being near me, each evening, until I learned that he will not actually jump on me and kill me.

That's the 'behaviourist' or 'behaviour therapy' way of understanding what happened. But there is another way of understanding this process, and it's this:

When I was a little child, I was full of anger at my parents. I had to do something with that anger, to prevent it coming out in our home, and provoking them into attacking me and killing me. I guess my anger at them, for their mistreatment of me – including severe beatings for minor infringements of their rules – was so intense that, if I could not dump this anger - it would cause me to hit them in the way they were hitting me. So, one day, when I was about three or four years old, my sister suggested that our neighbour's dog was a danger to me, and so I projected all of my anger into that dog, so it felt like it no longer belonged to me. Then, I noticed angry dogs everywhere I went, and felt terrified of them. But I felt *no* anger towards my parents, no matter how badly they treated me. I needed them to keep me at home, so I could survive. I did not want them "giving me to the gypsies" which my mother threatened to do when I was not cooperative with her.

This is a process called projection of our own negative side into our environment, and fearing it from afar.

Another way of seeing this situation is this:

Because of my experience in my family of origin, I came to look at dogs, and other children, as threats to my survival. We could think of this as a kind of 'non-conscious framing' of dogs and children.

Whenever I saw a dog, or another child, I looked at them through a particular frame or lens, which suggested this meaning:

"This dog/child is dangerous".

As a result of this kind of *non-conscious framing*, I felt nervous, anxious, worried, apprehensive, avoidant, of all dogs and all children.

This is also a helpful way to think about your own anxieties.

When you see, or anticipate, something that makes you anxious, we can infer that, *somewhere in the basement of your brain-mind*, a *frame* (or way of perceiving) is *being applied* to your perception. You are seeing what you automatically, habitually, *expect to see*, because of the *frame* through which you are (non-consciously) perceiving it.

Here is the good news. Whatever you once learned to *frame as a 'fearful thing'* you can now learn to *re-frame as a 'safe thing'*, (assuming it is actually safe!) And that is what this chapter is designed to do for you: To teach you to re-frame those things which are causing you to feel anxious, so that they *begin to show up* as a little less frightening every day, until one day you wake up and find you are over that particular anxiety. Or you have at least reduced it to realistic and tolerable proportions.

~~~

The material in this chapter has previously been published in a number of books by the E-CENT Institute, because it is one of the central models of E-CENT counselling. In the presentation below, we have emphasised problems of anxiety.

Brief explanation

The Nine Windows Model of E-CENT[4] counselling is a way of helping individuals to rethink and re-frame their upsetting or distressing problems, without engaging in *confrontation* and/ or *conflictual arguments* with them.

It can be used to reduce and control anxiety, anger, depression, and to produce a calm state of body-mind.

The Windows Model consists of an experiment, in which the person needing help is asked to *imagine* how their problem would *look and feel*, when viewed through nine different window frames (or lenses) – each of which provides a slightly different 'context' for the problem.

The context is provided by a philosophical statement (or belief), such as 'life is difficult'; or 'some things are beyond my control'.

---

[4] This model was developed by me, Jim Byrne, between 2007 and 2010, and originally consisted of just four windows, mostly derived from Buddhist sutras and moderate Stoical principles. I then expanded it to five and then six windows, but had to modify it because one or two extreme ways of reframing had crept into the system, mostly from Buddhism. Then it increased to eight windows, and very recently I added number nine.

And the person is asked to look at a *specific problem* - which is disturbing or distressing them - through those nine different windows, or contexts, frames, or philosophical lenses - as if they are true beliefs.

What follows is a brief introduction to each of the nine frames, windows, or perspectives.

Here's how it works:

Think about a current problem that you have, which makes you feel anxious, and which is serious enough to require urgent treatment.

Try to create a visual image or representation of that problem. (For example, you could imagine yourself being told you have a particular illness; or you could see yourself standing in front of an audience, about to give a challenging presentation; or you could see yourself clearing your desk, after being told you've lost your job).

Then look through each of the following nine 'windows' in turn, (as if looking at that serious problem). In practice, the first six of these windows are most relevant to problems of anxiety. Also, ask yourself the questions suggested:

Window No.1: The frame around this window says:

"In life, there are certain things I can control, and certain things that are beyond my control".

Looking at my chosen problem:

*- Am I currently upset because I am **trying** to control something that is **beyond** my control?*

For examples:

  o   *Other people are beyond my control; though some of them may be more or less open to being influenced by me.*

  o   *The economy is beyond my control; as is government policy [today, and for the foreseeable future!]*

  o   *The health of the nation, and communicable diseases, are beyond my control – though I can take self-protective precautions.*

  o   *The things that happened to me in my early childhood are definitely beyond my control. But I can control how I think about what they meant, using my adult intelligence, instead of my early childhood feelings. And so on.*

- If I <u>give up</u> trying to control what is clearly beyond my control, how much less anxious would I feel? (Normally, a lot! All other things being equal.[5])

- If I am not trying to be perfectly safe, in an unsafe world, how much calmer would I feel? (Normally, a lot! All other things being equal!)

*- And, if I take the time to do the Two-Columns activity, described in Chapter 2 above, how much more **(realistic) control** would I be likely to feel?* (Normally, a significant amount! All other things being equal!)

~~~

Window No.2: The frame around this windows says:

"Life is difficult for <u>all</u> human beings, at least some of the time, and often much of the time".

Therefore, since I am a human being, life is sometimes going to be difficult for me, as it is when I am confronted by my current problem.

---

[5] "All other things being equal", in this context, means: Provided I am getting enough good quality sleep; avoiding caffeine and junk foods; eating the right kinds of food; taking regular physical exercise; and so on.

If my problem is one in which somebody is acting illegally towards me, I should seek legal help. If they are acting immorally against me, I have to ask myself if I can stop them, and if not, I should consider putting myself beyond their influence or control.

Once I have taken care of my legal and moral situation, I should ask myself:

- So why must life not be difficult for me (in this problem situation)? Why must I (alone, among humans) be exempted from threats and dangers?

Since I am human, it follows that I will experience anticipation of threats and dangers! (And if I cannot control and eliminate them, then I will have to learn to accept them – without subjecting myself to sadistic, illegal or immoral victimization!)

- Is there any reason why I should be exempt from having to face threats or dangers? (The sensible answer is this: 'No!')

- Is there any good reason to believe that I cannot <u>cope</u> with having to face this current threat or danger? (No, especially if you are well rested, well fed, well exercised; etc.)

~~~

Window No.3: The frame around this window says:

"Life is much less difficult when I avoid picking and choosing what happens to me; or how it happens; or if I pick and choose more modestly, sensibly or reasonably."

- So, if I am experiencing difficulty right now (in relation to the threat or danger I am viewing through this window), doesn't that mean I must be (unrealistically) picking and choosing? (If I accepted the difficulty I am facing, I would not feel so anxious!)

- And isn't it true that life would be much less difficult if I were to pick and choose more moderately, more modestly, more realistically. (For example, when I was

unrealistically choosing that Sonny not exist in my road, I felt extremely anxious. But once I shifted the focus to choosing that things be the way they are – "I'm the kind of person..." – my anxiety gradually receded and eventually disappeared.)

- *How can I change my choices and preferences in order to show that I am picking and choosing realistically and reasonably and modestly?* (I must keep my expectations in line with everyday *reality*.)

~~~

Window No.4: The frame around this window says:

"Life is both difficult and non-difficult".

- *So if I am very anxious, might it not be because I am exclusively focusing on the* **threats and dangers** *in my life, and overlooking those bits of my life which are* **not threatening or dangerous** *(for which I could be grateful)?*

- *What happens to how I feel if I add back in the 'missing', non-threatening bits of my life?* (You will feel a lot less anxious!)

- *I must make a list of those positive things I have in my life for which I could feel grateful, such as my eyesight or hearing; my ability to walk or talk; and so on.* (Those non-difficult things, for which I can feel grateful, represent no threat or danger to me).

~~~

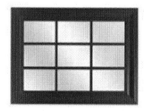

Window No.5: The frame around this window says:

"Life could always be **very** *much more difficult than it currently is for me".*

- *So am I making the mistake of thinking it is already (and always) 100% bad?*

- *Or as frightening, threatening and dangerous as it could be?* (What if a crocodile was eating my rear end off, in addition to my current problems? What percentage badness would that be?)

- *Think of some things that I may lose **later in life** – which represent potential future threats or dangers – but which I still currently **have**. Such as*

- *my hair,*

- *some of my teeth,*

- *my unwrinkled skin.*

- *My youthfulness, or whatever).*

How does that make me feel? (When you focus on the things for which you can be grateful, right now, you take the focus off the things you are worrying about!)

- *Write down three things for which I can be grateful right now.* ('Count your blessings'!)

~~~

Window No.6: The frame around this window says:

"Life is a school which obliges us all to learn how to survive and grow. So, I must pay attention, and learn quickly".

- *Which **aspect(s)** of my current problem should I pay attention to?* (Use attention directors, like: (1) the WDEP model[16]; (2) the Egan (Skilled Helper) Model[17]; (3) Dr De Bono's CoRT tools[18]18 below; or read Appendix G to get a better understanding of your emotions).

- *Is this problem a repeating pattern? If so, why do I keep getting to this point? Am I creating or attracting this problem by some unhelpful behaviour or thought/ feeling/perceiving pattern of my own?* (Remember my problem with Sonny. It was my early childhood experiences; my anger at my parents; and my projection of my anger into dogs; that caused my problem with Sonny!)

*- What **positive lesson** could I learn from my current negative situation(s)? I must write about this, and write down the answer(s).* (The positive lessons that I learned from the humiliation and fear of Sonny were: That any problem of anxiety can be resolved, if you *acknowledge its existence*; if you tell yourself *the truth* about it; if you *bravely* accept yourself with all your imperfections, such as your fears and phobias! And if you do the necessary *work* to solve the problem!)

- If there was an independent witness present, observing me and how I relate to this threat or danger, what would they conclude? (Write down your answer. It could help to solve your problem. This is the beginning of clarifying the nature of the problem; and facing up to solving it).

~~~

The six windows covered up to this point are probably the most important ones for dealing with problems of anxiety. The next three windows may help when there are secondary problems of depression or shame or non-acceptance of yourself. Or when your anxiety causes you to want to quit on your goals.

Here they are:

Window No.7: The frame around this window says:

*"I'm okay, exactly the way I am (in terms of appearance, social status, efficiency, and effectiveness, general behaviour, etc.); as long as I am in the habit of acting **morally and legally"**.*

And, if I accept myself being the way I am, I am less likely to become anxious about how other people might judge me!

But before I practice Window No.7, as a philosophy of life, I might tend to judge myself negatively when I notice some limitation of my appearance, social status, efficiency, effectiveness, general judgements, public behaviours, and so on. I might also reject myself (or not accept myself) if I notice that I am more anxious than I believe I should be!

- In what ways am I judging myself negatively? Do I beat myself up for not being able to solve this (present) problem of anxiety? Do I blame myself for having this problem? (I was ashamed of my fear of Sonny. But I bravely faced up to my apparent cowardice, and solved the problem. "I'm okay", I told myself; "I accept myself one-conditionally[6]; and I would accept myself today, even if I still had a significant fear of dogs!")

- How justified are any negative judgements that I make of myself (given that I am a fallible, error-prone human)?

- How could I learn to accept myself more thoroughly, kindly, and charitably? (I must not accept myself <u>completely unconditionally</u> – independently of my moral and legal actions in the world. But I must learn to accept myself <u>one-conditionally</u>, and that one condition is that I always act as a moral being, following the Golden Rule, of treating other people as well as I would want them to treat me, if our roles were reversed).

~~~

Window No.8: The frame around this window says:

*"You're okay (meaning 'you, other people'), exactly the way you are (in terms of appearance, social status, efficiency, effectiveness, etc.); as long as you are in the habit of acting **morally** and **legally**".*

- In what ways am I judging you (another person) negatively?

- How justified are those judgements (given that you [another person] are a fallible, error-prone human)?

- How could I learn to accept you [other person] more thoroughly, kindly, and charitably? (I must not accept you <u>completely unconditionally</u> – independently of your moral and legal actions in the world. But I must learn to accept you <u>one-conditionally</u>, and that one condition is that you appear to act as a moral being,

---

[6] And the one condition that I apply to myself and my behaviour is this: I will accept myself completely, so long as I always strive to act morally and legally in every situation.

following the Golden Rule, of treating other people as well as you would want them to treat you, if your roles were reversed).

~~~

Window No.9: The frame around this window says:

"Winners never quit – but they certainly don't persist in banging their heads on the same section of the wall that obstructs their progress".

- Some people quit too soon, or too easily, and therefore fail to win the prize that they desired.

- Some people keep going, striving and persisting, and they do (often) achieve the prize that they were after.

- And some people keep going, and going, and going, despite the fact that they are clearly flogging a dead horse. This is a form of losing, and failing, and self-disregard or self-abuse!

- I must try, try and try again – <u>within reason</u> - to succeed; but not necessarily in the same (unworkable) relationship; or the same (unrewarding or intolerable) business or employment; or on the same path through life.

- Winners are life-long learners, and they have the courage to act on their earned wisdom!

- How can I decide when to persist and when to quit? (I could try using the CoRT tools developed by Dr Edward De Bono[18], applied to my current problem situation).

- Is my current problem a result of bashing my head on the wrong section of wall?

- Is it time to quit on some person, or organization, or some object or thing, or goal, in order to resolve my current problem?

~~~

Reflection: Did this process, of viewing a current problem from nine different 'directions' or perspectives - or through nine different 'lenses', or 'frames' - change how it looks and feels to you? (Normally it will! And the first six of those windows will have helped, more than the final three, with problems of anxiety and panic.)

~~~

We can summarize the Nine Windows in the following illustrations:

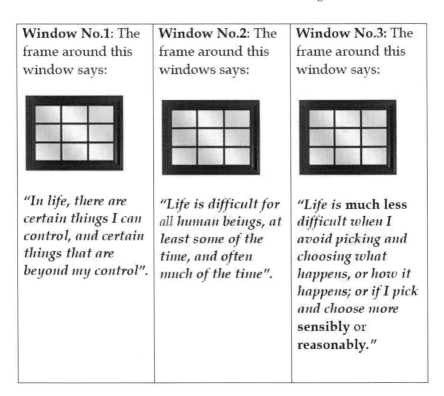

Window No.1: The frame around this window says:	Window No.2: The frame around this windows says:	Window No.3: The frame around this window says:
"In life, there are certain things I can control, and certain things that are beyond my control".	*"Life is difficult for all human beings, at least some of the time, and often much of the time".*	*"Life is* **much less** *difficult when I avoid picking and choosing what happens, or how it happens; or if I pick and choose more* **sensibly** *or* **reasonably.***"*

Window No.4: The frame around this window says:	Window No.5: The frame around this window says:	Window No.6: The frame around this window says:

"Life is both difficult and non-difficult".	*"Life could always be very much more difficult than it currently is for me".*	*"Life is a school which teaches you how to survive and grow. Pay attention. Learn quickly".*

Window No.7: The frame around this window says:	Window No.8: The frame around this window says:	Window No.9: The frame around this window says:

"I'm okay, exactly the way I am (in terms of appearance, social status, efficiency, and effectiveness, etc.); as long as I am in the habit of acting morally and legally".	*"You're okay (you other people), exactly the way you are (in terms of appearance, social status, efficiency, effectiveness, etc.); as long as you are in the habit of acting morally and legally".*	*"Winners never quit – but they certainly don't persist in banging their heads on the same section of the wall that obstructs their progress. And they don't stay in self-destructive situation when they are free to leave".*

~~~

If you review those nine windows – and especially the first six - every day, for 30, 60, 90 or preferably 120 days, you should be able to re-wire your brain with *a self-supporting philosophy of life*, which will help you to be more resilient in the face of any future threats or dangers. And it will help to clear up your current problems with anxiety and panic.

But you have to do the homework, diligently, systematically, for significant period of time, to gain the benefits, because it takes time to re-wire your non-conscious brain-mind. What you are striving to do, by reviewing the nine windows over and over again is the slowly change your non-conscious, habitual perceptions/feelings/thoughts, which are all of a piece.

As Paul McKenna expresses it: "*Repetition* is the mother of self-change".

~~~

Chapter 4: Jacobson's Progressive Muscle Relaxation, for anxiety problems

By Renata Taylor-Byrne, March 2020

~~~

This chapter originally appeared as Chapter 15 of Byrne (2020)[19]. It teaches a system of muscle relaxation which switches off the flight response, which is the physical basis of feelings of anxiety.

Introduction

> *"Why use sedatives and tranquilising drugs with their many side effects, when nature has provided a built-in device free from all such defects (a built-in tranquiliser)?"*

> Oscar G. Mayer, (In Jacobson, 1980).[20]

~~~

Progressive muscle relaxation is a technique that will greatly improve the quality of your life, including your resilience in the face of life's difficulties! It will reduce your anxiety, boost your energy, make you sleep better at night and improve your sports abilities. Furthermore, it will make you less susceptible to heart attacks, and high blood pressure; and it will boost your immune system; to name just a few of the benefits you can gain from practicing this system of relaxation on a regular basis.

The creator of this technique was Dr Edmund Jacobson (1888 – 1983). He was a physiologist, and physician in psychiatry and internal medicine. He spent seventy years researching and developing the key insights of scientific relaxation, based on observing tension within the human body. Starting in 1908 at Harvard University, followed by Cornell University, and after that Chicago University, he then set up his own institution in Chicago called the Laboratory for Clinical Physiology.

What Dr Jacobson developed was a simple technique which, if practised daily, reduces physical tension throughout the body-brain-mind.

'Why is this a valuable process?' you might ask.

And my answer: Because the reliable, measurable reduction in levels of physical tension, which you get if you do the exercise daily, has *beneficial effects throughout* the body-mind. People have more energy, less illness, reduced anxiety and depression; and this slowly transforms people's self-confidence. They are able to sleep better and to banish insomnia; and their memory reliably improves.

This is a crucial point: most people don't realise that they become *increasingly physically tense* as they try to solve the daily problems of their lives. This tension uses up lots of their physical energy.

Because of this phenomenon, of accumulation, or building up of physical tensions, day in and day out, people develop anxiety, depression, and a range of physical illnesses: such as high blood pressure, heart attacks, peptic ulcers, spastic colon and nervous indigestion.

The process of progressive tension works like this: As we handle the daily tasks and challenges of life: like work, commuting, and managing the home; physical tension slowly builds up in our bodies as the day progresses. And this accumulating tension is added to by a steady bombardment of bad news via mobile phones, the TV and newspapers.

This accumulated tension interferes with our ability to get to sleep reasonably quickly, to recharge our batteries. And if we have poor quality sleep, we begin the next day feeling tense before our work challenges even begin!

In an effort to escape from the demands of our lives; and to relax and enjoy ourselves; we go on holidays. But this strategy can easily backfire as we experience the challenges of air, road and rail travel, and/or hotel and accommodation hassles. People increasing turn to drugs of one sort or another - (including alcohol and/or street drugs, or pharmaceutical drugs from their doctor) - to escape their tense and stressed life situations.

What Dr Jacobson has demonstrated over the decades is this: You can switch off, or gradually reduce, the tension of daily stressors and strains by learning how to *relax* your muscles, which automatically relaxes your central nervous system, including your brain-mind. Progressive muscle relaxation (PMR) is like taking a natural, internally available tranquilizer!

In addition to taking care of the tension of the daily grind, progressive muscle relaxation can also be used (doubled up) at times of particularly high stress and strain, to switch off anxiety and panic symptoms, in contexts like the following:

- job interviews, making presentations, dealing with difficult people;

- before examinations, or auditions, or taking a driving test;

- or taking part in sports events and other areas of skill performance.

Progressive Muscle Relaxation (PMR) defined

> *"Nature does not excuse us when we display ignorance of the laws of health".*

> Jacobson (1963).[21]

~~~

In this chapter I will define Progressive Muscle Relaxation and describe its development as an efficient and very effective relaxation technique which has been thoroughly tested for its therapeutic power.

Examples of case studies showing its ability to heal very serious health problems will be described; and some recent research studies will show that it is highly relevant for our present, high-stress culture.

Then the topic of insomnia, and how daily progressive muscle relaxation can greatly help, will be explained. The final part of the chapter will be a description of the technique which you can try out for yourself, and further information about the benefits including my own feedback on having experimented with the technique for the past five months.

~~~

(1) The definition of Progressive muscle relaxation

> "We must learn tension control just as we learn French, the pianoforte or golf. Nature favours us with instincts which our parents readily turn to account to teach us to walk in infancy. However (nature) does not teach us to control ourselves, else we might have fewer addicts to sedatives, tranquilisers, alcohol and such (drugs)".

(Jacobson, 1963, page 29).[22]

~~~

Progressive muscle relaxation (PMR) is a technique whereby a person (a client) sees a relaxation therapist, and slowly learns, through the tensing and releasing of body muscles, to *not do anything at all* to their muscles. Relaxation is the *total* absence of any muscle movement in the body.

Jacobson elaborates on this point like this: "According to my experience, those who preach 'relaxation exercises' have not quite understood that to relax is simply **not to do**; it is the total absence of any muscular exercise". (Jacobson, 1980, page 34)[23].

He considered relaxation to be the complete physiological *opposite* of being excited or upset.

Matthew Edlund, M.D.[24] has described Jacobson's technique as being 'paradoxical' because you start to become relaxed *without* making any effort to become relaxed. Paradoxically, you focus on muscle tension at first, and then switch off the tension to leave yourself in a state of relaxation.

Jacobson's clients included engineers, journalists, lawyers, doctors, bankers, dentists and people from all the current businesses and professions which were operating in America from the 1920's up to the 1980's. When his first book - which was entitled "Progressive relaxation" - was published in 1929, he was told by the workers and printers at the Chicago University Press who produced his book, that they *in particular* experienced a great deal of tension. And later in his career he came across union members in the garment and other industries, and assembly line workers, who displayed evidence of extreme tension.

His theory was that clients experienced tension because they had hyperactive bodies and minds, and the build-up of tension in the body resulted in the following symptoms:

- anxiety, and high blood pressure,

- cardiovascular disorders, and nervous indigestion,

- peptic ulcers and spastic colon.

People were trying to cope with a very fast and constantly changing society – even in those much slower than today, days - and the problem was that their efforts to cope were using up lots of energy.

This energy, which is called *adenosine triphosphate*, comes from the food we eat. And Jacobson compared it to the petrol supply in a car. Just like the petrol in a car's tank, we have a limited amount of "personal petrol" (or fuel) which we need for our brain, nerves and muscles, and it comes directly from the food we eat.

This energy supply is used up by the activities we do to achieve our goals. When we have a job to do, we use some of our 1,030 skeletal muscles, which we contract and relax as necessary, in order to get things done.

But what Jacobson learned from experience of seeing clients was this: None of the doctors who had dealt with his clients, before they came to him, had told them about the need to *control their energy usage* as they lived their lives.

Those clients were well versed in the reality of running a business or profession. Thus they knew that, if they spent too much money, they would risk damaging their business, and, potentially, bankruptcy.

But they had *no idea* that they needed to manage their own *personal* supply of *physical energy*. Here is what Jacobson found:

"I have had experience with the top management of some of the (American) nation's most successful corporations. The officials conducted business duties with outstanding efficiency and success, yet spent their personal energies quite extravagantly.

"I was shocked to find that 40% of the top executives of one leading corporation had blood vessels that were beyond cure. They were paying with their lives for (unregulated) energy expenditure." (Jacobson, 1980, Page 12).

~~~

(2) How our muscles become tense and cause problems for us

When we perform any activity, we use our muscles, by contracting (or tensing) them. This reduces the length of the muscle fibres temporarily.

Within the muscles there are two sets of nerves:

- One set of nerves transmits information *to* the muscles, and:

- The other set of nerves takes information *from the muscles to the brain and the spinal cord.*

The information transmitted from the muscles via the nerves is electrical in nature, but it moves more slowly than the electricity we use in our daily lives.

When we tense our muscles, in order to carry out some act, we spend personal energy and this is in the form of increased nerve impulses. As stated earlier, this personal energy, which we burn up in our brains, muscles and nerves, is called *adenosine triphosphate.* Jacobson (1980) states: *"At every moment you depend on your personal energy expenditures – namely you burn adenosine triphosphate in your muscle fibres, in your nerve cells and fibres and in your brain cells and fibres. In this burning of fuel you resemble a car or an aeroplane, which likewise burns fuel in order to move".* (Page 11).

Furthermore, the energy that people use up as they go about their daily lives (which has to be acquired through the food they have eaten) can be measured with electrical machines.

Jacobson created a machine called an 'integrating neurovoltmeter' which simply means a way of measuring *muscle and nerve tension* of different intensities. It was able to measure mental exertion down to one ten-millionth of a volt. As people become tenser, there can be an increase from 1 to 70 electrical discharges per second, from nerves and muscles.

He described human beings as having a brain-nervous-muscular system which is a very complex "electrochemical-mechanical integrated system" which serves people as they go about their working lives. But nature, although *providing* ways in which people can control and manage the energy they use up in the course of daily life, *doesn't* show human beings *how to do that.*

People have to find out for themselves about energy conservation, and that was what Jacobson wanted to help them with.

They need to understand that tensions would build up in their bodies and cause serious health problems if they didn't learn to manage this process. Jacobson made the study of tension in the human body, and the reduction of it, his life's work.

He gives an example in his (1980) book, titled 'You Must Relax', of how three different people - a soldier in a battle, a student working in an examination room, or a runner taking part in a marathon, would all have high levels of physical tension.

And if these people were wired up so the electrical impulses could be recorded, then this high level of physical tension would be confirmed by the results, showing a high frequency of electrical impulses.

And if these three people were to go to a more peaceful environment, and have a rest, lying down, there would *in most cases* be a reduction in the electrical impulses recorded on the equipment.

But this *doesn't always follow* because there are people who have highly active, high pressure lives and when they try to switch off, they are unable to do so, because the nervous stimulation messages that they receive from their muscles and nerves has become normal (or habitual!) for them.

A closer look at how tension and stress builds up in our bodies

If we don't give ourselves time to *relax and recover* after we have exerted ourselves - (for example by doing a hard day's hard day's work; tackling a sudden problem; dealing with an accident; or any one of the many challenges that humans of all ages meet regularly) - then we can cause problems for ourselves.

Here's why we have to relax: Our bodies have developed through centuries of evolution, so that we are able to handle stressors, and then *recover* from them quickly, by calming down and resting. We've got a very efficient, in-built system for handling pressure. It's called the 'fight or flight' response, and our bodies react with the release of stress hormones which help us cope with the problems that arise.

But once the problem has passed, we have an automatic recovery system which kicks in, and this is called the 'rest and digest' system. Meyer, quoted at the start of this chapter, described it as our 'inbuilt tranquiliser." These two different, but inseparable, types of responses are part of our autonomic (meaning 'automatic') nervous system, which protects our body-mind through appropriate activations and deactivations of our energy release system.

The autonomic nervous system makes sure that, after we have dealt with a sudden crisis or stressful event, our digestion *slowly* returns to normal; our breathing slows down, as does our heart rate; and we get back to full energy conservation mode.

But if we *don't* give ourselves time to recover in-between these stressful events, we stop the natural recovery process from taking place. Our bodies experience more and more stress without this safety valve, or recovery stage, to dissipate it. Then there is a gradual accumulation of *excessive tension* in our muscles, and stress hormones in our blood and body tissues.

That is where Jacobson's Progressive muscle relaxation can help us.

"Tension disorders are more common than the common cold" stated Jacobson in his 1980 book.

He concluded, from his professional experiences, that many disorders of the body are a *direct* result of physical tension.

For examples: states of fear and anxiety; high blood pressure; nervous indigestion; heart problems; and peptic ulcers.

His goal was to show people how to *manage* their bodily energy carefully, so that they could reduce their physical tension levels.

He set up an organisation in Chicago called the Foundation for Scientific Relaxation. It was a non-profit organisation and it provided training for doctors and other professionals involved in health education.

Dr Martin Turner and Dr Jamie Barker - authors of 'What business can learn from Sport psychology', (2014)[25] – are convinced that *daily practice* of Progressive Muscle Relaxation (PMR) is needed before you can experience the benefits in reduced stress levels. (In other words, it's not enough to do it *occasionally*!)

They recommend *checking your heart rate* before and after the practice of the technique, which will provide you with reassuring information that the technique is actually working.

And they also conclude that PMR will improve your performance in different areas of your life and your work.

One of their findings is this: *"After a week's practice you will notice an increase in your ability to self-regulate"*... (Defined as *"managing your actions, thoughts and feelings so you achieve your valued goals'* - RTB.)... *and begin to see the value in integrating muscle relaxation into part of your preparation for important performance situations, or alternatively as an integral part of your daily routines".* (Turner and Barker, 2014: page 173).

Case studies: Several examples of how progressive muscle relaxation can help

(1) The first example. A case of anxiety in times of war:

Jacobson gives a description of the use of his 'scientific relaxation' technique (Jacobson, 1980) and explains how, during the Second World War in America, USA Navy cadets, aged 19-22 (straight from schools and college), were involved in flying aircraft during warfare against enemy planes. Imagine how anxiety-inducing that would be!

As a direct result of the continuous flying missions that the cadets had to complete, (which they couldn't withdraw from – [remember *Catch 22*]), as well as other challenges, the cadets started having nervous breakdowns and other indications of the strain – meaning accumulated physical and mental tensions - that they were under.

As an experimental solution, the US navy decided to send five of its officers (nicknamed the 'Navy Five') to Jacobson's Education Department, based in his Laboratory for Clinical Psychology in Chicago. There they got instructor training in how to teach Progressive Muscle Relaxation (PMR), for 6 weeks; so that they could then go back to their bases and train the new intakes of cadets in progressive muscle relaxation (PMR), and the principles of scientific relaxation.

The message that Jacobson wanted to get across was this:

"Scientific relaxation is not just lying down or sitting in a quiet manner with good intentions. It's as technical an undertaking as running a plane, which many of the cadets were striving to learn". (Page 33)

But how could Jacobson and his colleagues make sure that the 'Navy 5' instructors were *really* learning to relax? They would have to measure their starting tension levels, and their ending relaxation levels.

Fortunately, this had already been catered for, in an earlier period of Jacobson's work. In order to measure the level of physical tensions in the bodies of his clients, Jacobson and his colleagues, with the collaboration of the Bell Telephone Company Laboratory, had created *a tension measuring device* called an 'integrating neurovoltmeter'. This measuring equipment was so sensitive that, even if a muscle looked relaxed, any slight tension could be recorded, down to *one millionth of a volt of electricity.*

The evidence from the results produced by the electrical equipment showed clearly that the Navy instructors were learning to relax their muscles.

The instructors *also* needed to learn that *physical exercise*, on the one hand, and *muscle relaxation*, on the other, were **two separate processes**. For example, Jacobson had established that, if you worked all day in an office, stuck behind a desk, even though you were not moving around and exercising, you were still using your body muscles; even though the movements were not as apparent as those of a manual worker or sportsperson. Therefore, he was able to conclude that, someone who *looks* physically inactive can have *unseen* levels of tensions in their muscles.

After their training period in Chicago, the Navy instructors returned to their **Pre-flight training bases** in different parts of the US. They then, in turn, taught 95 officers the skills of relaxation training, so they could become instructors also; and in the next seven months, 15,700 cadets were instructed in relaxation skills.

The *American Journal of Psychiatry* published the results of the training, which were summarised as follows:

- *The anxious nervousness and fatigue amongst the cadets was reduced, and they reported much better sleep.*

- In addition, when the accident rates of the untrained cadets were compared with those of the trained cadets, *the accident rates were lower with those cadets who had received the training.*

- There was also *a high level of appreciation for the relaxation training* from the cadets, their instructors and from people who had simply seen the beneficial effects of the training on the young cadets.

~~~

(2) An individual example:

In 1980, Jacobson wrote about Mrs Hardy, a client that he treated with PMR. She had been suffering from cyclothymic depression. (This is a type of mood pattern which is characterised by alternating, short episodes of depression and hypomania; in a milder form than that of bipolar disorder). Her depression had lasted for several years. She was worried about her age and how long she would live, and she was convinced that she would never be able to stop worrying about it. As a result, she had very high levels of physical tension. (This suggests her depression was preceded by *anxiety* and *tension!*)

Jacobson taught her to notice when she was tensing the muscles in her body, and how to stop tensing them. And gradually, as a result of daily practice, she began to spot the signs of tension in her body and when she was tensing her muscles unnecessarily. This allowed her to desist from tensing, which left her body in a state of relaxation.

She learned this new **relaxation habit** lying down; and also in her daily life with her family, as she cooked, cleaned and ran the home. And as she did this awareness exercise, she realised that no-one was forcing her to tense up part of her body. She had been doing it herself all the time.

Jacobson (1980) stated: *"She was doing something with her muscles just as definitely as if she were sweeping a room or washing the dishes. Anxiety was* **an act** *which (at least in part) she was performing and need not perform."* (Page 40. **Emphasis added**).

What she was doing with her muscles became apparent to her when she had a very low level of tension in her muscles and she discovered the following:

"… To her surprise, perhaps for the first time in years, she found herself free for the moment from the severe anxiety which previously had oppressed her constantly." (Jacobson, 1980).

As she continued with her treatment, she was advised to keep practising the muscle relaxation exercises. And the outcome was that she stopped worrying about the difficulties of getting older.

When her level of tension was measured electronically, it confirmed her progress – she was able to go back to the job that she had been doing, handle money problems easily, and she was able to join her husband in his business.

The final comment on how she had changed as a result of the relaxation exercises was expressed by Jacobson as follows:

"She became free of the fears that had held her as a slave. She became confident, self-assured and cheerful."

~~~

(3) The third example:

Jacobson also describes a client who came to his clinic: *"Towards the end of World War 1, a patient who came from the United States Army, described how his parachute failed to open when he pulled the cord. He fell to earth and the parachute fell on top of him and broke his back."*

The surgeons in the US army were able to treat his injuries successfully but he was left with persistent pain which didn't reduce in its intensity. So the man travelled to Jacobson's Chicago clinic for treatment. He was given several months of Progressive Muscle Relaxation (PMR), and daily practice was *essential* to help his pain management. The result was that he slowly experienced a reduction in the pain from his injuries, and one day, feeling better, he visited a golf course (which he had never done before) to see what the sport was like.

He started trying out the game, on the golf course. And as he did so, his behaviour was observed by several golf professionals. They watched his movements and they became convinced that he possessed a natural flair for the game and encouraged him to learn to play golf. He took their advice on board and started learning to play properly. The result: *"...he became one of the outstanding golf professionals of the country"*. (Jacobson, 1978, page 143).

Recent research studies

Because so much of Jacobson's own research was conducted up to the 1970's, I want to present two recent research studies which confirm the power of Positive Muscle Relaxation (PMR):

(1) PMR and Anxiety: Research in Greece in 2019

The most recent research study, that I could find, was conducted in Greece, in January 2019, with 50 long-term unemployed people.[26] They had been suffering from anxiety disorders, and the participants were split up into 2 groups. One group of thirty individuals were put on an 8 week progressive muscle relaxation training programme, and the control group did not receive any training.

At the start of the research study, the participants' level of stress, anxiety, depression, integrity; their health–related quality of life; and their sense of safety and security; were all measured. And at the end of the research, the result was that the intervention group (which had the training in PMR) had improved results in all those aspects of their functioning which had been measured by the researchers.

So, even though the intervention group had statistically higher levels of depression, anxiety and stress *before* the intervention, they gained a significant reduction in those levels because of the PMR; whereas in the control group, no significant difference was observed.

Between the two groups, the differences were statistically significant. To summarise the findings, the intervention group showed a *decrease* in the evidence of depression, anxiety and stress; the quality of their life and general mental health had improved; and they felt more of a sense of coherence about their lives.

~~~

(2) PMR and pain: Research in Egypt in 2018

A research study which took place in 2018 is another example of the power of PMR: After having a caesarean section, a lot of women suffer pain, disturbed sleep, and difficulty moving and walking. A research study was undertaken at the Damanhur National Medical Institute in Egypt with a group of women - 80 in number - to see if Progressive Muscle Relaxation (PMR) could help improve their recover from their operations.[27] The research study took the form of a randomised, controlled clinical trial, and 40 women were assigned to a study group and 40 women were assigned to the control group. The women in the study group were shown how to do PMR, and then did it themselves. The results appeared to be quite conclusive:

- When the quality of the sleep experienced in the two groups were compared, 62.5% of the PMR group had nourishing sleep, compared to 5% of the control group.

- The level of pain they experienced by the control group was described by them as being at a level of 70%. On the other hand, in the PMR group, pain was 'significantly absent' from the whole of this group.

Therefore the conclusion made by the research team was that PMR significantly reduced pain and made women's physical activities less painful and restrictive, and there was a definite improvement in sleep quality. The researchers concluded in their report that their findings were similar to others in the same area of research: That the pain that mothers who had experienced caesareans was reduced by PMR through the operation of several body systems.

They observed that it reduces the stress hormones of epinephrine (adrenaline), catecholamines and cortisol.

Also, the deep breathing technique used, increases the oxygen levels in the body, and reduces the oxidative factors, and as a result of this, less pain is experienced.

PMR can also:

- restrict the reaction of the sympathetic nervous system (the 'Fight or flight' response)

- and stimulate the parasympathetic response (the 'Rest and digest' part of the autonomic nervous system)

- by restricting the feedback pathway from the brain-mind to the muscles; and as a result, *block* the biological response to pain.

As a consequence, it will normally lower the heart rate, the level of blood pressure and the metabolic rate.

The outcome of the research study, the researchers concluded, was that post- caesarean women who practiced the PMR technique have lower post caesarean pain, a better quality of sleep and a reduced level of restriction on their physical activities than those who received just the routine nursing care.

~~~

And there are several case studies of PMR being used to cure problems of anxiety, available on the Internet today. For examples: Li, Wang, Tang, et al. (2015); Ramasamy, S., Panneerselvam, S., Govindharaj, er al. (2018); McCloughan, LJ, Hanrahan, SJ, Anderson, R. and Halson, SR. (2016); and several others.

How progressive muscle relaxation helps with insomnia

"The reason you can't sleep is because some of your muscles are tense when they shouldn't be. Who is responsible for this tensing? Your grandmother? Your boss? No – you are responsible – you are doing it".

(Jacobson, 1978, page 93)

~~~

(This statement by Jacobson is a little harsh, and unrealistic, given that human beings are largely non-conscious creatures of habit, who are initially wired up by the socialization processes they experience in their family of origin, and their early schooling. A more realist stance would be this: *The reason you can't sleep is because some of your muscles are tense. Let's teach you how to relax them!*)

~~~

Jacobson described several factors that made it difficult for people to get a decent night's sleep. These included:

- having anxieties, cares and worries,

- over-arousal from modern life,

- discomfort about decisions which they had taken, which activated their conscience, and:

- dietary stimulants like tea, alcohol, or lack of food.

Another factor is the job occupations that people have. Many people's jobs keep their minds constantly and fully engaged in their daily work; and being mentally very busy during the day, without breaks, creates tension in the body, and this tension doesn't suddenly evaporate from people's bodies at bedtime.

Jacobson goes on to say: *"You may want to state that when you are tense, you just can't help it. That is what is called a 'good alibi'. If you want to continue to be tense, and need an excuse to do so, all I can say is that your excuses are excellent".* (Jacobson 1978, page 93).

This however is a little harsh, because human beings are largely non-conscious creatures of habit. Jacobson shares with Albert Ellis this tendency towards blaming the (largely non-conscious) client for choosing to stress themselves. This is untrue and unscientific thinking.

Unless and until you are shown that you can tense your muscles; that you are tensing yourself (unwittingly); and how to *stop* tensing yourself; nobody has the right to blame you for your tension.

Jacobson knew from all the years of research that he had undertaken, that when a person relaxes completely, they fall asleep automatically. And clients who suffered from insomnia were over concerned with not sleeping, moving around in bed repeatedly, reorganising their bedding, and generally keeping up tension levels in their bodies. He states: *"What prevents slumber and keeps us awake is quick changes."* (Jacobson 1978, page 106)[28].

He further stated that he had observed a lot of sleepless people and seen that they altered their body positions *repeatedly*, and this was counterproductive because constant movements simply kept the insomnia going. (But he failed to notice that this was not voluntary action, but habitual patterns of movement).

His research findings suggested that individual would fall asleep more quickly and easily at night if they stuck to the daily pattern of practising the PMR relaxation strategies. A tense body with tense muscles will predictably prevent sleep for a long time during the night.

But if you learn to become aware of and to deliberately *let go of* tension in your muscles, slowly you will become more and more relaxed, and you will get the full benefits of a good night's sleep in time. (Aim for at least 8 hours of sleep every night). The more relaxed you are, the quicker you will be able to get to sleep and achieve the mental nourishment that only sleep can give the body.

If you have had insomnia for several years then Jacobson's realistic advice is that you will recover from it less quickly than someone who has had it for a relatively brief period of time: *"If you've got severe, chronic insomnia what you most require is a long course in nervous re-education"*, he stated (Jacobson 1963, page 111).

At this point, Jacobson is being more realistic. Human beings are creatures of habit, and the longer we practice a habit for, the longer it is likely to take us to change that habit.

How to practice the PMR technique

Here are some brief guidelines for doing the PMR practice:

Choose a place where you can be alone for 15 – 20 minutes, for daily practice. Make sure that the room is quiet, and warm enough; and there are no loud sounds to distract you.

Now follow this sequence of activities:

1. Lie on a beach mat or bath towel on the floor; or on a long couch or settee.

2. What you are going to do is *tense up* and then *relax* each of the main muscles of your body, for a count of 5 seconds; and then release the muscles, and focus on the pleasant feeling of relaxation for a count of 10 seconds[7].

Do not tense any muscle to the point of causing pain or a muscle strain. (If you feel a muscle is cramping, stop tensing for a few seconds and try again. If you get cramp in any let muscle, get up and walk around until it goes.)

This process, of tensing and relaxing, helps to educate your body and mind about the distinction between the *feeling* of tension and the *feeling* of relaxation.

Here is the sequence to follow:

(a) Focus your attention on your toes, and curl them. Feel the tension in your toes; hold it for a count of 5 seconds; and relax. Feel the sensation of relaxation for a count of 10 seconds.

(b) Now focus your attention on your feet, and press them both forward, as far as the toes will go. Count to 5 seconds, and then relax completely for 10 seconds.

(c) Next, pull your toes and feet back as far as they will go, to tense your lower legs. Count to 5 seconds, and then relax for 10 seconds. Savour the feeling of relaxation.

---

[7] If you are not used to counting seconds, try this (American) method: Using a normal pace of (silent, mental) speech, count: "One thousand and one; One thousand and two; One thousand and three; One thousand..." etc.

(d) Tense your thigh muscles, by lifting your heels a few millimetres off the floor while keeping your legs straight and tense; hold it for 5 seconds, and relax to the count of 10 seconds.

(e) Now breathe out completely, and contract your abdominal muscles. Hold it for 5 seconds; and relax. Savour the relaxation response for 10 seconds.

(f) Tense your chest: Breathe in until your lungs are full. Tense the muscles of your upper chest and upper back. Count to 5 seconds, and then relax for 10 seconds.

(g) Now raise your shoulders as if trying to get them to reach your ears. Hold it for 5 seconds; release suddenly; and enjoy the feeling of relaxation for 10 seconds.

(h) Next, make fists with your two hands, to tense your hands and forearms. Count to 5 seconds while tensing; and then relax them for 10 seconds.

(i) Tense the front of your upper arms (biceps). Make fists, and fold your arms – keeping your elbows by your sides - so as to try to touch your shoulders with your fists. Hold this muscle tension for the count of 5 seconds; and then release suddenly, and savour the sense of relaxation for the count of 10 seconds.

(j) Tense the back of your upper arms (triceps). With your arms straight, make two fists. Face the back of both fists towards the floor, and straighten both arms as hard and straight as you can. Feel the tension in your triceps for the count of 5 seconds; and then relax to the count of ten seconds.

(k) Tense your neck by pushing your head backwards against the surface you are resting on. Count to 5 seconds, and then relax for 10 seconds.

(l) Now tense your jaw: Bring your teeth together very firmly by biting hard, and pull back the corners of your mouth (but avoid straining or paining your jaw muscles). Count to 5 seconds, and then relax for 10 seconds.

(m) Then, press your lips together tightly, while trying to smile. This will tense your lips and face muscles. Hold it for the count to 5 seconds, and then relax to the count of 10 seconds.

(n) Now press your tongue against the roof of your mouth, behind your front teeth, to tense your tongue and throat. Hold it for the count of 5 seconds; and then relax for 10 seconds.

(o) Squeeze your eyes tightly shut, to tense the muscle around them; and hold the tension for 5 seconds. Then relax for 10 seconds.

(p) Now tense up your forehead by raising your eyebrows. Hold the tension for 5 seconds, and then relax for 10 seconds.

~~~

This whole process will most likely take you six or seven minutes to complete.

When you have done it, treat yourself to a further ten or fifteen minutes of rest, while you savour the feeling of relaxation throughout your body.

I suggest that 15 minutes would be the minimum amount of time for the whole process. When you have finished tensing and relaxing the different parts of your body, then just lie still.

You may find you fall asleep quite naturally and this is a good way to combine learning about your body tension and releasing it, and having a daily siesta. You will feel refreshed, and with renewed energy, after the PMR process is complete. And, of course, you can do supplementary PMR in bed at night, if you are having difficulty getting to sleep.

This is crucial point: For this technique to work, and provide maximum benefit, you need to do this *every day*. Try to make sure you do not miss a session. You will get an energy boost from this relaxation technique; plus big benefits for your heart and blood pressure; and for your stress and anxiety levels. To establish the habit, it is best to have a definite start time – which is the cue to begin. (See Appendix F on habit change).

~~~

The 'abbreviated' progressive muscle relaxation technique

Jacobson's progressive muscle relaxation technique (PMR) has been recognized and acknowledged by health care professionals throughout the world as being very effective in many different healthcare contexts. It is a technique that anyone can learn and use for themselves, and this increases their sense of self-efficacy and control over their bodies. It's also a lot cheaper than drugs and doesn't have the negative side effects that drugs have!

Progressive muscle relaxation technique (PMR) teaches the client to raise their awareness of the muscles in their body; then as they *notice* the tension, slowly letting go of it, in each of the main muscles of the body. If this is done regularly (daily is best), the client become more and more able to spot the tension in their muscles as it arises. And the more they practise, the more they can automatically spot and release unnecessary tension.

A modification was made to Jacobson's PMR technique by Joseph Wolpe (commonly pronounced as 'Welpay'); a South African psychiatrist. This was because Jacobson's original training of his clients in the relaxation process took a long time and was very detailed about the exact procedure for relaxing the muscles. The original version of progressive muscle relaxation stipulated an exercise requirement of one hour a day; and over 50 training sessions (about three muscle groups per session) were considered necessary.

After mastering the basic relaxation exercises, then 'differentiated relaxation' could be added.

This means that to get more benefit for your body and mind, you could experiment with the use of progressive muscle relaxation in everyday life (e.g. when reading and writing at work or when driving a car).

It was recommended that you should use the necessary movements to carry out a daily task, and any muscle groups that were *not needed* to do the activity, were to remain as relaxed as possible.

Practising the full progressive muscle relaxation technique every day, in the way Jacobson recommended, would mean that it could take 3–6 months before a client had learned the technique, so Joseph Wolpe altered the process by reducing its length.

Wolpe, practiced psychiatry in the US; specialised in behaviour therapy; and created a treatment to help desensitize patients with phobias by *exposing them to their fears gradually*, one step at a time).

Wolpe[29] built upon the research findings of Jacobson, and made it clear that relaxation was an *essential* part of systematic desensitisation, which was the name of the treatment he created.

Systematic desensitization has helped many people recover from fear and panic attacks. He used progressive muscle relaxation (PMR) but considered that a shorter version would be more practical for his clients.

So progressive muscle relaxation was re-named as 'abbreviated progressive muscle relaxation training' (APMRT) and this quicker form is still used today, as it is more practical and easy to accomplish, once a person has learned the technique; and it is still very beneficial for the body.

And the version described above is closer to Wolpe than it is to Jacobson.

Conclusion

In this chapter, I have defined PMR (Progressive Muscle Relaxation), and described how and why our muscles become tense and cause us all kinds of health problems. I then cited three case studies which show how effective PMR is when measured scientifically. Then I presented two case studies from 2018 and 2019, which also confirm PMR's effectiveness for the treatment of a range of social/emotional/pain problems. I then looked at the way PMR helps with insomnia.

Subsequently, I described the process of doing PMR so you can do it yourself. And I referred to the fact that Joseph Wolpe has argued for the use of a quicker, easier approach to PMR/desensitization. However, the guidelines that I have offered in this chapter are a quick version of PMR, taking as little as 15 to 20 minutes per day.

Here is a list of some more of the most powerful benefits of PMR that I mentioned in the first part of this chapter; this time from Maria O'Toole (2005). In her encyclopaedia, she states that, when individuals use PMR on a regular basis, they find that:

- there is a reduction in anxiety levels;

- the ability to concentrate is enhanced;

- panic attacks take place less often, if at all;

- creativity and spontaneity are elevated;

- there is an increased feeling of being able to manage emotional mood states;

- people are able to become more adept at facing up to sequenced fearful situations; and finally:

- they have higher levels of self-esteem!

~~~

During the five months in which I (Renata Taylor-Byrne) have been experimenting with doing daily PMR, I have found that:

- the quality of my sleep has improved; and

- my sense of well-being and autonomy has increased;

- my anxiety level has reduced.

Furthermore:

- I have more energy

- My sleep-efficiency has improved: (which means the amount of time that I'm asleep, each night, is higher now, as a proportion of the total amount of time that I'm in bed). And:

- I also fall asleep more quickly than I used to, because I can quickly scan my body for signs of tension and relax any tense muscles, using the knowledge gained from daily practice of Jacobson's/Wolpe's PMR technique.

~~~

At the start of this chapter I quoted the words of Oscar Meyer, a lifelong friend of Edmund Jacobson. I truly agree with his view that, with daily progressive muscle relaxation, we can bring about the use of our 'inner tranquiliser'; which makes us more resilient. I strongly recommend that you give it a try and enjoy the very real benefits!

~~~

Copyright © Renata Taylor-Byrne, Lifestyle Coach/Counsellor

Hebden Bridge, April 2020

~~~

Chapter 5: Dr Jim´s Stress and Anxiety Diet

By Dr Jim Byrne, April 2020

The material in this appendix is extracted from Part 3 of Taylor-Byrne and Byrne (2017).

~~~

Sometimes, your anxiety and panic symptoms may be largely, or significantly, coming from your poor diet and inadequate nutrition.

Sugar, caffeine and alcohol are probably the main culprits; but also junk foods; low nutrient foods; and lack of particular vitamins and minerals - especially selenium; B-vitamins; and omega-3 fatty acids.

~~~

Because I was sensitized to the gut-brain-mind connection – from the earliest days of my counselling career - through my own personal experience of diet and ill health (specifically Candida Albicans overgrowth in my guts), I was alert to new research coming out about similar unconventional insights; including the information that

- trans-fats are linked to problems with lack of control of anger[30];

- caffeine causes a build-up of stress hormones, and can trigger anxiety and panic attacks;

- and research showing that British prisoners who were switched to a diet high in omega-3 fatty acids experienced a reduction in aggressive incidents, fights, etc., with their fellow prisoners.

Furthermore, I occasionally got a depressed or anxious client who had no apparent psychological problem which could be identified as the cause or stimulus for their emotional state; but they were often on a high sugar and yeast diet, and were, in fact, suffering the effects of Candida Albicans overgrowth[31]. Once they changed their diets, in ways that I recommended, their depression and anxiety problems cleared up.

So I learned about the gut-brain-mind connection the hard way; the personal way; and from published research studies; and I also collected empirical evidence of the truth of those insights from my counselling practice!

...

Sections 1 and 2 have been deleted:

3. No universal agreement regarding diet

As far as I can tell, after years of personal research, there is no universal agreement about the precise kind of diet which will promote or reduce stress, although we have some pretty good ideas of some of the major culprits, and some of the main forms of 'best practice'.

As suggested by many other sources of nutritional information, it is advisable to eat lots of fresh fruit and vegetables (if you know you can *tolerate* the fruit!). And, actually, this guideline should be expressed the other way around: Eat *lots of vegetables* and *less* fruit. Fruits contain sugars, and even though they are 'natural sugars', they can still cause problems for our blood-sugar management system. So do not over-consume them. (High GI [glycaemic index] foods push our blood sugar levels too high. See section 4[b] above. And high GI fruits will feed unfriendly gut bacteria, like Candida Albicans, which can result in problems with anxiety, panic and depression; irritability and anger).

Sugars also occur naturally in vegetables, and some people are so sensitive to sugars that they have to reduce their consumption of those vegetables which are highest in such elements as fructans, oligosaccharides, disaccharides, monosaccharaides, and polyols.

These elements are normally referred to by the acronym of FodMaps; and there are some online information sites regarding the nature of FodMaps, and which foods contain them.

~~~

4. Schools of thought on diet

There are many schools of thought on diet and health; perhaps several dozen; or even more. There are many different types of diet in circulation today. ... Vegetarian diets; the Atkins, Ketogenic and Paleo diets (high in meat and fats, and low in carbs); Mediterranean diets; Scandinavian (Nordic) diets; Semi-vegetarian diets; Raw-food diets; Wholefood diets; Macrobiotic (bean) diets; Weight control diets; Low-calorie diets and high calorie diets; Very low calorie diets; Low-carbohydrate diets and high carb diets; Low-fat diets and high fat diets; Crash diets and detox diets. And, of course, the *Metabolic typing diet* ([Atkinson, 2008[32], pages 50-54]: which I tried but found both unhelpful to me, and difficult to implement).

Dr Atkinson's general (non-metabolic typing) advice is probably sound: He suggests that we:

#Avoid trans-fatty acids (found in junk foods);

minimize (meaning 'eat in moderation') saturated fats (found in meat[8], dairy, [organic] eggs and seafood products); avoid refined carbohydrates (like white bread, white rice, white pasta, cakes, biscuits, sweets, bottles of juice and pop drinks, and most breakfast cereals);

avoid sugar (including the sugars found in junk and processed foods);

avoid artificial sweeteners;

avoid refined soya products (because refined soya is [no joke!] seen as unfit for feeding to piglets, as it damages their guts!)

restrict salt consumption to six grams (or one-eighth of an ounce) per day;

---

[8] But beware meat: *The China Study* found that the people who ate the most meat were had the most disease; while the people who at the most vegetables had the best health! (Campbell and Campbell, 2006).

avoid or limit mercury-laden fish. (The only really safe fish left on the planet is Wild Alaskan salmon!) Occasional sardines, or a piece of white fish may be tolerable, but levels of pollution are very high indeed! And some people suffer from adult-onset fish-allergy, which is visible on their skin, but which most likely also affects their moods and emotions. So do not overdo the fish consumption. Two fish meals per week is probably optimal.

Eat at least five portions of vegetables and fruit per day (seven or eight would be better!) But again, there are no 'totally safe' foods. Some vegetables contain high levels of various *sugars* (fructans, oligosaccharides, disaccharides, monosaccharides and polyols [collectively called FODMAPS]); and others contain excessive amounts of *lectins*; both of which can cause inflammation in the bowel

Drink filtered water – at least six to eight glasses per day, to stay hydrated.

Eat as much of your food from organic sources as possible.

And, take nutritional supplements, including a complete multivitamin complex, B-complex, omega-3 fatty acid supplement (like krill oil or cod liver oil)[33]; and friendly gut bacteria (like Acidophilus).

"Your health and mood is intimately linked to the food choices that you make". Dr Mark Atkinson (2008)

~~~

There is *no universal agreement* about what works for anybody, and some researchers now believe that a diet has to be personalized to the individual, because we each have an individual history of environmental effects which impact our genes.

Many experts recommend the **Mediterranean diet -** high in vegetables, fish and olive oil, and low in meat consumption[34]. See, for example: www.nhs.uk/Livewell/Goodfood/Pages/what-is-a-Mediterranean-diet.aspx.

Or (occasionally, but *not* long-term) the *Paleo diet* - high in meat, fish, vegetables, fruit; and excluding (most) grains and dairy. See: thepaleodiet.com/what-to-eat-on-the-Paleo-diet/)[35]. (But this diet probably involves eating *too much meat*, according to Dr Michael Greger (2016)[36]. Meat (which is mostly grain fed) contains a lot of the essential fatty acid (omega-6), but it seems from Dr Greger's argument that we should not have too much of this fatty acid – even though it's essential. It seems we need to watch the ratio of omega-3 to omega-6. (See Simopoulos, 2002)[37]. So the emerging Nordic diet may be worth considering; or the Mediterranean diet, because they both favour fish over meat, with the Nordic involving more fish.

Eating organic foods is one way of minimizing the chemical pollutants that get into our bodies and impair our ability to function healthily in the face of the pressures and strains of daily life, according to Bart Cunningham, PhD.[38] There is also recent research which suggests a link between trans-fats (including hydrogenated fats in processed foods) and aggression, irritability and impatience.[39] And caffeine and sugar will increase your tendency towards anxiety and panic.

5. Stress management advice

The Stress Management Society gives the following advice: "*If you want a strong nervous system, boost your intake of vitamins B, C and E, together with minerals magnesium and zinc. The best source of these nutrients is from food, rather than supplements. So eat a balanced diet of meat, nuts, seeds, fresh fruit and vegetables and oily fish. If you need to snack during the day, try pumpkin or sunflower seeds and fruit, particularly (greenish) bananas. Fresh organic food is the best source. If you can't get fresh, frozen vegetables are a reasonable alternative as much of their nutritional content is retained.*" [40]

We suggest you follow most of this advice, except for the supplementation of vitamins and minerals. Unless you are on a wholly organic diet, your food will be largely denatured and devoid of much nutritional value; you may not know what to eat in order to have 'a balanced diet'; and it you cook your food, you will lose some of the nutrients that are in it; therefore you need to use vitamin and mineral supplements of a good, natural-source quality.

The Stress Management Society also rightly emphasizes the importance of drinking lots of water over the course of the day:

"If you want to deal with stress, drink water. It hydrates every part of the body and brain and helps you to better cope with stressful situations. A good rule is to take a few sips every 15 minutes. The best source is room-temperature still water bought in glass bottles (some plastic bottles can leach chemicals into the water inside) or use a jug filter system that you fill from the tap."

(Stress Management Society, 2012/2016).

---

6. Proportions of food groups

How much protein, carbohydrate and other foods should we eat? There is a lot of emphasis today on having five (six, or seven) portions per day of fruit and vegetables. Before that particular campaign began, the Department of Health (in Britain) and many nutritionists were recommending that about fifty to seventy percent of our daily intake of food should come from complex carbohydrate, such as brown rice, pasta, wholemeal bread, millet, potatoes, and so on. (And this kind of ratio is maintained in the US to this day). About twenty-five percent (they said) should be unsaturated fats, from sources like oily fish, nuts, seeds, cold-pressed oils, like olive oil, flaxseed oil, and so on.

And ideally you need about fifteen percent of your food intake to be in the form of protein sources such as grass fed meat, (especially liver); fish (especially oily varieties [which contain more omega-3 fatty acid], though some white fish is very good for the brain); and eggs (preferably organic free range). Keep the meat proportion low and the fish proportion high, to reduce the omega-6/omega-3 ratio (Simopoulos, 2002).

Increasingly, we see recommendations that about 80% of your dinner plate should be vegetables, with a small amount of protein. Or, in the case of current UK guidelines: 35% grains and legumes; 35% vegetables and fruit;

and the remaining 30% split into three groups: milk and dairy foods (10%); meat, fish and alternatives (10%); and foods containing fat, and foods containing sugar (10%).

The best and safest sources of protein are probably wild Pacific salmon, or wild Alaskan salmon; grass fed lamb; organic, free range chicken; and organic eggs.

7. Food combining, or not

Some theorists believe that combining complex carbohydrates with a protein can reduce stress and provide a solid fuel for daily energy requirements: (Atkinson, 2008: page 57). This, however, contradicts the *Hay Diet*, which recommends keeping carbohydrates and proteins separate, in meals separated by at least four hours! (However, there does not seem to be any scientific studies supporting the Hay approach to food combining – although Renata and I have found it very helpful in reducing indigestion, and promoting efficient elimination).

Others argue that too much carbohydrate, especially refined forms, could cause stress (e.g. Gangwisch, J. et al. (2015) in *ScienceDaily*, 2015)[41]. On the other hand, oily fish, like salmon, mackerel and sardines, with green vegetables and complex carbohydrate are believed to be particularly beneficial. There *are* scientific studies to support the claims about the impact of oily fish on the reduction of panic attacks. For example, Perretta, 2001, page 90).[42]

Cunningham (2001) maintains that fast foods, which are normally high in fats and sugars "...*are stressful to our systems*". (Page 201)[43]. So eliminating fast foods would seem like a sensible precaution as part of a stress management programme. And getting rid of sugar and salt in general from our diets is sometimes said to be a good idea, though some theorists think *a small amount of salt* is needed by the body to function normally. In general, however, western diets are overloaded with salt and sugar, and a vast reduction seems to be called for, as high blood sugar levels are bad for stress levels, and high salt levels are implicated in heart attacks and strokes (according to some experts, and some studies). And caffeine, sugar and alcohol are stressful to the body-brain-mind.

The **Ph Diet** is an interesting one, which emphasizes the general guideline that about 75% of the content of each main meal should comprise vegetables. Pasta, rice and potatoes should never be taken as more than a *small* side dish!

Avoid pizzas, burgers and other processed foods. Additionally, as Nicki Woodward writes:

"Acidifying foods should be reduced in the diet as much as possible".

According to C Vasey, author of The Acid-Alkaline Diet...

"These foods are primarily rich in proteins, carbohydrates and/or fats. Cheese, vegetable oils, hard animal fats, bread, pasta, white sugar all fall into this category".[44]

Sugar and sugary foods are bad; avoid processed foods (especially pastries, pastas and white bread); salt; and minimize saturated dietary fat (as in meat, cheese and eggs).

8. Drinks and drinking

As a general rule, we can definitely say that you could benefit from minimizing your consumption of caffeine (coffee, tea, cocoa, and cola drinks). Also, avoid sugary drinks (like colas, sodas, pops and power drinks/energy drinks). All of these drinks tend to stoke the build-up of anxiety. And avoid alcohol, if you have Candida overgrowth problems. And minimize it otherwise, which means about one unit of alcohol three times per week. Preferably red wine with a meal.

Green tea is good for you. Camomile tea is very calming of the central nervous system.

Minimize milk, as it contains high levels of lactic acid, which is a sugar that feeds candida, and thus triggers depressed feelings. (Very little research has been done, apparently, on the effect of milk upon the emotional states of *adult* humans. However, a significant degree of research has been done on the effect of milk, via migraine reactions, on *children's moods and behaviours*, and the effects can be quite negative and disruptive of brain-mind functioning)[45].

It is important to drink at least six or eight glasses of water per day, preferably mineral water, or a combination of mineral water and filtered water. (Tap water is bad for your health, because of various forms of pollution, like heavy metals and agricultural chemical run-off).

Avoid sugary cola and pop drinks. And minimize alcohol consumption, as suggested above. (Alcohol can trigger anger, aggression, and suicidal ideation and self-harm acts; and it feeds the unfriendly bacterium, Candida Albicans). Perhaps one unit of alcohol three times per week might be tolerable (especially a red wine). More than that and you will damage your health. Alcohol is a depressant which also disturbs your sleep, which has a negative effect upon your mood the following day. Some nutritionists are concerned that 'green smoothies', or regular 'fruit smoothies' may be bad for us, because they give us a quick spike of sugar (fructose and other forms) which raises our stress level. (For example: Dr Thomas Campbell recommends that you, *"Use your mouth and your teeth the way nature intended and put the smoothies aside or have them just as treats."*[46]

9. Fats and oils

Fats are one of the three macronutrients, which are essential for physical and mental health. The other two are protein and carbohydrates. We also need two micronutrients: vitamins and minerals. And we need water.

We need fat for current energy needs; plus energy storage (for later use); and for the building and rebuilding of our cells, including our brain cells; and to produce myelin, which is essential for transmitting signals from brain cell to brain cell. And certain essential fatty acids (EFA's) are important for brain and emotional health.

But even though we need fat, we can also have *too much*.

Most of the important questions about fat remain unanswered (according to Campbell and Campbell, 2006)[47]. The 'diet wars' are as much about fat as any other macronutrient or food group.

Butter is probably quite bad for you (because it is 100% animal fat, and animal fat (and animal-based foods in general) are bad for our general health [according to the China Study, by Campbell and Campbell, 2006]). And margarine is even worse (even though it is vegetable fat – and even though vegetable fat tends to promote health while animal fat reduces it [Campbell and Campbell, 2006: pages 66, and 129-130]). And the reason for the problem with margarine is the chemicals that are used to harden it and colour and flavour it. Most margarines are made from, or contain, trans-fatty acids, which are bad for your body and brain. Some of the chemical processes used in the manufacture of margarine (like bleaching!) are clearly not good for human health! (Source: The Real Food Guide (2017))[48].

A McDonald's Double Cheeseburger is 67% animal fat, and whole cow's milk is 64% animal fat. Very small amounts of animal fat are probably going to be okay, but we have to keep it low. (Campbell and Campbell, 2006).

So small amounts of extra virgin olive oil dribbled on your (gluten free) bread might be better (as demonstrated by the Mediterranean diet), but keep the quantity to about one teaspoon per day, as processing fats uses up your body's water content, which results in dehydration. (You could also try Extra Virgin Coconut Oil, which is solid at room temperature, and can be spread like butter. [However, Patrick Holford[49] recommends cold-pressed seed oils, like flaxseed oil or hemp oil]. But, again, watch out for dehydration by keeping oil consumption low [or you could significantly increase your water consumption?!]).

Avoid all trans-fats, which are found in junk foods, processed food, and most take-way foods. (See Part 1 of this book, section 4(a), above).

According to Campbell and Campbell (2006), we should probably keep our total fat consumption below 30% (although this has not been established as a 'vital threshold'). It is also difficult for us to figure out how much fat we are eating in any case! It's not easy, since all of the main food groups, in the UK National Food Guide, and the US Food Guide Pyramid (renamed My-Pyramid), contain some fat. So, as a general guideline, it is probably best to keep your animal product consumption low, since there is *a strong parallel between increasing animal products and increasing total fat consumption*. And there is also a strong link between increasing the consumption of animal products and increasing disease! (Campbell and Campbell, 2006: page 83, and page 129-130).

We recommend that you keep your dairy products and meat consumption low or very low. You should probably aim for less than 10% of your total calorie consumption from this food group. (You will still be getting plant based fats from the other food groups, and plant based fats are probably better [based on the results of the China Study]).

Make sure you get at least as much omega-3 fatty acid as omega-6. Again this is difficult to calculate and maintain, because most of our foods contain lots of omega-6 fatty acids, and very few contain much omega-3. The best way to do this is to eat oily fish (like salmon, mackerel, tuna and sardines) at least twice each week. And eat lots of nuts and seeds on a regular basis. Since it is very difficult to measure the fats we are eating, it is probably best to choose a good, healthy, balanced diet, like the Mediterranean or the Nordic diets, and stick to those general guidelines. Perhaps also get cookbooks for those diets, and try to be guided by the types of food recommend therein. (But mainly go for plant based foods, and keep meat and dairy products very low).

What about other uses of oils in the kitchen?

For salad dressings, it is probably best to use olive oil.

And what about frying? We tend not to fry anything. I (Jim) usually poach our salmon fillets, in herb-flavoured water, instead of frying them.

But what do the experts say? One BBC blog reported on some recent frying experiments (by Professor Martin Grootveld, at De Montford

University) like this: *'Firstly, try to do less frying, particularly at high temperature. If you are frying, minimise the amount of oil you use, and also take steps to remove the oil from the outside of the fried food, perhaps with a paper towel.*

'To reduce aldehyde (which are noxious chemical products of the frying process) go for an oil or fat high in monounsaturated or saturated lipids (preferably greater than 60% for one or the other, and more than 80% for the two combined), and low in polyunsaturates (less than 20%).

'He thinks the ideal "compromise" oil for cooking purposes is olive oil,

> *"because it is about 76% monounsaturates, 14% saturates and only 10% polyunsaturates - monounsaturates and saturates are much more resistant to oxidation (which produces trans-fats) than are polyunsaturates".'* (Source: Mosley, M., 2015)[50].

If we (Renata and Jim) - very occasionally - fry anything, then we add some butter to the olive oil, which is even better at resisting the oxidation process (which is what produces the aldehydes). And rapeseed oil and goose fat were also found by Prof Grootveld's study to resist the oxidation process (and thus produced a healthier friend food result).

10. Never skip breakfast

Don't skip your breakfast, no matter how late or busy you might be, as you need a solid supply of *food-derived-glucose*, **burning slowly** throughout the morning, to keep your blood sugar level at a suitable and fairly constant level. Porridge or cooked fish make a good, slow-burning breakfast; or wholemeal brown toast and organic eggs. Make sure you eat at least three nutritious meals every day; and have a light snack mid-morning and mid-afternoon, to keep your blood sugar level up. Always eat in a relaxing environment. And avoid simple sugars, as they are seen to over-boost blood sugar levels, precipitating insulin release, and a quick fall back in blood sugar levels, thus reducing energy, concentration, and potentially boosting stress levels via the release of adrenaline.

Some people are so sensitive to sugar that they cannot even cope well with fruit sugar, and those individuals fare better on a diet of seven portions of vegetables per day, and no fruit at all.

The worst kind of breakfast is no breakfast at all!

The next worse kind of breakfasts is one of refined carbohydrate and simple sugars, such as white toast, or any kind of bread made from refined flour; sugary cereals; jams and marmalades; and so on.

The best kind of breakfast (according to some theorists) consists of complex carbohydrate, such as porridge or muesli, combined with a couple of pieces of fresh fruit (if you can tolerate the fructose), such as apples or bananas. (However, in relation to carbohydrate consumption, watch out for *gluten intolerance* in yourself - and it is advisable to only eat gluten-free breakfast cereals (complex, not refined or processed). Also watch out for food intolerances - allergic reactions - and eliminate those foods to which you are currently allergic). You can always consult a nutritional therapist regarding what to eat for your particular needs and problems.

A couple of times per week, a protein breakfast would be good, such as grilled mackerel, kippers, or traditional (organic) bacon and egg, etc. It is best to eat like a "king/queen" at breakfast, to fuel your morning's work. Then have a reasonable lunch, to carry you through the afternoon. And finally, have a light meal in the evening.

PS: Some months back, for several months, I had salad for breakfast, with nuts and seeds and some low-sugar berries. And I seemed to thrive on that!

11. Snacks, supplements and raw food

Mid-morning and mid-afternoon, it is important to have both (small) snacks and (10 minute) naps. The best forms of snacks are probably a handful of nuts or seeds, and a piece of fruit, with a bottle of mineral water or a herbal tea. Brazil nuts are particularly high in selenium and magnesium, which are both calming. Dr John Briffa believes that just three or four Brazil nuts per day can stabilize the moods of anxious individuals.[51]

If you prefer to take a magnesium supplement, then 250 to 400 milligrams per day is probably a good level to take. Some theorists believe milk is particularly helpful, because its calcium content is calming. However, it also contains lactose, which is a form of sugar, and it has been shown to cause emotional problems (Brown, 2017); so watch the consumption level. And the Paleo theorists think dairy products cause inflammation in the guts, which can then cause mood swings. (Plus, 80 or 90% of the serotonin in our bodies is, apparently, produced in our guts!) There is no doubt that many people are lactose intolerant, and we have included a reference to research that shows milk can have a negative impact on mood, emotions and behaviours in children, and, by implication, in adults also.

Raw food is very important, as much cooked food is very low in nutritional content, and especially enzymes, which are essential for digestion: so at least one salad meal per day would seem to be sensible. Furthermore, eating lots of salad vegetables seems like a good idea. (The Chinese would not agree with that, as they think the digestion process is aided by lightly stir-frying vegetables.)

12. Find out for yourself

However there really is no alternative to experimenting with these ideas, and trying to map the effects of particular kinds of food on your energy level and your mood. We do know from scientific studies that caffeine and alcohol are particular causes of concern, in that they stimulate the sympathetic nervous system, pushing your stress level up, causing irritability and anger, anxiety, panic attacks, depression and insomnia. (Perretta, 2001, page 88)[52].

Smoking also tends to increase stress levels, and some recreational drugs are also stressors. Therefore, many alternative health practitioners and nutritionists advocate giving up smoking; reducing alcohol consumption to one unit every other day, or less; avoiding stimulants; and restricting your intake of caffeine to two cups of fresh ground coffee per day, or four cups of tea: (Cunningham, 2001)[53].

Dr John Briffa recommends *complete elimination* of caffeine for individuals who are *"on the anxious side"*. We recommend that you reduce or eliminate smoking; alcohol consumption; and breathing polluted air.

Most practitioners recommend consuming less than two units of alcohol every other day, as a maximum, for men, and half of that for women - (although the latest idea is that there is no such thing as 'a safe level' of alcohol consumption).

It is also advisable to slowly get off tobacco completely. Marijuana has also been implicated in the causation of panic attacks and paranoia. And sugary foods trigger anxiety and panic as an aftereffect of the body's reaction to excess sugar.

13. Supplements and healthy foods

Because modern methods of agriculture have resulted in reduced levels of nutrition in our foods, and many of those foods are further denatured by the food-processing industry, you are strongly advised to take a good quality multivitamin and mineral supplement, plus a full spectrum B-complex, plus iron, magnesium and calcium. Omega-3 fatty acids, in the form of cod liver oil or krill oil. Probiotic supplements are also helpful; plus the amino acid, L-Theanine. You could also try valerian root and liquorice root to calm your central nervous system.

You will also benefit from extra vitamin C (at least one gram per day, and perhaps up to three grams, preferably in powder form).

Perretta (2001) recommends the following foods in particular: avocado; mushrooms; spring greens and spinach; liver; millet; guava and papaya. And a friendly bacteria supplement will support your gut health. And other theorists recommend wild salmon, shrimp, tuna, halibut, yogurt, eggs, cheese, lamb, venison, turkey, grass-fed beef, carrots and green, leafy vegetables.

~~~

14. Finale

Green vegetables are recommended by many nutritionists, and the British Department of Health. And don't forget the oily fish! It aids all brain functions, including managing stress. Best oily fish: Wild Alaskan salmon, (or Wild Pacific salmon) which is available fresh (chilled) or in tins. Also, tinned sardines, which can be with tomato sauce for taste purposes; grilled fresh mackerel; or trout.

And finally, lettuce is a natural tranquillizer[54], so it seems sensible to eat lots of it; and drinking Chamomile tea may also calm the nervous system, and reduce insomnia[55]. But be careful. Everything we put in our digestive system has the potential to produce side-effects; and some investigators have reported anecdotal evidence that Chamomile tea can interfere with antidepressant medication! (See 'Health Unblocked' blog[56]). (Not that we can recommend antidepressant medication, which seems to be no better than a placebo, and has some very nasty side effects which will, predictably, affect a high proportion of the users of these drugs. 'Food is the best medicine'!)

~~~

If you want to check out the areas of agreement and disagreement among medical practitioners on the subject of diet and emotional wellbeing, then take a look at this debate: 'Sugar, Gluten, Paleo, Vegan: 3 Doctors Debate The Best Way To Eat', here: http://www.mindbodygreen.com/ revitalize/ video/sugar-gluten-paleo-vegan-3-doctors- debate-the-best-way-to-eat

And remember: This is not *medical* advice. It is *educational* information. For medical advice, please see your medical practitioner, GP, or holistic, complementary or alternative health physician; or your health coach. For professional advice and help with your diet, please see a registered nutritional therapist or nutritionist.

~~~

Chapter 6: Sleep and anxiety

By Renata Taylor-Byrne (Copyright, 2020)

This chapter has been written as an original contribution to the present book. Many of the ideas in this chapter were developed in my book on sleep science (Taylor-Byrne, 2019). And some of them appeared in a co-authored chapter (5) of Byrne (2018c).

~~~

"Poor sleep itself can dramatically worsen mood, and has been linked to depression and anxiety". Dr Chris Winter (2017, Page 19)[57]

~~~

"People who don't get enough (sleep) are twice as likely... to feel anxious..." Patrick Holford (2008), Page 203; supported by Pearson et al (2006)[58].

~~~

Introduction

Anxiety and sleep bear a 'chicken and egg' relationship to each other. If you are anxious at bedtime, it will be very difficult to get to sleep and stay asleep. And if you get an inadequate night's sleep, in terms of duration or depth of sleep, then you are highly likely to have emotional management problems the following day, including the possibility of heightened levels of anxiety.

In this chapter I will explain the ways in which your sleep patterns can affect your anxiety level, by *reducing it*, or *increasing* it; and present evidence of sleep's crucial role.

The information is organised into four parts:

- Firstly, how our sleep affects our anxiety levels.

- Secondly, a set of strategies which you can use immediately to start improving the quality of your sleep, and thus reducing your anxiety.

- Third, a summary of the key learning points thus far; and:

- Fourth: Six key strategies for protecting your sleep.

~~~

We have already defined anxiety as linked to tension, worried thoughts, and physical changes, such as increased blood pressure; and also a sense of dread, heightened vigilance, and the desire to run away or escape.

Bear in mind that anxiety is a bodily reaction that is an in-built part of how we manage the challenges and pressures of our daily lives.

It is part of being a human animal, and it helps to keep us alive.

As Dr Chris Winter states:

"Vigilance and anxiety can be important reactions. Without them we couldn't awaken to the smell of smoke at night and react to save ourselves and our family. We would simply be too sleepy. Anxiety makes the world go round ... I don't want my surgeon to be a laid back individual. I want her to be a tense bundle of nerves." (Page 81).

However, anxiety levels can get too high; and *without* the regular nourishing and rejuvenating recharge of a decent night's sleep, we can become overly-anxious.

The natural *safety response* of our bodies can become imbalanced or over-reactive.

In the next section, below, I will present two major explanations as to why we need good sleep so that our anxiety levels don't get too high:

How does our sleep affect our anxiety level?

There are at least *two key ways* in which sleep helps us *recover* from the concerns and stresses that we have each day:

(a) Dreams help us process the day's challenges and stressors

"REM (rapid eye movement sleep) takes the painful sting out of difficult, even traumatic emotional episodes you have experienced during the day, offering emotional resolution when you awake the next morning." (Walker, 2017, page 207).

Matthew Walker (2017)[59] – who has done decades of research on sleep and dreaming - considers that rapid eye movement (REM) sleep, which we have every night when we dream, offers a form of *overnight therapy*. That is the theory he has developed after years of research.

Walker's theory – based on taking thousands of MRI[9] scans of sleeping brains - is that the process of rapid eye movement sleep has the power to *reduce* the painful impact of harsh, emotionally upsetting events that have taken place during the day. When we wake from sleep the following morning, there is a reduction in the emotional pain that we experienced.

So, if you felt threatened today, in various ways, resulting in anxious feelings and apprehensions; when you go to sleep tonight, your sleeping brain will rerun those experiences, *without* the emotional content because of the blocking off of noradrenaline (which is a stress hormone); so that, when you awake tomorrow morning, you will no longer have those apprehensions and worries. You can begin again with a (relatively) blank slate.

MRI scans of activity in two parts of the brains of sleeping research subjects - the hippocampus and amygdala - gave researchers the clue that it was *highly likely* that while human beings were dreaming, memories of an emotional nature were being processed.

---

[9] MRI = Magnetic Resonance Imaging, a way to look inside the body and brain, to see what is going on.

So, significantly, one of the brain's stress chemicals, noradrenaline, was shut off whilst this emotional memory processing activity was taking place, Walker (2017) speculated that this *could* mean that distressing memories were being 'rerun' in a peaceful and low stress brain area.

To check out the validity of his theory, Walker and his colleagues assembled a group of young people, all of whom were in a good physical condition, and split them up into two groups. Both groups were shown emotionally – arousing images, while they were in an MRI scanner. The scanner registered their brain's reactions to these images.

The second part of the experiment involved the showing of the same emotion – arousing images, but this time there were two changes: the research participants were asked about their emotional reactions to the images (at the second viewing) and there was a time interval of 12 hours between the two events.

But also there was a further difference: One group saw the images in the evening, and then the following day, after they had a restful sleep. The other group saw the images in the morning and then 12 hours' later on the same day, (in the evening), they were shown the images again.

From the feedback given by the 2 groups, it merged that the group who saw the 2 sets of images in the same day had no chance to mentally digest their negative experiences. States Walker:

"Their deep emotional brain reactions were just as strong and negative, if not more so, at the second viewing compared with the first, and they reported a similarly powerful re-experiencing of painful feelings to boot." "(Page 210)

However, the group who had been able to have a night's restful sleep in between the 2 viewings, reported a marked *reduction* in their emotional responses to the images. The MRI scans also showed a big drop in the reaction to what was seen, in their amygdalas (the part of the brain where emotional and painful feelings are registered). And there was also, Walker states: *"...a reengagement of the rational pre-frontal cortex of the brain after sleep that was helping to maintain a dampening brake influence on emotional reactions."*

Overall, the research findings show that:

- It is *essential* for us humans to have *sufficient dream (REM) sleep*;

- This is *required* for us to be able to *fully restore ourselves* from the stresses and challenges of the previous day.

Which will moderate our anxiety levels, and sustain our emotional intelligence.

~~~

(b) Inadequate sleep reduces our brain's ability to control anxiety and worry

There is a connection between a lack of sleep and our brain's ability to control our *tendency to worry*. In other words, *lack of sleep* makes us worry more and become more anxious.

According to researchers at the University of California, at Berkley, sleep loss increases feelings of anxiety, especially among individuals who are prone to worry. (Nauert, 2018)[60]. The Berkley research report begins like this:

"UC Berkeley researchers have found that a lack of sleep, which is common in anxiety disorders, may play a key role in ramping up the brain regions that contribute to excessive worrying."

*"Neuroscientists have found that sleep deprivation **amplifies** anticipatory anxiety by firing up the brain's amygdala and insular cortex, regions associated with emotional processing. The resulting pattern mimics the abnormal neural activity seen in anxiety disorders."* (Anwar, 2013)[61].

The researchers also suggest that if you can *fix* your sleep problems, you can also *reduce* your anxiety condition.

But how can you fix your sleep problems so that you get high quality sleep, awakening refreshed and recharged each morning, ready for the challenges of the day with a calm body and mind?

~~~

Here are some practical strategies for your guidance:

Strategies to improve the quality of sleep, and reduce anxiety

(a) Cut down on watching or reading bad news

We strongly recommend that you minimize your exposure to daily newspapers, news programmes on TV and radio, and horror stories on the Internet. Plus gossip about stressful news stories.

Why?

You may think that it is *harmless* to read or hear bad news. Or that it's very important to be *well informed!*

But you are a human animal, and you are very likely to respond with distress, concern and anger at much of what you read and hear in news sources. Your body will become tense and stressed, and this will affect your ability to sleep properly.

News bulletins are transmitted all day, every day. Bad news - (and most of the news *is* bad) - arouses *fear* in us, and *needless aggression*, or depression; and we become stressed the more we read or hear about the many wars, tragedies and natural disasters that take place all over the world.

And these are most often things over which we have *no control whatsoever.*

So we have no outlet to relieve our feelings – there's usually *nothing* we can do to improve or help with natural disasters/ criminal behaviour/ ruthless exploitation of humans by their fellow-humans; and so on.

Dr Andrew Weil, in his book, *'Natural Health, Natural Medicine'* (1995)[62] wrote:

"Is it really necessary to know about murders in a distant city or about the latest oil spill or the hideous acts of terrorists? My experience is that a great deal of the most upsetting news is of no relevance to our daily lives, and that when an event is important enough to concern us, we find out about it soon enough."

What Dr.Weil prescribes for his patients is a *'Newsfast'*, so that people can recover from the constant stress arousal effect that bad news has on the body.

And in his book he reminds people to: *"Be aware that news producers select and edit events for journalistic **value**.....stories that **cause anxiety** and **concern** over developments yet to come, have **greater journalistic value** than those that do not."*

When we hear about bad news and read about it constantly, here's what happens: *it creates anxiety and mental turbulence* in our bodies! Our body instantly reacts by turning on the 'fight or flight' response of the autonomic nervous system. Daniel Reid (2003)[63] puts it very concisely: *"When you 'don't worry' your adrenal glands don't secrete stress hormones such as cortisone, which suppress immune response and enervate the nervous system with hypertension".* (Page 319)

So why not give up your news addiction today? Ration yourself to a few key news events every week – such as only reading the Sunday paper(s); only watching the TV news when there is a local or regional emergency you need to know about; and so on.

Too much bad news is bad for sleep. *Because* of the bodily changes taking place, resulting from stress hormones released by bad news, the individual trying to get to sleep is *overstimulated*, which makes sleep much more difficult or even impossible to achieve.

The takeaway message from this information is that if we don't *manage* our intake of bad news, our ability to get a sound night's sleep will suffer, with a knock on effect on our daytime levels of anxiety.

~~~

(b) Alcohol disrupts sleep

"Alcohol is hell on your sleep..."

Winter, 2017, (page 118) [64]

~~~

You may find it difficult to believe, but alcohol *doesn't* help you to sleep! There are two ways in which it actually *destroys* sleep:

Firstly, one of the by-products of alcohol is aldehyde (formed by the oxidation of alcohol) and this blocks a very important part of sleep – rapid eye movement sleep (REM) sleep! This means that no dream sleep (which is very nourishing for the brain) will take place, and problems of poor concentration and fatigue will happen the following day; as well as increased tendencies towards anxiety.

Secondly, alcohol actually *breaks up* sleep, and people wake up frequently, at very short intervals, but because of the brevity of those awakenings, they aren't remembered by the person. But they *are* picked up by brain scans in sleep labs! And because the sleep is broken up, it's not beneficial in the way that normal sleep is; and the full recharging of the alcohol user's energy doesn't take place because their sleep is constantly interrupted.

To summarise the key learning point about alcohol:

It creates problems because of the suppression of rapid eye movement (REM) sleep, which is essential for *processing* the emotions of the day. Without sufficient REM sleep you will enter a new day carrying much of the stress and anxiety and unresolved emotional problems of the previous day.

~~~

(c) Nicotine, found in cigarettes, cigars and pipe tobacco, has several negative effects on sleep:

One negative effect of nicotine is that it speeds up our central nervous system. Nicotine is a stimulant, which means that it acts as *a stressor* on the body. The effect of nicotine on the body is stimulating for the smoker, and that's because the heart starts beating faster, and adrenaline is released into the bloodstream.

The second negative effect is that nicotine activates the stress response. This is because what has been stimulated into action, by ingesting nicotine, is the 'fight or flight' response, and this response makes us tense up our bodies, ready for action. That is why smoking before bedtime will make it difficult to get to sleep: because the nicotine activates the stress response.

Fourthly, nicotine breaks up the 'architecture' of our sleep process. And this means that it affects the *specific pattern* that our sleep follows, which has evolved over thousands of years. This sleep pattern is the pre-ordained, biological sequencing of distinct stages of sleep that we experience during the sleeping process – including shallow sleep, rapid eye movement sleep, (REM), and NREM sleep (Non-rapid eye movement sleep).

Why is this a problem? Nicotine causes fractures in the sleeping process. Consequently, it takes you *longer* to get to sleep if you smoke. And when you *do* get to sleep, you have less slow-wave sleep, (called deep sleep) which is an important loss, because slow wave sleep is *nourishing* for the body and brain[10]. So you awake tired and edgy, and prone to an anxious response to minor problems.

A final point to make here is to inform you of the research findings produced in China in relation to drinking and smoking by adolescents: The less well they slept, the more likely they were to drink alcohol or smoke.[65]

~~~

(d) Caffeine seriously disrupts sleep

Caffeine is a problem because it stops sleep's ability to heal us from anxiety-arousing thoughts and worries. It is a very popular drug, present in tea, coffee, soda, cola, ice-cream, energy drinks, chocolate, pain-killers and weight reduction tablets. And decaffeinated drinks still have caffeine in them. (A 'decaffeinated' coffee drink has roughly 15% to 30% of the amount of a regular cup of coffee, which is definitely not free from caffeine).

And caffeine sticks around for a long time in the body!

A single dose of caffeine takes between five and seven hours to reduce by half, and this means that if someone drank a caffeine-containing drink with an evening meal, then the caffeine would *still* be affecting their brain (at half its original strength) in the early hours of the morning, with a potentially negative effect upon their attempt to sleep. And a further five to seven hours later, the caffeine would be reduced to 25% of the original strength. And during this process sleep could be disrupted, if the original dose of caffeine was strong enough.

A fascinating piece of research was conducted in the 1980's by NASA - (which is the US National Aeronautics and Space Administration) - which was an investigation into the toxicity of stimulant drugs such as caffeine, LSD, amphetamine (speed) and marijuana. The results showed what happened to spiders' attempts to make a web, when injected with a size-appropriate amount of each of those drugs mentioned. The shocking effect of the caffeine injection was apparent in the picture of the webs constructed under the influence of this drug.[66]

The following experiment shows how powerful this stimulant drug is: Christopher Drake, PhD (Associate Professor of Psychiatry and Behavioural Neurosciences at Wayne State University of Medicine in Detroit), ran an experiment into the effects of coffee.[67]

The participants were given caffeine at three different times of the day:

- Six hours before bedtime,

- Three hours before bedtime, and:

- Immediately before bedtime.

All of them showed noticeable effects of the caffeine on their sleep. So even if you have caffeine six hours before bedtime, it will still have a *measurably negative impact* on your sleep.

The results of this experiment are very important, because they show that people *don't realise* they are experiencing negative effects upon their sleep, from the caffeine they drank before bedtime.

They also don't take into account the negative effects of caffeine taken earlier in the day.

But *because* they haven't had enough nourishing, deep sleep, they feel tired. This makes them reach for a coffee, to 'wake them up'. And this coffee leads to poorer sleep on the following night. And so the sleep debt builds up. Shawn Stevenson (2016)[68] describes this process as: *"The vicious cycle of sleep deprivation."*

Two of the hormones which are released under caffeine's influence are adrenaline and cortisol, common stress hormones, which also play a part in affecting people's sleep: the adrenaline switches on our 'fight or flight' response, which is a very powerful protective response of our bodies to the threat of attack. It causes an increased heart rate, high blood pressure and rapid, shallow respiration, and our body temperature increases and causes sweating.

And if there is too much cortisol (a steroid hormone which is released in response to stress) in someone's body, then this affects their ability to sleep at night, and affects the stomach, which is very sensitive to stress hormones. It can cause anxious feelings and a nervous stomach, and feelings of paranoia and panic.

The worst kind of caffeine is **synthetic caffeine**: *Synthetic* caffeine, unlike the caffeine in tea and coffee, is a different substance altogether. It is found in energy drinks, and it comes mostly from large factories in China. The

Nazis created it in 1942, and then subsequently it was manufactured by Monsanto. It is a combination of different types of chemicals. Here is how Dr Mercola[69] describes its effects:

"Just one-fourth of a teaspoon can make your heart race and bring on anxiety. Drink enough energy drinks, one after another quickly enough, and you could find yourself in serious trouble... One tablespoon of synthetic caffeine is equivalent to drinking 50 cups of coffee."

Can you imagine the effect of 50 cups of coffee on your attempt to find sleep? And imagine how many multiples of 5-7 hours it would take to get that over-stimulant out of your system? Energy drinks are clearly very bad for the body, on the basis of this research finding by Dr Mercola. And just imagine how much less anxious a person would feel if they stopped drinking those 'energy drinks'?

~~~

(e) Light, especially blue light is a problem (including from mobile phones, lamps and laptops)

New electronic gadgets can be really appealing and very attractive and efficient, and many people can be influenced into buying them, without being fully aware that the price tag for the gadget might be *more* than financial. There can be a severe physical cost due to the disruptive effects on your sleep.

The evidence for this is shown in the details of an experiment into the effects of iPads and other electronic equipment that use LED lights, (such as mobile phones, and lap top computers) on human beings.

What is LED light?

LED stands for Light Emitting Diodes.

A light-emitting diode is a special kind of diode that glows when electricity passes through it. They are commonly used to illuminate computer screens, iPads, iPhones, etc.)

"Evening blue LED lights have twice the harmful impact on night-time melatonin suppression than the warm, yellow light from old incandescent bulbs, even when their lux intensities are matched." (Walker, 2017)

The blue light, which is emitted by the LED lights, is very powerful (twice as powerful as an ordinary light bulb). But it is also twice as powerful at inhibiting the *release of melatonin* in our bodies/brains in the evening - (and melatonin is *essential* for the onset and maintenance of sleep).

Most people may not be aware that they are making it difficult to sleep by using these devices at night.

Human sensitivity to blue LED light

As human beings, we have a sensitivity to blue LED lights. This sensitivity within us causes a health problem. Here is an example:

Four researchers, Anne-Marie Chang, Daniel Aeschbach, Jeanne F. Duffy and Charles A. Czeisler, decided to find out what the effect of our sensitivity to LED light has on the ability of people to get a good night's sleep, if any.[70]

The research experiment was conducted in 2014. The four researchers, mentioned above, got together a group of adults who didn't have any health problems. Those adults took part in two different processes in which the experimental conditions were different.

The experiment lasted for two weeks in a tightly-controlled laboratory experiment. What the researchers found was that the result of reading on an iPad before going to sleep, as compared to reading a paper-based book, held back the release of melatonin by *over 50%*.

This meant that there was a *delayed* release of melatonin - (the hormone that signals the brain-body to sleep) - by up to three hours. Consequently, their melatonin didn't arrive until early in the morning, instead of late at night.

In other words, when they had read an iPad, it took much longer to get to sleep than when they read a paper-based book. And the negative effect on their melatonin levels lasted for days.

The researchers came to the following conclusion:

"Overall, we found that the use of portable light-emitting devices immediately before bedtime has biological effects that may perpetuate sleep deficiency and disrupt circadian rhythms, both of which can have adverse impacts on performance, health, and safety."

So, if we want to sleep well, get good quality REM sleep, and avoid feeling tired and anxious the following day, we should avoid using any source of LED light after teatime each evening.

~~~

(f) Sleeping pills make the problem worse

> *"Here's some very straightforward advice (about sleeping pills): stop using them. Right now."*

> Nick Littlehales, (2016)[71]

~~~

Many people take sleeping pills if they are suffering from lack of sleep or insomnia, and appear to be convinced that they will help them to get a decent night's sleep.

The case against sleeping pills

On the other hand, Nick Littlehales (2016), who is a leading sleep coach for many world famous top sports teams and athletes, states that one of the *first* jobs that a sports club will request him to do, when they call him in, is to get the sportsmen and women *off* sleeping tablets, because of the drain on the body's energy that they inflict.

There is considerable evidence that it's not possible to take a pill which will eliminate your sleep problems. Dr Chris Winter (2017)[72], explains that he has never seen a research study that shows clear evidence that sleeping pills increase people's sleep by more than a few minutes.

He has also never seen evidence that people get to sleep more than just a couple of minutes quicker than they would without them. So why do millions of people take them?

~~~

Popular lies about sleeping pills

Firstly, he considers that there is a great deal of false and misleading information being transmitted to the American public about sleep. (And what happens in the US today, happens in the UK tomorrow!) The message, repeated regularly by the media, is that if you have difficulty sleeping, all you have to do is take a pill and your problem is solved. Many people believe the popular, public image of sleeping pills as being a normal, risk-free way of getting to sleep at night; because this idea is presented to them repeatedly by the media and the medical profession.

However, taking sleeping pills makes the process of achieving natural sleep much harder, because people become accustomed to taking pills as their first line of defence. But to really solve a sleep problem, they would have to make more of an effort, in examining their lifestyle, and making some lifestyle changes, which seems tougher for them than just putting a pill in their mouth.

An illustration of the strength of the allure of sleeping tablets is that, in 2014, around the globe, people spent *$58 billion dollars* on sleep aid products.

There can be side effects to using sleeping tablets which you may not be aware of:

Arianna Huffington (2017, Page 49)[73] states:

"As so many of us burn out in our efforts to keep up in today's high pressure, always-on world, we've made it easier for the pharmaceutical industry to tighten its grip on us... instead of questioning how we live our lives, we fall prey to the sophisticated marketers that promise us health, happiness, sleep and energy".

In her book, Arianna Huffington (2017) quotes several short examples of the effects of a sleeping medication called Ambien, also known as

Zolpidem. People can sleep walk, or drive in their sleep, run over others and kills them, and worse!

Apparently *the wording on an Ambien packet*, warning the purchaser of the drug about the possible side-effects, is as follows:

"After taking Ambien you may get out of bed while not being fully awake and do an activity that you do not know you are doing. The next morning you may not remember that you did anything during the night." (Huffington, 2017, page 53).

And of course, sleeping pills prevent proper processing of the day's events during sleep, and exhaustion and anxiety may occur the following morning.

~~~

What's wrong with prescribing sleeping pills?

Walker also clarifies that sleeping pills don't provide anyone with restful, rejuvenating sleep. People do go to sleep after taking them. But what is actually going on is this:

- The pills affect the brain in ways that *modify* the *activity* of the brain cells, and thus they share the same way of affecting the body-brain-mind as sedatives do. Sleep takes place, but it is light in nature and there is no nourishing slow-wave sleep taking place.

What is the drawback of not getting enough slow wave sleep? During slow wave sleep there is a reduction in levels of cortisol (which reduces physical tension and anxiety levels), heart rate and blood pressure.[74] None of this happens when people are taking sleeping tablets.

Conclusion

The part played by sleep in helping us handle the challenges we face every day is huge. But how do we ensure we get it?

Here are the key learning points from this chapter followed by six key strategies for protecting your sleep.

Summary of key learning points

1. Respect your sleep needs – make sure that you get a good eight hours' sleep a night, every night. This will ensure that your body has enough time to have dream sleep, in which the anxiety arousing events of the previous day are processed and reduced in intensity.

2. Control your reading or listening to bad news – it will affect your body and mind negatively, and arouse your anxiety and stress levels. And most of it is beyond your control, so don't drain your energy by over-consuming it.

3. If you want to *undermine* the quality of your sleep, the best way to do that is to drink alcohol during the late afternoon and/or in the evening; and/or caffeine from mid–afternoon onwards. Either of or both of those drinks will certainly keep you awake; and if you get to sleep; they will wake you up again later, especially in the case of alcohol.

And caffeine can be in many different types of drinks, such as tea, coffee, 'sports drinks', colas, fizzy drinks, and cocoa and chocolate. With those substances in our body, a decent night's sleep will definitely be prevented or undermined!

And the next day, you will have a sleep debt which will lower your emotional intelligence; spoil your concentration; and make it difficult for you to learn new information or skills.

4. We humans evolved to deal with threats in a physical way, and if we aren't physically active and have exercise of *some* kind, on a daily basis, then we get a build-up of stress hormones in our bodies. And if we *don't* also give our bodies time to 'rest and digest', all the stress hormones we have accumulated stays in our bodies and blocks our ability to sleep.

People who sleep badly are found to have high levels of stress hormones in their bloodstream, which shortens the amount of time they get sleeping, and reduces the nourishing element of the sleep that they *do* have.

5. Controlling the level of light in your bedroom plays a key role in making sure that you get a decent night's sleep. This is because of the way our body clock functions. We are affected by the reduction of light when dusk arrives. From the pineal gland in our brains, melatonin is released into our bloodstream, and it sends a strong signal to the brain that sleep is arriving shortly. Melatonin *in itself* doesn't bring about sleep, but it *signals* to the brain regions that *do* generate sleep, that sleep must be started.

The problem is that melatonin can be held back from being released if there is too much light in the sleeping environment – specifically, in the evening. This means that bright lights can *hold back* the release of this hormone and sleep won't take place until the early hours of the morning, if too much exposure to computer screens, phone screens or bright lights, (especially LED lights), takes place in the evening or during the night.

Controlling the light level in the sleeping environment is therefore a really crucial part of having a decent nights' sleep. People are increasingly 'parking' their mobiles outside their bedrooms so that their sleep won't be affected by the light from the screen.

6. If you have a demanding job, and/or a family to care for, you need a high level of energy to deal with all the challenges involved in those roles. But you need *more* than just physical energy – you also need a good level of emotional intelligence (in order not to wreck your relationships at work or at home). Experiments have shown that, without sleep, our ability to *regulate* our emotions is reduced and weakened. This means that our ability to control our emotions, moods, anxiety level and/or behaviours is reduced, and we have less self-control. Our anger management, empathy, and accurate appraisal of non-verbal communication skills are impaired, with damaging results.

~~~

Six key strategies for protecting your sleep

Firstly, exercise is essential! If you want to have deep, nourishing sleep then you had better do something about the stress chemicals that are in your bloodstream. Stress hormone release is a natural response to the environmental pressures that you are living under. To adapt to the challenges and unpredictability of life, the best technique is to use the response to stress that was *inbuilt* into us as we evolved as human beings thousands of years ago: Physical activity is the best method, because it burns up the stress hormones which are triggered in us by pressure, stress, strain, threats, dangers, and so on.

As human animals, we have evolved to go out every day and engage in physical activity so that we can secure food for ourselves and our families. We also need to *move* our bodies throughout the day, and then rest and recover, as dusk arrives and night darkness approaches. In that way, the frustrations and challenges that people face in their lives are *processed* by physical exercise during the day and this exercise removes the stress hormones from our bodies. And exercising ensures that we have guaranteed for ourselves a very good night's sleep. And during that restful sleep, the stresses and strains of the day are processed, so that we can start all over again the next day with a relatively clean slate – relatively anxiety free.

Secondly, relaxation techniques are another very effective way to improve your sleep. When we relax, we are turning on the 'rest and digest' part of our autonomic (automatic) nervous system, called the *parasympathetic* nervous system.

Your 'relaxation response' is an inbuilt de-tensing, balancing and energy-recharging process, against the effects of the 'fight or flight' response. It relaxes your body, repairs it and helps it to recover from stressful events.

But how do you switch on your 'relaxation response'? You do it by sending messages to your body from your brain, to relax! Benson (1977) considered that because human beings in the modern world are living and working in environments that call for *"continuous behavioural adjustment"* (page 46), this has very negative effects on our blood pressure, making it rise.[75]

However, what he found was evidence that patients suffering from high blood pressure could *lower* their blood pressure by bringing on their "relaxation response" in themselves. And relaxation techniques that reduce the negative effects of the 'fight or flight response' have been very helpful for people who have difficulty getting to sleep.

Alternately tensing and relaxing the different parts of your body means that you can slowly spot the difference between how your body feels when it is *relaxed*, and when it is *physically tensed up*. (See Chapter 4 for an introduction to *Jacobson's Progressive Muscle Relaxation technique*). This increased awareness of your body state helps you to know when to intervene, when you feel your body tensing up, and therefore you can start to drop your tension level as you realise that it is not needed.

When your body is relaxed, your mind is relaxed. And when your body-mind is relaxed, it is easy to get to sleep and to stay asleep. So relaxation can get you to sleep, which will reduce your tendency towards anxiety. But, additionally, physical relaxation switches off the stress response, and lowers your anxiety level directly.

Third: Taking naps will benefit your health and build up your sleep quota. We have an inbuilt, *fundamentally biological* pattern of sleep and rest, which is described as 'bi-phasic', meaning that there are *two* phases to our sleep urge; or *two* times every day when human beings are genetically hard-wired to feel the need for sleep:

- The main one begins in the evening, and lasts throughout the night until after dawn has arrived.

- And the second one occurs in the mid-afternoon, after a lunch-time meal. We experience a drop in energy and alertness *regardless* of the culture that we were brought up in, or the part of the world that we live in. If this daily pattern of energy reduction is accepted and integrated into our working lives, then there are massive benefits - for employers and employees, in terms of productivity and creativity – and also in terms of physical and mental health.

How long should a nap be? There's no universal agreement about how much of a nap you need for it to be effective. Walker (2017) suggests that we aim for 45 to 90 minutes, which is between one half and one full sleep cycle.

On the other hand, Dr Carl Bazil, who runs the Sleep Disorders Centre at Columbia University Medical Centre, says you'll benefit if you have a nap for about twenty minutes.[76]

What you get from a napping period is the chance to catch up on lost sleep, boost your mental energy reserves and recharge your batteries for dealing with people and unexpected challenges, constructively and skilfully. Emotional intelligence is increased, and moods are stabilized.

Fourthly: daily meditation is a simple process which will help you sleep better. The good news is that practising meditation will calm down your body and mind; reduce your anxiety; and help you to sleep better.

If you sit in a meditation posture, and observe your breathing – (See Appendix C, below) - it will slow down your body and mind, which switches on the 'rest and digest' side of the autonomic nervous system. (Which switches off anxiety).

If you practise meditation, which brings on the 'relaxation response', for ten to twenty minutes every day, it will enhance your well-being; improve your sleep; and reduce your anxiety. There will be a reduction in the activity of your sympathetic nervous system. And it will be much easier to fall asleep at night, as you have reduced activity in your nervous system.

Also, meditation increases melatonin - an essential hormone for good quality sleep – which helps us to get to sleep more quickly, and for a prolonged period of time. Melatonin is also necessary for non-rapid eye-movement sleep (NREM), and rapid eye-movement sleep (REM) to take place (which facilitates the processing of emotional experiences).

And, when you are meditating, you are focusing your mind in the present moment, so you cannot at the same time be 'off in the future' feeling anxious about potential threats and dangers.

Fifth: Manage your diet. If you improve our diet, your sleep will improve. In the view of Dr Sara Gottfried, processed drinks like diet soda/ colas/ pop can cause a great deal of damage. We also suffer when we consume agricultural chemicals (from non-organic foods); food additives and preservatives; and chlorinated water; all of which can damage your intestinal bacteria, which disrupts the chemistry of sleep.

There are also several foods and medicines that can destroy the melatonin that we need to sleep well at night. These include: caffeine, tobacco, alcohol; chocolate (in particular, dark chocolate); aspirin; B complex tablets taken close to bedtime; and antidepressants and tranquilisers, such as Prozac.

If you want to eat the right food to help you sleep, you should focus on vegetables, fruits, nuts, seeds, grains (or pseudo grains), and proteins (like organic eggs, feta cheese, and oily fish like salmon and mackerel); and other types of healthy food. But you should also take food supplements as needed, in particular, calcium and magnesium; omega-3 fatty acids; and tart cherries or cherry juice. (See Chapter 5 and Appendix B).

Finally, you need to *process* **stressful events that have happened to you,** which may still be stuck inside of you, causing you stress, which will block your ability to sleep at night. Stress hormones don't naturally *disappear* with the passage of time, if you do nothing about them. You have to *act* to get rid of them!

But how do you reduce your stress?

Exercise is number one priority: move around; walk; practice yoga or Chi Kung; or swim, or go to the gym (but not late in the evening).

Managing your mind to calm it down is probably next. (See Chapter 3 above, on re-framing; and Appendix E, below, on journal writing).

Physical relaxation helps. (See Jacobson's Progressive Muscle Relaxation, in Chapter 4, above; and Appendix A below, on anti-anxiety breathing).

Having a nap helps;

- exercise helps;

- happy relationships help;

- the right kind of diet and exercise makes a big difference;

- and creating the right sleeping environment is also important.

Then there is the idea of 'processing your stuff'; which means getting it off your chest, and out of your mind.

- Keeping a diary or journal is a good way to process your stressors.

- And getting worries and problems off your chest by talking them through is a great help.

You can do that with a close friend; a trained pastoral or mental health counsellor; or a private counsellor/ coach/ mentor. All of these processes can help you to experience peace of mind, which will quickly improve the quality of your sleep. This will work wonders for your anxiety level, reducing it a great deal; before, during and after the sleep process itself!

Sweet dreams!

~~~

Renata Taylor-Byrne, Lifestyle Coach/Counsellor, Hebden Bridge, April 2020

~~~

Chapter 7: Physical exercise for anxiety reduction

By Renata Taylor-Byrne and Jim Byrne (Copyright © 2017/2020)

~~~

> *"Exercise strengthens the entire human machine – the heart, the brain, the blood vessels, the bones, the muscles. The most important thing you can do for your long-term health is lead an active life."*
>
> Dr Timothy Church (2013)[77].

~~~

Preamble

There is lots of evidence that physical exercise can and will reduce your anxiety level. Indeed, some theorists would claim that physical exercise is by far the best approach to working at reducing your anxiety level. (See Sapolsky, 2010).

In Taylor-Byrne and Byrne (2017), we looked at the effects of various approaches to exercise on the emotions of anxiety, anger and depression. In a later book, we summarized much of that research: (Byrne, 2018). In this chapter, we will present some extracts from Chapter 4 of Byrne (2018), specifically related to managing anxiety.

Most of this material results from research done by Renata Taylor-Byrne for our 2017 book.

Physical exercise and emotional wellbeing

Part 2 of Taylor-Byrne and Byrne (2017) was about the relationship between physical exercise and emotional well-being; and the power of exercise to reduce the incidence of anxiety, anger and depression.

Sitting down for long periods of time is now recognized as being linked to both physical disease and emotional disorders.

When we get up and move around, we force our lungs to draw in more oxygen, which is good for us; and we force our lymphatic drainage system to work, which eliminates toxins from our bodies. And provided the movement is not linked to stressful situations, physical movement will burn off stress hormones, including those that drive anxiety.

Thirty minutes of walking per day – in the freshest air you can access - is the minimum that we recommend to lift your mood and reduce your feelings of anxiety or anger. One hour would be significantly better. And the ideal place to walk is near trees and/or a body of water. Alternatively you could walk around a local park, or on minimally polluted roads. (Avoid walking in air polluted by car exhausts).

Exercise and the stress response

In Taylor-Byrne and Byrne (2017), the effectiveness of exercise in reducing stress, in all its forms, was explored. The opinions of the NHS in the UK and the Mayo Clinic in America were cited; and two forms of exercise which are highly rated (Chinese and Indian), were examined.

Normally, when we experience stressful events in our daily lives, if we also have an *active* lifestyle, this physical activity can burn off the stress hormones which would otherwise accumulate in our bodies.

In an emergency (or an apparent emergency), our internal protective mechanism, called the *'fight or flight response'*, will normally mobilise our body-brain-mind, by pouring very powerful stress hormones into our system to empower us to get moving and to resolve the problem we are faced with, in a physical way. This is called *activation of the **sympathetic** system*. The *sympathetic system* gets us into action!

We automatically either fight our way out, or flee; or sometimes freeze.

When we get to a safe place, or have resolved the emergency, and can breathe more easily, the *'rest and digest'* system kicks in and our bodies slowly return to a relaxed state and our digestion returns to normal.

This is called *activation of the **parasympathetic** system*. The *parasympathetic system* calms us down!

Anxiety and physical activity

But if we don't give our bodies a chance to work off the stress hormones, with physical activity, then tension can build up, which can trigger anxiety; and this can accumulate and become a habitual anxiety problem (which some would call 'an anxiety disorder'. But it should not be given such an apparently 'medical' label!) This habitual state of anxiety means that we can feel stressed even when there is no danger in our immediate environment.

An important part of the solution to feeling excessive stress and anxiety is to keep yourself physically fit.

But it is a mistake to think that, because you have a physically demanding job, or housework, that you don't need to exercise.

If your job or housework is itself stressful, it will not be reducing your physical stress level.

Also, it's a mistake to think that competitive sports – like squash, golf, and forms of racing – will help to de-stress your body-mind. This will not happen because competition increases the stress response!

Furthermore, it's best to do eastern than western forms of exercise, because yoga and Chi Kung, for examples, switch on the rest-digest side of the nervous system, as soon as you begin to exercise; while western gym-based exercise systems push up the fight-or-flight response for the whole duration of exercising. (It is only later that western exercise systems allow the stress response to fall away).

And it is also a mistake to exercise after teatime each day, because that will tend to keep you awake well past your normal sleep time, which will tend to trigger anxiety the following morning.

So always try to exercise at the start of the day, or at least before teatime; such as sometime in the afternoon.

Research evidence

How effective is exercise at reducing stress?

This question was answered by the research findings produced by Joshua Broman-Fulks (2008) who recruited two groups of students, 54 in total, and got them exercising[78].

Both sets of students had generalised anxiety disorder and high levels of anxiety, and they normally exercised less than once a week.

One group ran on treadmills (at 60–90% of their maximum heart rates) and the second group walked on treadmills at a rate that was equal to 50% of their maximum heart rates. Each of these two groups had six sessions of the exercise (twenty minutes in length) spread over two weeks.

As a result of the exercise sessions, both groups of students became less sensitive to anxiety, and the more physically demanding exercise produced beneficial results in a shorter period of time.

But why did the exercising work?

In a nutshell, the exercise reduces the tension levels in your muscles (stopping the *anxiety feedback loop* going to your brain). So you stop feeling (psychologically) anxious about feeling (physically) anxious! Or, you stop having *psychological feelings* about your *physical sensations*.

...

Exercise for stress reduction

Dr Robert Sapolsky, who is a professor of biology, neuroscience and neurosurgery at Stanford University in America, has been studying stress management for many years and uses exercise as his favourite way to manage stress.

He points out that one virtue of keeping to an exercise regime, in addition to reducing your stress level, is this:

Whatever the type of exercise might be, when it is regularly practiced, it is very good for providing individuals with a sense of achievement and self-efficacy.

In addition, he makes two key points:

*(1) The stress reducing benefits of exercise will **wear off** if they are not repeated; and:*

*(2) If you do not want to exercise, but are **forced** to do it, then it won't help your health. It has to be **voluntary**, and **personally enjoyable!***

Sapolsky (2010) writes: *"Let rats run voluntarily on a running wheel and their health improves in all sorts of ways. Force them, even when playing great dance music, and their health worsens."* (Page 491)[79].

Finally he recommends that you have a consistent, regular pattern for a prolonged period of time (a minimum of twenty to thirty minutes per session, several times a week) and that you don't overdo it (because it is possible to harm yourself while exercising. For example, by pulling a muscle. This is a particular problem with 'hard' [Western] exercise; and much less of a problem with 'soft' [Eastern} exercises, like yoga and Chi Kung).

Yoga and Chi Kung for emotional self-management

We wanted to look at specific approaches to physical exercise in our earlier book – (Taylor-Byrne and Byrne, 2017). Although brisk walking has been shown to reduce depression and anxiety symptoms, we wanted to look at some of the more formal systems which claim to help with emotional problems.

Therefore, we examined evidence about the value of Qigong (Chi Kung) and yoga, and found that they both have lots of evidence supporting their ability to help people manage anxiety, anger and depression. (See Taylor-Byrne and Byrne, 2017). The best way to get started with either yoga or Chi Kung is to find a public class in your neighbourhood (when the coronavirus pandemic has passed); or view some relevant video clips on YouTube.

We also advocate the use of brisk or relaxed walking, because it is so easy to do, and does not cost anything. We advise against jogging, especially on hard surfaces, because of the damage it does to knee joints.

Press ups and sit backs are a good way to strengthen arms and core muscles; and also to lift your mood. Swimming is a good form of general workout, which is good for body and mind.

Competitive sports tend to push up stress levels; but friendly games and sports can be fun and mood enhancing.

But in general, Eastern 'soft' exercise systems (like yoga and Chi Kung) have bigger up-side advantages, and smaller down-side disadvantages, than Western 'hard' exercise.

...

~~~

Chapter 8: Conclusion

This book began by defining anxiety, and how you can quickly and easily get it under control. This included a discussion of how to manage panic symptoms as well.

We then moved from the general to the specific, with a discussion of nine ways to reframe, or re-think/re-feel, any threat or danger, so that it shows up as less anxiety-arousing. The first six of those frames are particularly helpful for reducing anxiety.

Then we looked at the power of relaxation of your muscles to switch off tension in your body, which will then switch off anxiety feelings in your mind.

Diet, sleep and physical exercise are also important ways of managing your mental strength, and minimizing feelings of anxiety or panic. And those areas of lifestyle self-management were covered in detail in Chapters 5. 6 and 7.

We also referred to the resources in the appendices, below, which will teach you:

- how to use conscious breathing to reduce your anxiety;

- more information on nutrition for emotional control;

- meditation as an anti-anxiety practice;

- three strategies to control worry;

- journal writing to calm your nerves;

- how to change those habits that are linked to your anxiety level;

- and further discussion of how to understand and control your emotions, including anxiety.

~~~

References

Abbas, A. & Haider, A. (2013). 'Generalized anxiety disorder: Can we rest now?' *Pak J Neurological Sciences, Vol.8(1)* - March 2013.

Aftab A, Bhat C, Gunzler D, et.al. (2017) 'Associations among comorbid anxiety, psychiatric symptomatology, and diabetic control in a population with serious mental illness and diabetes: Findings from an interventional randomized controlled trial'. *International Journal of Psychiatry Med. 2018 May; 53(3):* 126-140. doi: 10.1177/0091217417749795. Epub 2017 Dec 27.

Abel, J. L., & Larkin, K. T. (1990). 'Anticipation of Performance among Musicians: Physiological Arousal, Confidence, and State-Anxiety'. *Psychology of Music, 18*(2), 171–182. https://doi.org/ 10.1177/ 0305735690182006

Alternative Health (2017) (The) 'Hay Diet'. A blog about food combining. Available online: https://www.althealth.co.uk/help-and-advice/ diets/ hay-diet/. Accessed: 11th October 2017.

Author unknown (1973/2015) *The Dhammapada.* (Taken from Juan Mascaró's translation and edition, first published in 1973). London: Penguin Books (Little Black Classics No.80)

Amen, D. (2012) *Use your brain to change your life.* London: Piatkus.

Amen, D.G. (2013) *Use Your Brain to Change your Age: Secrets to look, feel, and think younger every day.* London: Piatkus.

Anwar, Y. (2013) 'Tired and edgy? Sleep deprivation boosts anticipatory anxiety'. *Berkley News* (University of California). Online: http://news.berkeley.edu/ 2013/06/25/anticipate-the-worst/. Accessed: 22nd January 2018.

Atkinson, M. (2008) *The Mind Body Bible: Your personalised prescription for total health.* London: Piatkus Books.

Aurelius, M. (1946/1992) *Meditations.* Trans. A.S.L. Farquharson. London: Everyman's Library.

Baikie, K.A., and Wilhelm, K. (2005) Emotional and physical health benefits of expressive writing. *Advances in Psychiatric Treatment, 11:* 338-346.

Ballantyne, C. (2007) 'Fact or Fiction?: Vitamin Supplements Improve Your Health'. *Scientific American* (Online): http://www.scientificamerican.com/ article/fact-or-fiction-vitamin-supplements-improve-health/ May 17, 2007. Accessed 26th April 2016.

Baran, J. (ed) (2003) *365 Nirvana: Here and now.* London: HarperCollins/ Element.

Bargh, J.A. and Chartrand, T.L. (1999) 'The unbearable automaticity of being'. *American Psychologist, 54(7):* 462-479.

Barratt, J.S., Irving, P.M. Shepherd, S.J., et al. (2009) Comparison of the prevalence of fructose and lactose malabsorption across chronic intestinal disorders. *Alimentary Pharmacology and Therapeutics, 2009; 30(2): 165-74.*

Beck, C.J. (1999) *Everyday Zen.* London: Thorsons.

Beezhold, B. L., Johnston, C. S., & Daigle, D. R. (2010) 'Vegetarian diets are associated with healthy mood states: a cross-sectional study in Seventh Day Adventist adults'. *Nutrition Journal, 9,* 26. http://doi.org/ 10.1186/ 1475-2891-9-26

Benson, H. with Klipper, M. (1977) *The Relaxation Response,* London: William Collins Sons &Co. Ltd.

Benton, D., and G. Roberts (1988) Effects of vitamin and mineral supplementation on intelligence in schoolchildren. *The Lancet, Vol 1 (8578),* Pages 140-143.

Bjarnadottir, A. (2016) 'Why Refined Carbs Are Bad For You'. By Adda Bjarnadottir, MS | September, 2015. Available online: https://authority nutrition.com/why-refined-carbs-are-bad/. Accessed: 10th June 2016

Blumenthal, J.A., Smith, P.J., and Hoffman, B.M. (2012) 'Is exercise a viable treatment for depression?' *American College of Sports Medicine Health & Fitness Journal.* July/August; Vol.16 (4): Pages 14–21. doi: 10.1249/01.FIT.0000416000.09526.eb.

Bond, F.W. and Dryden, W. (1996). Why Two, Central REBT Hypotheses Appear Untestable. *Journal of Rational-Emotive & Cognitive-Behaviour Therapy,* 14(1), 29-40.

Borchard, T. (2015) '10 Ways to Cultivate Good Gut Bacteria and Reduce Depression'. *Everyday Health Blog.* Online: http://www.everyday health .com/columns/therese-borchard-sanity-break/ways-cultivate-good-gut-bacteria-reduce-depression/

Bowlby, J. (1988/2005) *A Secure Base.* London: Routledge Classics.

Boyd, D.B. (2003) Insulin and Cancer. *Integrative Cancer Therapies.* Dec 2003. *Vol. 2 (4):* Pages 315-329.

Bravo, J.A., P. Forsythe, M.V. Chew, E. et.al. (2011) Ingestion of Lactobacillus strain regulates emotional behaviour and central GABA receptor expression in a mouse via the vagus nerve. PNAS 2011 108 (38) 16050-16055; published ahead of print. August 29, 2011, doi:10.1073/pnas.1102999108

Bretherton, I. (1992) 'The Origins of Attachment Theory: John Bowlby and Mary Ainsworth'. *Developmental Psychology 28:* 759.

Brewer, S. (2013) *Nutrition: A beginners guide.* London: Oneworld Publications.

Briffa, J. 'High Anxiety', *Observer Magazine,* 19th June 2005, page 61.

Broman-Fulks, J.J., and Storey, K.M. (2008) Evaluation of a brief aerobic exercise intervention for high anxiety sensitivity. *Anxiety Stress Coping. 2008 Apr; 21(2):* Pages 117-28. doi: 10.1080/10615800701762675.

Byrne, J. (2009a) Rethinking the psychological models underpinning Rational Emotive Behaviour Therapy (REBT). E-CENT Paper No.1(a). Hebden Bridge: The Institute for E-CENT. Available online: https://ecent-institute.org/e-cent-articles-and-papers/

Byrne, J. (2009b) 'The 'Individual' and his/her Social Relationships - The E-CENT Perspective'. E-CENT Paper No.9. Hebden Bridge: The Institute for E-CENT. Available online: https://ecent-institute.org/e-cent-articles-and-papers/.

Byrne, J.W. (2016) *Holistic Counselling in Practice: An introduction to the theory and practice of Emotive-Cognitive Embodied-Narrative Therapy.* Original edition. Hebden Bridge: The Institute for E-CENT Publications.

Byrne, J.W. (2018a) *How to Write a New Life for Yourself: Narrative therapy and the writing solution.* Hebden Bridge: The Institute for E-CENT Publications.

Byrne, J. (ed) (2018b) 'CBT and drugs aren't working: How Effective is Cognitive Therapy and Cognitive behavioural Therapy?' A brief review of five pieces of evidence. Online: https://abc-counselling.org/cbt-and-drugs-arent-working/

Byrne, J.W. (2018c) *Lifestyle Counselling and Coaching of the Whole Person: Or how to integrate nutritional insights, physical exercise and sleep coaching into talk therapy.* Hebden Bridge: The Institute for E-CENT Publications.

Byrne, J. (2019a) *A Major Critique of REBT: Revealing the many errors in the foundations of Rational Emotive Behaviour Therapy.* Hebden Bridge: The Institute for E-CENT Publications.

Byrne, J. (2019b) *Facing and Defeating your Emotional Dragons: How to process old traumas, and eliminate undigested pain from your past experience.* Hebden Bridge: The Institute for E-CENT Publications.

Byrne, J.W. (2019c) *Holistic Counselling in Practice: An introduction to the theory and practice of Emotive-Cognitive Embodied-Narrative Therapy. Updated edition (2).* Hebden Bridge: The Institute for E-CENT Publications.

Byrne, J.W. (2020) *The Bamboo Paradox: The limits of human flexibility in a cruel world.* Hebden Bridge: The Institute for E-CENT Publications.

Byrne, J.W. (2020/In press) *Recovery from Childhood Trauma: How I healed my heart and mind - and how you can heal yourself.* Hebden Bridge: The Institute for E-CENT Publications.

Cameron, J. (1992) *The Artist's Way: A spiritual path to higher creativity.* London: Souvenir Books.

Campbell, T. (2014) 'Are smoothies good or bad?' *Newsletter: Centre for Nutrition Studies.* Available online: http://nutritionstudies.org/are-smoothies-good-or-bad/. Accessed: 16th October 2017.

Campbell, T.C. and Campbell, T.M. (2006), *The China Study: Startling implications for diet, weight loss and long-term health*. Dallas, Tx: Benbella Books.

Cardwell, M. (2000) *The Complete A-Z Psychology Handbook. Second edition.* London: Hodder and Stoughton.

Cervio, E, Volta, U, Verri, M. et al. (2007) 'Sera from patients with celiac disease and neurologic disorders evoke a mitochondrial-dependent apoptosis in vitro'. *Gastroenterology. 2007; 133*: 195–206

Chang, A., Aeschbach, D., Duffy, J.A. and Czeisler, C. A. (2015). Evening use of light-emitting eReaders negatively affects sleep, circadian timing, and next-morning alertness. *Proceedings of the National Academy of Sciences of the United States of America.* January 27, 2015. *Volume 112 (4)* Pages: 1232-1237. Available online: https://doi.org/ 10.1073/ pnas.1418490112.

Christensen, L. (1991) The roles of caffeine and sugar in depression, *The Nutrition Report 1991*: 9(5 Pt.1): Pages 691-698.

Coates, G. (2008) *Wanterfall: A practical approach to the understanding and healing of the emotions of everyday life.* An online e-book. Available at this website: http://www.wanterfall.com/Downloads/Wanterfall.pdf. Section 1: The origins of emotions.

Coffman, M.A. (2016) 'The Disadvantages of Junk Food'. A blog post at the 'Healthy Eating' website. Available online at this url: http://healthy eating.sfgate.com/disadvantages-junk-food-1501.html. Accessed on: 30th April 2016.

Collings, J. (1993) *The Ordinary Person's Guide to Extraordinary Health.* London: Aurum Press Ltd.

Cunningham, J. B. (2001) *The Stress Management Sourcebook.* Second edition. Los Angeles: Lowell House.

Damasio, A. R. (1994). *Descartes' Error: Emotion, reason and the human brain.* London, Picador.

Darwin, C. (1872/1965) *The Expression of the Emotions in Man and Animals.* Chicago: University of Chicago Press.

De Bono, E. (1995) *Teach Yourself to Think.* London: Viking/Penguin.

Dhammapada – See Author unknown, above.

Di Sabatino, A. and Corazza, G.R. (2009) 'Coeliac disease'. *Lancet. 2009; 373:* 1480–1493

Drake, C., Roehrs, T., Shambroom, J. and Roth, T. (2013). Caffeine Effects on Sleep Taken: 0, 3, or 6 Hours before Going to Bed. *Journal of Clinical Sleep Medicine.* November 15, 2013. *Volume 9 (11)* Pages: 1195-1200; published online November 15, 2013. Available online: https://dx.doi. org/10.5664%2Fjcsm.3170.

Duhigg, C. (2013) *The Power of Habit: Why we do what we do and how to change.* London: Random House.

Edlund, M. (2011) *The Power of Rest: Why Sleep alone is not enough.* New York: Harper Collins.

Ekman, P. (1993) 'Facial expression and emotion'. *American Psychologist, 48 (4):* Pages 384-392.

Ellis, A. (1958). Rational Psychotherapy, *Journal of General Psychology,* 59, 35-49.

Ellis A. (1962). *Reason and Emotion in Psychotherapy,* New York, Carol Publishing.

Enders, G. (2015) *Gut: The inside story of our body's most under-rated organ.* Scribe Publications.

Epictetus (1991) *The Enchiridion.* New York: Prometheus Books.

Erwin, E. (1997) *Philosophy and Psychotherapy: Razing the troubles of the brain,* London, Sage.

Esterling, B.A., L'Abate, L., Murray, E.J. and Pennebaker, J.W. (1999) Empirical foundations for writing in prevention and psychotherapy: Mental and physical health outcomes. *Clinical Psychology Review, 19(1):* 79-96.

Evans, D. (2003) *Emotion: A very short introduction.* Oxford. Oxford University Press.

Fernandez, C. and Liz Hull (2015/2016) 'Food firms won't join once-a-week warning from pasta sauce maker: They claim their dishes ARE safe to eat every day'. (Dolmio and Uncle Ben's both put warning on their savoury cooking sauces). Published: 15 April 2016. Updated: 16 April 2016. Available online at: https://www.dailymail.co.uk/news/article-3542592/Food-firms-won-t-join-week-warning-pasta-sauce-maker-claim-dishes-safe-eat-day.html

Ford, R.P.K. (2009) 'The gluten syndrome: A neurological disease'. *Medical Hypotheses, Volume 73, Issue 3*: Pages 438 - 440.

Freeman, D. and Freeman, J. (2012) *Anxiety: A very short introduction.* Oxford: Oxford University Press.

Freke, T. (1999) *Zen Made Easy.* Godsfield Press.

Frey, W. H., Hoffman-Ahern, C., Johnson, R. A., et.al. (1983) 'Crying behaviour in the human adult'. *Integrative Psychiatry, 1*, 94–100.

Gangwisch, J. et al. (2015) 'High Glycaemic Index Diet as a Risk Factor for Depression: Analyses from the Women's Health Initiative'. *American Journal of Clinical Nutrition, August 2015.*

Gerhardt, S. (2010) *Why Love Matters: How affection shapes a baby's brain.* London: Routledge.

Gesch, C B. et al (2002) Influence of supplementary vitamins, minerals and essential fatty acids on the antisocial behaviour of young adults. *British Journal of Psychiatry 81*: Pages 22–28.

Gilliland, K. and Andress, D. (1981) Ad Lib caffeine consumption, symptoms of caffeinism and academic performance. *American Journal of Psychiatry, Vol 138 (4),* Pages. 512-514.

Glasser, W. (1984) *Control Theory: A new explanation of how we control our lives.* New York. Harper and Row.

Glasersfeld, E. von (1989) 'Learning as a constructive activity'. In Murphy, P. and Moon, B. (eds) *Developments in Learning and Assessment.* London: Hodder and Stoughton.

Glasser, W. (1999) *Choice Theory: A new psychology of personal freedom.* New York. HarperPerenial.

Gobbi, G, Bouquet, F, Greco, L et al. (1992) 'Coeliac disease, epilepsy and cerebral calcifications'. *Lancet. 1992; 340:* 439–443

Goldacre, B. (2007) 'Patrick Holford's untruthful and unsubstantiated claims about pills': http://www.badscience.net/2007/09/patrick-holdford-unsubstantiated-untruthful/ Accessed 14th April 2016.

Goldacre, B. (2012) *Bad Pharma: How drug companies mislead doctors and harm patients.* London: Fourth Estate.

Golomb, B.A., Evans, M.A., White, H.L., and Dimsdale, J.E. (2012) 'Trans-fat consumption and aggression'. *Online: PLoS One. 2012; 7(3):* e32175. doi:10.1371/journal.pone.0032175. Epub 2012 Mar 5.

Goodyer, P. (2018) 'Preventing depression - Can food rules help?' Online: http://www.smh.com.au/lifestyle/diet-and-fitness/preventing-depression--can-food-rules-help-20151022-gkfolu.html

Goyal, M., Singh, S., Sibinga, E.M.S., et al. (2014) Meditation Programs for Psychological Stress and Well-being: A Systematic Review and Meta-analysis. *JAMA Intern Med.* 2014; 174(3): Pages 357–368. doi:10.1001/jama internmed.2013.13018

Grant, D. and Joice, J. (1984) *Food Combining for Health.* Wellingborough: Thorsons.

Greger, M. (2015) *How Not To Die: Discover the foods scientifically proven to prevent and reverse disease.* London: Macmillan.

Griffin, J. and Tyrrell, I. (2003) *Human Givens: A new approach to emotional health and clear thinking.* Chalvington, East Sussex: HG Publishing.

Hadjivassiliou, M., Gibson, A.; and G.A. Davies-Jones, et al (1996) 'Does cryptic gluten sensitivity play a part in neurological illness?' *The Lancet, Volume 347, Issue 8998,* 10 February 1996, Pages 369-371

Hadjivassiliou, M., Williamson, C.A, and Woodroofe, N. (2004) 'The immunology of gluten sensitivity: beyond the gut'. *Trends Immunol. 2004;* 25: 578–582

Hadjivassiliou, M, Mäki, M, Sanders, DS et al. (2006) Autoantibody targeting of brain and intestinal transglutaminase in gluten ataxia. *Neurology. 2006; 66:* 373–377

Hadjivassiliou, M, Aeschlimann, P, Strigun, A, et.al. (2008) 'Autoantibodies in gluten ataxia recognise a novel neuronal trans-glutaminase'. Ann Neurol. 2008; 64: 332–343

Hadjivassiliou, M., Sanders, D.S.; and Grünewald, R.A., et al (2010) 'Gluten sensitivity: from gut to brain'. The Lancet Neurology, Volume 9, Issue 3, Pages 318 - 330.

Hadjivassiliou, M., Sanders, D.S, and Grünewald, R.A., et.al. (2010) 'The neurology of gluten sensitivity'. Lancet Neurol. 2010; 9: 330–342

Halmos, EP, Power, VA, Shepherd SJ, et al. (2014) 'A Diet Low in FODMAPs Reduces Symptoms of Irritable Bowel Syndrome'. Gastroenterology, 2014; 146(1): 67-75

Hayes, N. (2003) Applied Psychology (Teach Yourself Books). London: Hodder and Stoughton.

Hellmich, N. (2013) 'The best preventative medicine? Exercise'. Online: dailycomet.com. Accessed: 18th June 2016

Hobson, R.F. (1985) Forms of Feeling: The heart of psychotherapy. London: Routledge. Page 88.

Holford, P. (2008) How to Quit without Feeling S**t. London: Piatkus. and:

Holford, P. (2010) Optimum Nutrition for the Mind. London: Piatkus.

Hölzel, BK, Carmody, J., Vangel, M., et al. (2011). 'Mindfulness practice leads to increases in regional brain gray matter density'. Psychiatry Research: Neuroimaging, 2011; 191 (1): 36 DOI: 10.1016/ j.pscychresns. 2010.08.006

Huffington, A. (2016) The Sleep Revolution: Transforming your life one night at a time. London: Penguin. Random House, UK.

Ismail,N., Taha, W., and Elgzar, I. (2018) 'The effect of Progressive muscle relaxation on Post-caesarean section pain, quality of sleep and physical activities limitation'. International Journal of studies in Nursing. Vol 3, No.3 (2018). ISSN (online) DOI: https://doi.org/10.20849/ijsn.v3i3.461.

Jacobson, E. (1963) Tension Control for Businessmen. CT. USA: Martino Publishing.

Jacobson, E. (1978) *You Must Relax: Practical methods of reducing the tensions of modern living. Fifth edition, revised and enlarged.* London: McGraw-Hill Book Company.

Jacobson, E. (1980) *You Must Relax.* London: Unwin Paperbacks.

Karell, K; Louka, AS, Moodie, SJ et al. (2003) 'HLA types in celiac disease patients not carrying the DQA1*05-DQB1*02 (DQ2) heterodimer: results from the European Genetics Cluster on Celiac Disease'. *Human Immunology. 2003; 64:* 469–477

Kashdan, T. and Biswas-Diener, R. (2015) *The Power of Negative Emotion: How anger, guilt and self-doubt are essential to success and fulfilment.* London: Oneworld Publications.

Kiecolt-Glaser, J.K., Belury M.A., Andridge, R., et.al. (2011) 'Omega 3 supplementation lowers inflammation and anxiety in medical students: A randomised, controlled trial'. *Brain, Behaviour, Immunity, Vol.25 (8).* Pages 1725-1734

King, D.S. (1981) 'Can allergic exposure provoke psychological symptoms? A double-blind test'. *Biological Psychiatry, Vol. 16(1):* pages 3-19.

Koskinen, O, Collin, P, Lindfors, K, et.al. (2009) 'Usefulness of small-bowel mucosal transglutaminase-2 specific autoantibody deposits in the diagnosis and follow-up of celiac disease'. *J Clin Gastroenterol.* 2009;

Landsman, J. (2015) The link between gum disease and Alzheimer's. Blog post on Natural Health 365. Online: http://www.naturalhealth365 .com/alzheimers-disease-oral-health-1552.html. Accessed 20th May 2016.

Lawrence, F. (2004) *Not on the Label: What really goes into the food on your plate.* London: Penguin Books.

Lazarides, L. (2002) *Treat Yourself, With Nutritional Therapy.* London: Waterfall 2000.

LeDoux, J. (1996). *The Emotional Brain: The mysterious underpinnings of emotional life,* New York. Simon and Schuster.

Lewis, T., Amini, F. and Lannon, R. (2001) *A General Theory of Love.* New York: Vintage Books.

Li, Y., Wang, R., Tang, J., et al. (2015) 'Progressive muscle relaxation improves anxiety and depression of pulmonary arterial hypertension patients'. *Evidence-based Complementary and Alternative Medicine: eCAM*, 2015, 792895. https://doi.org/10.1155/2015/792895

Littlehales, N. (2016) *Sleep: The myth of 8 hours, the power of naps, and the new plan to recharge body and mind*. London: Penguin, Random House.

Lock, R.S.; D. Pengiran Tengah; D.J. Unsworth; et.al. (2005) 'Ataxia, peripheral neuropathy, and anti-gliadin antibody. Guilt by association?' *Journal of Neurol Neurosurg Psychiatry*. 2005; 76: 1601–1603

Mehrabian, A. (1981) *Silent messages: Implicit communication of emotions and attitudes*. Belmont, CA: Wadsworth (currently distributed by Albert Mehrabian, email: am@kaaj.com)

McCloughan, LJ, Hanrahan, SJ, Anderson, R. *et.al.* (2016) Psychological recovery: Progressive muscle relaxation (PMR), anxiety, and sleep in dancers. *Performance Enhancement & Health. Volume 4, Issues 1–2*, March 2016: Pages 12-17.

McGreevey, S. (2011) Eight weeks to a better brain: Meditation study shows changes associated with awareness, Harvard Science and MGH Communications. Friday, January 21, 2011, Source: http://news.harvard .edu/gazette/story/2011/01/eight-weeks-to...

Meracou, K., Tsoukas, K., Stavrinos, G., et.al. (2019) 'The effect of PMR on emotional competence, depression-anxiety-stress, and sense of coherence, health-related quality of life, and well-being of unemployed people in Greece: An Intervention study'. *EXPLORE, Volume 15, Issue 1*, January–February 2019: Pages 38-46. https://doi.org/10.1016/j.explore.2018.08.001

Mercola, J. (2010) 'Scientists Unlock How Trans Fats Harm Your Arteries'. (Health Blog). Available online: http://articles.mercola.com/ sites/ articles/archive/2010/11/16/scientists-unlock-how-trans-fats-harm-your-arteries.aspx. Accessed: 20th May 2016.

Mercola, J. (2013) 'Vitamin D — One of the Simplest Solutions to Wide-Ranging Health Problems'. Available online: http://articles.mercola.com/ sites/articles/archive/2013/12/22/dr-holick-vitamin-d-benefits.aspx. Accessed 15 June 2016.

Mercola, J. (2019) Pump up Your Performance With Artery-Loving Nitric Oxide *and* Help Fight Free Radical Damage ...'. Online blog: https://products.mercola.com/hydro-nitro/?

Mosley, M. (2015) 'Which oils are best to cook with?' 28th July 2015. BBC: News: Magazine, 28th July 2015. Online: http://www.bbc.co.uk/ news/ magazine-33675975

Mulligan, J. (1997) *Shopping Cart Soldiers.* New York: Scribner/Simon & Schuster. (Paperback novel).

Nauert, R. (2018) Sleep Loss Increases Anxiety – Especially Among Worriers. PsychCentral blog post. https://psychcentral.com/ news/ 2013 /06/27/sleep-loss-increases-anxiety-especially-among-worriers/56531.html

NHS (2007) Understanding alcohol misuse in Scotland: Harmful drinking 3 – Alcohol and self-harm'. 2007. NHS Quality Improvement Scotland. Available online at: http://bit.ly/TbBYAX. Accessed: 28th May 2016.

Noever, R., Cronise, J. and Relwani, R.A. (1995) 'Using spider web patterns to determine toxicity'. *NASA Tech Briefs 19, No.4 82.*

O'Connor, A. (2011) 'Lack of Deep Sleep Tied to Hypertension.' New York Times blog post: https://well.blogs.nytimes.com/2011/08/31/lack-of-deep-sleep-tied-to-hypertension/ (date accessed: 02/12/2018)

Ong, D.K, Mitchell S.B, Barrett J.S, et.al. (2010) 'Manipulation of dietary short chain carbohydrates alters the pattern of hydrogen and methane gas production and genesis of symptoms in patients with irritable bowel syndrome. *Journal of Gastroenterology and Hepatology. 2010 Aug; 25(8):* 1366-73

Owen, M.M. (2019) 'Breathtaking'. *Aeon Magazine.* Available online: https://aeon.co/essays/do-hold-your-breath-on-the-benefits-of-conscious-breathing.

Panksepp, J. (1998) *Affective Neuroscience: The foundations of human and animal emotions.* Oxford University Press.

Panksepp, J. and Lucy Biven (2012) *The Archaeology of Mind: Neuroevolutionary Origins of Human Emotion*: W.W. Norton and Company.

Pearson N.J, Johnson L.L, and Nahin R.L. (2006) 'Insomnia, trouble sleeping, and complementary and alternative medicine: Analysis of the 2002 national health interview survey data'. *Archives of Internal Medicine, Vol.166 (16)*. Pages 1775-1782.

Pennebaker, J.W. (1997) 'Writing about emotional experiences as a therapeutic process'. *Psychological Science, 8(3):* 162.

Pennebaker, J.W. (2002) 'Writing about emotional events: From past to future'. In: S.J. Lepore and J.M. Smythe (eds) *The Writing Cure: How expressive writing promotes health and emotional well-being.* Washington, DC: American Psychological Association.

Perlmutter, D. (2015) *Brain Maker: The power of gut microbes to heal and protect your brain – for life.* London: Hodder and Stoughton.

Perretta, L. (2001) *Brain Food: The essential guide to boosting brain power.* London: Hamlyn.

Perricone, N. (2002) *Dr Nicolas Perricone's Programme: Grow young, get slim, in days.* London: Thorsons.

Pinker, S. (2015) *How the Mind Works.* London: Penguin Random House.

Pinnock, D. (2015) *Anxiety and Depression: Eat your way to better health.* London: Quadrille Publishing Ltd.

Plenke, M. (2015) The Science Behind Why We Should All Be Taking Naps at Work. Online blog (Mic): https://www.mic.com/articles/126102/naps-at-work-increase-productivity. Accessed: 18th April 2020.

Pollard, J. (2002) 'As easy as ABC'. *Life and Style. The Observer.* Sunday 28th July 2002. Available online: https://www.theguardian.com/lifeandstyle/2002/jul/28/ shopping. Accessed: 7th April 2018.

Prochaska, J.O., Norcross, J.C. & DiClemente, C.C. (1998). *Changing for Good.* Reprint edition. New York: Morrow.

Public Health England (2004) 'National Diet & Nutrition Survey: Adults aged 19 to 64'. Volume 5. London: Public Health England; with the Department of Health and the Food Standards Agency.

Raab, D. (2019) 'Calming the Monkey Mind'. *Psychology Today* blog; here: https://www.psychologytoday.com/gb/blog/the-empowerment-diary/201709/calming-the-monkey-mind

Ramasamy, S., Panneerselvam, S., Govindharaj, er al. (2018). Progressive muscle relaxation technique on anxiety and depression among persons affected by leprosy. *Journal of exercise rehabilitation*, 14(3), 375–381. https://doi.org/10.12965/jer.1836158.079

Ratey, J., and Hargerman, E. (2009) *Spark: The revolutionary new science of exercise and the brain.* London: Quercus.

Reid, D. (2003) *The Tao of Detox: The natural way to purify your body for health and longevity.* London: Simon and Schuster.

Ross, J. (2002) *The Mood Cure: Take charge of your emotions in 24 hours using food and supplements.* London: Thorsons.

Sansouci, J. (2011) Nutrition and anxiety. Healthy Crush Blog post. Available online: http://healthycrush.com/nutrition-and-anxiety/. Accessed 20th May 2016.

Sapolsky, R. (2010) *Why Zebras don't get Ulcers. Third Edition.* New York: St Martin's Griffin.

Schiffman, M. (1972) *Self-Therapy Techniques for Personal Growth.* Merlo Park, CA: Self Therapy Press.

Schmidt, D. (2017) Gum disease found to greatly increase risk of cognitive decline. Blog post. Available online at: https://www.naturalhealth 365.com /gum-disease-cognitive-decline-2233.html. Accessed: 15th April 2020.

Schmidt, K., Cowen, P.J., Harmer, C.J., et.al. (2014) Prebiotic intake reduces the waking cortisol response and alters emotional bias in healthy volunteers. *Psychopharmacology* (Berl.) (December 3rd 2014)

Schoenthaler, S.J. (1983) 'The Northern California diet-behaviour program: An empirical evaluation of 3,000 incarcerated juveniles in Stanislaus County Juvenile Hall'. *International Journal of Biosocial Research, Vol 5(2),* Pages 99-106.

Schoenthaler, S.J. (1983) 'The Los Angeles probation department diet behaviour program: An empirical analysis of six institutional settings'. *International Journal of Biosocial Research, Vol 5(2),* Pages 107-117.

Schoenthaler S., et al (1997) 'The effect of randomized vitamin-mineral supplementation on violent and non-violent antisocial behaviour among incarcerated juveniles'. *Journal of Nutritional & Environmental Medicine 7:* Pages 343–352.

Schoenthaler, S., and Bier I. D. (2002) 'Food addiction and criminal behaviour – The California randomized trial'. *Food Allergy and Intolerance. 731–746.*

Schore, A.N. (2015) *Affect Regulation and the Origin of the Self: The Neurobiology of Emotional Development.* London: Routledge.

Shepherd, S.J, Parker, F.J, Muir, J.G and Gibson, P.R. (2008) 'Dietary triggers of abdominal symptoms in patients with irritable bowel syndrome - Randomised placebo-controlled evidence'. *Clinical Gastroenterology and Hepatology. 2008; 6(7):* 765-771: http://www.sciencedirect.com/science/article/pii/S1542356508001511

Siegel, D.J. (2015) *The Developing Mind: How relationships and the brain interact to shape who we are.* London: The Guilford Press.

Simopoulos, A.P. (2002) 'The importance of the ratio of omega-6/omega-3 essential fatty acids'. *Biomedical Pharmacotherapy, Oct 2002, Vol.56 (8):* Pages 365-379.

Singh Khalsa, D. (1997) *Brain Longevity.* London: Century.

Smith, P.K., Cowie, H., and Blades, M. (2011) *Understanding Children's Development. Fifth edition.* Chichester, West Sussex: Wiley.

Stanfield, M. (2008) *Trans Fat: The Time Bomb in your Food: The Killer in the Kitchen.* Souvenir Press: London.

Stevenson, S. (2016) *Sleep Smarter: 21 Essential strategies to sleep your way to a better body, better health and better success,* London: Hay House.

Stress Management Society (2012/2016) Nutritional stress and health: The "Think 'nervous'" box. Available online: http://www.stress.org.uk/Diet-and-nutrition.aspx

Suzuki, S. (2006) *Zen Mind, Beginners Mind.* London: Random House.

Taylor-Byrne, R.E. (2019) *Safeguard Your Sleep and Reap the Rewards: Better health, happiness and resilience.* Hebden Bridge: The Institute for E-CENT Publications.

Taylor-Byrne, R.E. and Byrne, J.W. (2017) *How to control your anger, anxiety and depression, using nutrition and physical activity.* Hebden Bridge: The Institute for E-CENT Publications.

Teychenne, M, Costigan, S, Parker, K. (2015) The association between sedentary behaviour and risk of anxiety: A Systematic Review. *BMC Public Health, 2015.*

The Real Food Guide (2017) 'What is margarine and why is it bad for you?' An online blog: http://therealfoodguide.com/what-is-margarine-and-why-is-it-bad-for-you/

Tkacz, J., et al. (2008) 'Aerobic exercise program reduces anger expression among overweight children'. *Paediatric Exercise Science, 2008 Nov; 20(4):* Pages 390-401.

Tracy, B. (2004) *Goals! How to get everything you want – Faster than you ever thought possible.* San Francisco: Berrett-Koehler Publishers, Inc.

Turner, J.H. (2000) *On the Origins of Human Emotions. A sociological inquiry into the evolution of human affect.* Stanford University Press.

Turner, M., and Barker, J. (2014) *What Business can learn from Sport Psychology.* Oakamoor, USA: Bennion Kearny Ltd.

Van der Veen, F. M.; Evers, E.A.T., Deutz, N.E.P., Schmitt, J.A.J. (2006) Effects of Acute Tryptophan Depletion on Mood and Facial Emotion Perception Related Brain Activation and Performance in Healthy Women with and without a Family History of Depression. *Neuropsycho pharmacology, Vol.32, Issue 1,* Pages 216-224.

Volta, U, De Giorgio, R, Petrolini, N et al. (2002) 'Clinical findings and anti-neuronal antibodies in coeliac disease with neurological disorders'. *Scand J Gastroenterol. 2002; 37:* 1276–1281

Volta, U, De Giorgio, R, Granito, A. et al. (2006) 'Anti-ganglioside antibodies in coeliac disease with neurological disorders'. *Dig Liver Dis.* *2006; 38*: 183–187

Volta, U, Granito, A, Parisi, C. et al. (2009) 'De-amidated gliadin peptide antibodies as a routine test for celiac disease: A prospective analysis'. *J Clin Gastroenterol.* 2009.

Waite, M. (2012) *Paperback Oxford English Dictionary.* *Seventh edition.* Oxford: Oxford University Press.

Wallin, D.A. (2007) *Attachment in Psychotherapy.* New York: Guildford Press.

Waring, A. (2018) *Breathe with Ease.* Gravesend, Kent: Dot Dot Dot Publishing.

Watts, A. (1962/1990) *The Way of Zen.* London: Arkana/Penguin.

Walker, M. (2017) *Why We Sleep.* London: Allen Lane.

Weil, A. (1995) *Natural Health, Natural Medicine*, London: Warner Books.

Winter, C. (2017) *The Sleep Solution: Why your sleep is broken and how to fix it.* Melbourne: Scribe Publications.

Witt, P.N. and Rovner, J.S. (1982) *Spider communication: Mechanisms and ecological Significance.* New Jersey: Princeton University Press.

Wolpe, J. (1968) *Psychotherapy by Reciprocal Inhibition.* Redwood City, Cal: Stanford University Press.

Woodward, N. (2006) 'Stress, Diet and Body Acidification'. *Cellular Chemistry, Issue 130* - December. http://www.positivehealth.com/ article/ alkaline/stress-diet- and-body-acidification

Yu, W. (2012) 'High trans-fat diet predicts aggression: People who eat more hydrogenated oils are more aggressive'. *Scientific American Mind*, July 2012. Online: http://www.scientificamerican.com/ article/high-trans-fat-diet-predicts-aggression/

~~~

Appendix A: How to practise anti-anxiety breathing

The skill of ´belly breathing´ or 'diaphragmatic breathing'

By Jim Byrne, March 2020

~~~

Some theorists believe that correct breathing is central to good physical and mental health; and a cure for anxiety. (Reid, 2003[80]; Waring, 2018[81]).

"There is robust evidence that deep breathing reduces stress and any form of anxiety." (Owen, 2019)[82].

And that is why we are featuring conscious breathing in this book.

The subtitle of Owen's article, in *Aeon Magazine*, is this:

"From first cry to last sigh, we do it without a thought. Yet the benefits of conscious breathing are truly remarkable"

This takes our attention right back to the start of life. If you have ever handled a very young baby, say a few days or weeks old, you cannot help but have noticed that they breathe 'into their bellies'. Well, not literally. They breathe into their lungs. However, in order to fill their lungs fully, they push down their diaphragm muscle – which is a dome-shaped muscle between the bottom of the lungs and the top of the guts – thus expanding the capacity of their lungs. That pushes their bellies out like a balloon.

When I was a child, there was a common practice (in Ireland) of wrapping a 'binder' around babies' bellies, to prevent an *anticipated* rupture of the navel, resulting from the constant expanding of the belly during the baby's inbreath. This is no longer practiced, (and indeed probably died out in the late 18th or early 19th centuries in the UK), and there does not seem to be any problem of navels rupturing today; suggesting that the great expansion of the belly of a baby is perfectly natural and normal and safe.

In time, babies learn to hold their bellies in, and to breathe further up in the chest. This marks the onset of social anxieties of various levels of intensity. I have never met a teenager or twenty-something who breathes into their belly; because the resulting shape of the belly is considered socially unacceptable. And young soldiers are taught to stick their chests out, and breathe into the top of their lungs.

Later, in their thirties and forties, many men and women let their belly muscles go, through excess consumption of calories, and lack of physical exercise; but they still breathe further up in their chests.

Broadly speaking, belly breathing is relaxed, natural breathing; and upper chest breathing is anxious, unnatural breathing, which can be shallow and slow (or held); or it can be more like panting.

The earliest theorists to spot the problem of upper chest breathing, and the lack of conscious awareness of our breathing, were probably the Taoists in ancient China, and the Buddhists in India, and later in Japan; and some Sufi mystics in the Middle East.

For example, Reid (2003) quotes Sun Ssu-mo, a Tang dynasty physician, as writing this:

"When correct breathing is practised, the myriad ailments will not occur. When breathing is depressed or strained, all sorts of disease will occur".

Reid (2003) had earlier described our breath as the bridge between our body and mind. It is, after all, the only vital life function that can be controlled consciously. By understanding this fact, and consciously controlling your own breathing, you thus become capable improving your psycho-physical functioning. "At the same time", writes Reid, "it calms the mind, pacifies the emotions and banishes stress by switching off the 'fight or flight' action circuit of the autonomic nervous system, thereby stopping secretions of stress hormones such as adrenaline and cortisol". (Pages 90-91, Reid, 2003).

Owen (2019) draws attention to some additional theories and theorists, like this:

"...A prominent 14th-century Sufi[83], declared that: 'The more that one is able to be conscious of one's breathing, the stronger is one's inner life'."

Owen goes on to write that: "In the Taoist text the *Zhuangzi*, it is said that ordinary (wo)men breathe 'from their throats', but that the sage breathes 'from his/her heels' (with his/her whole body)." This is not quite explicit belly breathing, but it is at least conscious breathing of a very deep nature.

Owen (2019) then described the meditation teacher he met on a particular retreat, who was "...true to her Buddhist association: one of the Buddha's best-known discourses (the Ānāpānasati Sutta) is dedicated to 16 styles of meditative breathing, a practice that, according to the Zen master Thich Nhat Hanh, can enable us to 'look carefully, long, and deeply, see the nature of all things, and arrive at liberation'. In all forms of Buddhist meditation, the breath is used as an anchor with which to steady the ship of incessant and corrosive cogitation; endlessly directing your attention there aims at a 'one-pointedness' of mind that promises an end to suffering." Including the suffering of worry, anxiety and panic.

And, of course, Yoga, from India, is famously linked to the idea of the importance of breathing deeply and consciously. According to Owen: You might be familiar with the experience of going to a (yoga) class in need of a decent workout, and finding yourself cross-legged on the floor, placing a thumb over alternating nostrils for long stretches of time..." and breathing deeply.

How to practice belly breathing

To return to natural, conscious, deep breathing, in order to reduce your anxiety level, proceed like this:

1. Place a towel on a carpeted floor, and lie down. Keep your feet flat on the floor, and let your legs form an 'A' shape, with knees close together and pointing at the ceiling. Also, place a two-inch thick book under your head. This arrangement allows your spine to flatten onto the floor.

2. Place your left hand on your upper chest and the right hand on your belly, just below your rib cage.

3. Breathe slowly in through your nose. Push your diaphragm downwards as far as possible, which will push your belly out. (If you can't easily feel how to do this, at first, just persist, and it will become

obvious after a while. If it continues to elude you, take a look at a belly breathing video clip on YouTube!) Your left hand, on your chest, should remain still, while the right hand, on your belly, should rise significantly as you breathe in. Pause for one or two seconds.

4. Then release your breath, which will flow out quite naturally through your nose. Your right hand, on your belly, will move down to its original position, as your belly naturally returns to its normal level of flatness.

5. Repeat this process, breathing slowly and deeply, over and over again, for about 10 to 15 minutes per day. (To get the habit established, you can start off at three to five minutes per day).

It is not essential to practice this form of breathing on the floor. You could do it in an armchair, or even on a dining chair. Just stick to placing one hand on your chest, and one on your belly. Keep your spine erect. Always breathe through your nose; and hold the breath, for one or two seconds, at the end of both the in-breath and the out-breath.

~~~

What will you gain if you practice this form of belly breathing?

According to Daniel Reid (2003):

"Anxiety and anger evaporate into thin air, body and mind relax and release their tension, and a soothing state of calm flows like a wave through the entire system. A state of anxiety or anger simply cannot be sustained when the breath is consciously kept slow, deep and diaphragmatic, because deep breathing immediately switches the nervous system off the 'fight or flight' action circuit and shuts off the flow of stress hormones and neurotransmitters". (Page 91).

~~~

Appendix B: More on nutrition and emotions

The content of this appendix first appeared as Part 1 of our book on the link between diet and exercise, on the one hand, and anger, anxiety and depression, on the other: (Taylor-Byrne and Byrne, 2017)

~~~

Part 1: Diet, nutrition and the implications for anger, anxiety and depression management

By Renata Taylor-Byrne

> *"Unfortunately, in my experience, most people do not have a clue about how their physical health affects their cognitive and mental health".*

> Dr Daniel Amen[84]

~~~

1. Introduction

What we eat has a very powerful effect on our bodies and minds. And knowing and understanding how our body-mind *reacts* to the substances we feed ourselves is a crucial part of self-care.

For instance: (anxiety) can be caused by psychological reactions to (threats and dangers). But it can also be caused by certain kinds of body-brain chemistry problems, some of which can begin in the guts, and be related to bad diet, and lack of physical exercise. ...

...

Also, we can really benefit from knowing some of the latest ideas about where - (in our diets) - our depression, anxiety and anger can originate from; as developed by specialists who have devoted their lives to years of investigation into the workings of the human body and mind (or body-mind).

Firstly, then, in these pages, I will be defining nutrition, and what the constituents of a balanced diet are (in so far as that is possible), based on research evidence. (See Chapter 5, above).

Secondly, the views of health professionals, including medical doctors, neuroscientists, psychiatrists and nutrition researchers will be reviewed, in relation to the effects of the following substances on the body-brain-mind: transfats; sugar; alcohol; caffeine; processed food (and junk food); and gluten.

Thirdly, I will look at the question: Do we need supplements? The reasons for their usage will be considered; and arguments, from a few experts, will be presented, showing that it's not possible to gain all the nutrition we need from our food (under modern conditions of food production).

...

Finally, which diet is best for physical and mental well-being?

And which lifestyle practices complement and enhance the value of a healthy diet? Some of the research findings, which answer these questions, will be reviewed; and the key ideas of doctors, and other specialists - who know the interconnectedness of our dietary and lifestyle practices, on the one hand, and our physical and emotional states, on the other - will be summarised.

...

2. Why is nutrition important to the body-brain-mind?

Before we get to the link between nutrition and the health of the body and emotional well-being, we must lay some groundwork.

Firstly, what is nutrition?

According to the Oxford English Dictionary (2012)[85] it is the process of taking in and absorbing nutrients. Nutrients are those substances which are essential for life and growth. These nutrients are used by the body to maintain the growth, upkeep and reproduction of the cells.

Nutrition is very important for the body because without the energy we get from food we would not be able to move our bodies, or take part in any work activities, search for food, or communicate with other people. And we would quickly die, because our existence is not determined by our acts of will.

We are physical-social-animals, who are guided by innate emotions; who learn refined emotions from our family and schooling. We are body-mind-environment wholes, and we cannot think or feel independently of the use of brain food (like glucose, and essential fatty acids: [...]), which comes from our diet; (plus oxygen which is optimized by our physical activity, which promotes deep breathing).

Our full physical and mental development is dependent on the food that we eat. Without sufficient food we would not grow, our bodies would be stunted and our physical organs would be undeveloped; and the development of our brain would be irrevocably harmed.

We need high quality nutrition so that the body can repair itself, wounds can heal and cells can repair themselves as necessary. Our immune system needs a supply of high quality nutrients to keep it strong. In this way, viruses, infections and diseases can be kept out of the body.

There are many processes going on in the body and they need energy to work properly. Let's look at the example of the digestive system. Brewer (2013)[86] cites the amount of energy used up by the body when it is digesting food, which is 10% of the total energy gained from a meal. And our brains can use up to 40% of our consumed energy.

Nutrition is therefore crucial for the human body and brain. Without it, we could not survive or function in the world.

3. What would a *balanced diet* look like?

(And how do we know we are getting enough protein[87], carbohydrate[88], fats[89], and vitamins[90] & minerals[91]?).

There are lots of different diets around today, recommended for physical health, weight loss, weight gain, lower cholesterol, and so on. And increasingly, attention is turning to the link between diet and mood.

There is no universal agreement about the precise kind of diet which will promote good physical health and/ or stable moods and emotions; though elements of potentially 'good practice' and 'bad' practices are beginning to emerge.

It would be impossible to list, and discuss, in a book of this scale, all of the diets which are represented in the popular bookshops today. However, there are some important diets that we must at least touch upon in this book.

So let me just suggest the *rough* proportions of each food group that we ought to think about eating. You will need to adjust these proportions on the basis of how your body-brain-mind responds to particular foods:

Vegetables (mainly) with some fruit =	40%
(Wholegrain) Bread, other (wholegrain) cereals and (sweet) potatoes =	20%
Nuts, seeds, beans, organic eggs, wild Alaskan salmon, sardines, and (very occasional) meat (like a weekly lamb steak; or twice or three times weekly if grass-fed) =	25%

Milk and dairy foods (or oat or nut or rice alternatives) =	10%
Sugary foods =	5%

Avoid all transfats, and processed oils, and margarine. Minimal use of butter. Avoid all sugar and products with added sugar.

Avoid 'fish and chips' (because of the transfats and acrylamides), crisps, sweets, cakes, biscuits, processed foods (in packets, jars and cans, from supermarkets, etc.) Avoid white sliced bread, and soft sliced bread, even if it has been dyed to look somewhat brown. Buy wholegrain breads from artisan bakers (if you can tolerate grains at all!), rather than highly processed breads. Avoid or minimize alcohol and caffeine, sugary drinks, diet sodas and pops, and processed foods of all kinds.

The different emphases between our (personal) selection and proportions, on the one hand, and those of the UK NFG, on the other, reflects our researches on the subject over a number of years, and the fact that we cannot be lobbied by commercial interests! However, our ideas come from the books we've studied, and the theorists by whom we have been influenced. And the rule – that there is no *universal* agreement about diet and nutrition – applies just as much to *our ideas* as to the ideas of anybody else!

Our ideas also come from our own experiments, in trying different combinations of food, or different diets, and monitoring the effects upon our skin, mood and energy levels. And recently, one of us has had to give up *virtually* all grains – with the exception of two or three gluten free pies each week – because he (Jim) was suffering bad skin allergies and linked mood problems.

So you have to make your own mind up, by research and experimentation, and with professional support from your medical advisor/ GP/ alternative practitioner (although, it seems from *some* [anecdotal] reports that *at least some* GPs will not advise you on diet unless you ask – as they prefer to prescribe 'high-tech solutions' [like drugs] to their patient's problems).

You need to find out: *What works for you? What keeps you healthy? What causes reactions, in terms of energy or mood, or skin allergies, or digestive distress?*

And you need to face up to the fact that 'pills' cannot cure diseases which are caused by lifestyle 'sins', like eating junk foods and avoiding physical activity.

You might find some of the ideas in the following diets useful, interesting or helpful. From these, and other ideas in this book, you should try to craft your own *personalized diet* (which is discussed at the end of the section).

~~~

The Anti-Candida diet: Candida overgrowth in the large intestine has been linked to symptoms of depression and anxiety. The main components of this kind of diet involves the exclusion of sugary and yeasty foods. Junk foods and all forms of processed food should also be eliminated. Avoid bread and cheese, and all forms of fermented foods, including vinegar, beer, mushrooms. Also avoid foods which are loaded with antibiotics, like pig meats, factory-farmed chicken, non-organic eggs, and some others. Low carbohydrate foods are favoured, plus complex carbohydrates (like fresh vegetables, or gluten-free wholegrains); so using some elements of the Atkins or Paleo diets (below), *for a period of some weeks,* may often be indicated. But check with a qualified and recommended nutritional therapist, and avoid long-term use in case you suffer from nutritional deficiencies.

...

The 'FodMaps' diet: Most people are aware that sugars occur naturally in fruits, and that too much fruit can be bad for your blood-glucose level, triggering problems that could promote diabetes, plus fluctuating moods (as in manic depression). And sugar can also increase stress levels. But most people are probably unaware that many **vegetables** contain high levels of various kinds of sugars, which have been shown to be implicated in the causation of irritable bowel syndrome (IBS). This is where the 'FodMaps' diet can be helpful. FODMAP is the rather clumsy acronym for Fermentable Oligosaccharides, Disaccharides, Monosaccharides, and Polyols, which can be found in a range of vegetables. You can find lists of foods to exclude on a low-FodMaps diet in specialist books and on Internet blogs. Those kinds of low-FodMap diets have now been shown, scientifically[92], to control IBS symptoms, and some people have found them helpful for controlling Candida Albicans (which thrives on sugars of all kinds) - and of course, there is a link from Candida to depression, and so the low-FodMap diet can help to reduce and/or eliminate depression by reducing sugars and inflammation.

But make sure you get most of your nutrients (70% or more) from vegetables (40+%) and wholegrains (20% - if you can tolerate them); and try to get some nutritional expertise to support you, to avoid nutritional deficiencies. (One of us [Jim] has found he can no longer tolerate grains, because they cause him to have very sore and painful allergic reactions; and there is now evidence that allergic skin reactions can precipitate emotional/psychological problems; or rather, that the allergen provokes both skin reactions and mood reactions [See King, 1981][93]).

~~~

The Hay diet: This diet was developed by Dr William Howard Hay, beginning in 1904, as a way to cure himself from 'Bright's Disease' (which included high blood pressure, kidney disease, and a dilated heart), at a time when he had been told he would die from his condition. He saved his own life (and lost 50 pounds in weight, in just three months) by exploring the idea that some foods fight with other foods, and thus slow down the digestive process, allowing toxic waste products to linger much longer in the colon[94]. For example, he would argue that, if it takes a slice of bread X hours to travel from mouth to anus, and it takes a lamb chop twice as long to make the same journey, then combining the bread and lamb will take eight times as long, or more. (In actuality: *"Gut transit time is only 36 hours for vegetarians compared with 72 hours for meat eaters".* [Collings, 1993: page 29][95]. But Grant and Joice, 1984, would argue that those times could be significantly reduced by changing some of the food combinations eaten by both vegetarians and meat eaters!)

More generally, according to the Hay diet, if we combine starches and proteins in the same meal, then we slow down the digestive system to dangerous levels. Dr Hay's idea was that rapid elimination of waste products from the digestive system leads to a healthy body, while slow and sluggish elimination leads to ill health. There is no scientific evidence that this diet works, but there is anecdotal evidence. The authors of this present book have both used the Hay Diet, on and off, to varying degrees, for decades, and found it helpful in promoting efficient digestion.

(Efficient digestion is also taken up by Enders 2015. Dr Enders emphasizes chewing each mouthful of food at least 50 times, and using a squat toilet [or simulating a squat toilet], to promote efficient 'in and out' processes! To simulate a squat toilet, if you do not have one, simply put a foot stool, of say 6-9 inches in height, in front of your toilet; sit on the seat, and place your feet on the stool. It certainly accelerates the process!)

One website blog suggests that the Hay diet may be able to help with *"depression, schizophrenic and aggressive behaviours"*[96]. However, like the other diets in this book, you should not engage with this diet without the support of a qualified nutritionist, as nutritional deficiencies and insufficiencies may result from uninformed or ill-informed changes.

Because you can eat almost anything (apart from peanuts and margarine – and junk foods) on the Hay diet, so long as you combine them properly, there is less concern about the possibility of nutritional deficiencies.

~~~

Mediterranean diet: This diet, or versions of this diet, are eaten in many Mediterranean countries (such as Spain and Italy and parts of Greece) – and followers of the Mediterranean lifestyle also emphasize the importance of appropriate levels of physical exercise, and family mealtimes. According to some authors, the Mediterranean diet consists mainly of cereals, grains, vegetables, beans, fruits, and nuts, combined with moderate amounts of fish, cheese, olive oil; plus wine and a small amount of red meat (grass fed!) So it seems, on this basis, to be a high carbohydrate, low protein diet. However, we were unhappy with the looseness of this definition, and so we searched further, and found this: *"The Mediterranean diet is **a way of eating** rather than a formal diet plan. It* *features foods eaten in Greece, Spain, southern Italy and France, and other countries that border the Mediterranean Sea"*: (WebMD, 2017).

There are some studies which suggest that the Mediterranean diet can be helpful in managing moods and emotions, and especially in eliminating or preventing depression: (for example, Rahe, Unrath, and Berger, 2014).

The WebMD blog goes on to list typical components of the Mediterranean diet, as follows: "*The Mediterranean diet emphasizes eating foods like fish, fruits, vegetables, beans, high-fibre breads and whole grains, nuts, and olive oil. Meat, cheese, and sweets are very limited. The recommended foods are rich with monounsaturated fats, fibre, and omega-3 fatty acids.*"

The proportions are not mentioned, but it is precisely the proportions which matter here. Too much bread and whole grains, and not enough fish, and depression is the result! Similarly with too much meat and cheese, and not enough vegetables and fruits.

Omega-3 and omega-6 (unsaturated) fatty acids are essential for physical and mental health, and have to be obtained from our diet. The omega-6s are *more than adequately represented* in most modern diets. The omega-3s can be obtained from eating oily fish – like salmon, mackerel, sardines, and also from nuts and seeds. (The best seeds are flax, hemp, pumpkin, sunflower and sesame [Holford, 2010]). And/or you can supplement omega-3 from krill oil or cod liver oil. (...).

The evidence for the efficacy of omega-3 fatty acids in combatting heart disease, cancer and other physical diseases is patchy and conflictual (according to Greger, 2016; Campbell and Campbell, 2006); but the research evidence for the human need for omega-3 for brain health, and for mood and emotion regulation, is much more robust (Greger, 2016; Barasi, 2003; Perlmutter, 2015; Holford, 2010; Logan, 2004; Ross, 2003 [See quote in footnote][97]; Kiecolt-Glaser et al, 2011; Simopoulos, 2002; Schoenthaler, 1983a, 1983b[98]; and Gesch et al, 2002[99]). So make sure you get a good daily intake of omega-3 fatty acids, from food or supplements, or preferably both; and make sure you get more omega-3 than omega-6, by eating lots of oily fish, and minimizing your grain-fed meat consumption.

We recommend that you avoid grains that contain gluten. See the Mayo Clinic blog on alternative whole grains[100].

The Mediterranean diet is a good basis for beginning to develop your own personalized diet. But we will show later that the Nordic diet might have more to recommend it, because it contains more fish. (See Brewer, 2013, on the role of fish in preventing and/ or curing depression).

...

The Nordic/Scandinavian diet: The Nordic diet, which is eaten in Norway, Sweden, Finland and Denmark, is similar to the Mediterranean diet, in that it is about eating local, seasonal foods. It involves eating less meat than the traditional British or American diets, and instead eating lots of fish. Portions are relatively small, so they do not overindulge. And they eat home-cooked food, in a relaxed, family environment.

According to one blog: "*The Nordic Diet encourages an all-round healthy lifestyle including exercise, avoiding junk food, upping your fruit and veg intake and reducing the dairy and fat in your diet.*"[101]

According to a new book, by Trina Hahnemann, on the Nordic diet:

"*The Nordic Diet isn't a prescriptive weight-loss plan. It's about getting back to basics so that you can make a real difference to your health, waistline and happiness. But that does mean making a few changes to the way we eat now:*

"*Meals must be balanced with a focus on whole grains and seasonal produce.* (But, firstly: choose gluten free whole grains. See the Mayo Clinic guidelines in footnote 100 at the end of this book. And, secondly: watch out. High carb diets, of big portions, can build blood sugar levels to dangerous degrees, precipitating stress, mood fluctuations, and even type-2 diabetes! So, thirdly: we would prefer to focus on the fish, vegetables and fruit in this diet, and keep the grains low [if you can tolerate them at all]!)

"*Cooking from scratch is a must, including baking your own bread.*

"*Eat less often, avoid sugar, too much salt and junk food and exercise for at least thirty minutes every day.*

"*Up your fruit and vegetables - aim for six portions a day.*

"Eat veggie meals and fish twice a week at least; limit meat to three meals a week and cut back on dairy. (We think this point should be number 1, and not number 5! And fish three times per week would be better!)

"Enjoy cooking and eating! The kitchen should be the centre-point of your house and mealtimes should be shared with friends and family as much as possible.

"Take time over your food. Lay the table even if you're eating alone, sit down and eat slowly - a meal should take 30 minutes to eat.

"Food should be naturally healthy so you don't have to count calories".[102]

But will this help with your emotional self-management?

The *Sydney Morning Herald* (online) carries a report about new guidelines produced by the International Society for Nutritional Psychiatry Research which validates three standard diets which may help to alleviate or prevent depression: the Mediterranean, *Norwegian* or Japanese diets![103] And oily fish, high in omega-3 fatty acids are a big part of the Nordic diet (as we interpret it!), and this is good for brain health and mood control.

On the other hand, the Nordic diet may contain a little too much meat; and they favour grains over vegetables. We think you should reverse that priority. In general, we have detected some agreement around the following ideas:

The Nordic diet probably has a better balance of omega-3/omega-6 than the Mediterranean diet, and that is an advantage. We should aim to balance our omega-3 and omega-6 intake, so that it is close to 1:1. It could be a little higher, 2:1, or even 3:1. But lower is probably better. (...).

It is, however, very difficult to *calculate* how much of each of these essential fatty acids we are consuming, so a general guideline might be this: Keep your meat consumption super-low (below the Nordic level, and even possibly below the Mediterranean level [say one meat-based meal per 7-10 days {unless it's grass-fed, in which case two or three meals per week might be okay, according to the Nordic diet guidelines]); and keep your fish consumption (including oily fish) quite high (at about the Nordic level [of, say, two to three fish-based meals per week]).

(Another kind of fat – apart from omega-3 - which is important for cognitive and emotive functioning – including major depression, schizophrenia and bipolar disorder - is called 'phospholipids', which are used in building brain cell walls, and in promoting communication between brain cells[104]. The most important of these is probably phosphatidylserine. "It's manufactured by the body but can also be obtained through dietary sources such as meat, fish, white beans, barley, and soy lecithin. Notably, mackerel and cod, contain significant levels of phosphatidyl-serine")[105].

~~~

...

Vegetarian diet: Dr Michael Greger (2016: ix) presents evidence from his personal life - (in the case of his grandmother's health problems) - that giving up the meat-heavy, Standard American Diet (SAD), and adopting a vegetarian diet, combined with exercise, was able to transform her health and mobility. On the other hand there is at least one scientific study which suggests there is no solid evidence that a vegetarian diet is either better or worse for mental health (according to Michalak, Zhang and Jacobi, 2012)[106]. Then again, the China Study, a respectable 25-years study of the eating habits of thousands of people in China, suggested that animal-based foods are not necessary, while *people who ate the most plant based foods were the healthiest"*. (Campbell and Campbell, 2006).

And the China study seems to be supported by Beezhold, Johnson and Daigle (2010) – cited in Greger (2016), page 201 - who conducted a study with Seventh Day Adventists which seems to support the view that *"eating less meat isn't just good for us physically; it's good for us emotionally too"*. (Greger, 2016, page 201). One way to interpret the results was to assume that eating less meat reduced the amount of arachidonic acid[107] (which is an omega-6 fatty acid) in the body, thus ***reducing*** inflammation in general, including brain-based neuro-inflammation). (This is important because there are some studies which suggest that depression, and perhaps the other major emotional disorders, are linked to inflammation).

We could also use this research to justify a *low-meat diet*, rather than a completely vegetarian diet. (But there is no evidence that a completely vegetarian diet will worsen emotional states, provided B12 and omega-3 are acquired via supplements).

(But remember, with regard to vegetables, that the low-FodMaps diet suggests that some vegetables are too high in sugars, [for some people, {some of the time?}]; so we may have to be selective in the vegetables we eat if we are highly sensitive to sugars).

~~~

Personalized diet: The safest way to follow healthy diets seems to us to be this: Get a couple of good recipe books which emphasize the kinds of foods found in elements of the Mediterranean, Nordic, and Vegetarian diets; and Chapter 11 of the China Study, which emphasizes eight principles of food and health. And, if you can afford it, consult a good nutritional therapist.

According to Leslie Korn:

"No single diet is right for everyone. Each person has a different cultural-genetic heritage and therefore a different metabolism. Some people like the Inuit require mostly meat and fish, whereas people from India do well on a predominance of legumes, vegetables, fruits, and grains. Most people require a mix. However, that mix of food can vary greatly. Know your ancestral and genetic heritage and try to eat for your individual metabolic type". (Page 14, Korn, 2016).

But one thing we can safely predict, based upon scientific studies which are cited in this book: No race of people will ever exist who can, for long, remain physically and mentally healthy on a junk food diet; or an inadequate diet in terms of nutrients![108], [109].

Invest time and effort in shopping for raw ingredients, and spend time in the kitchen engaging in food preparation.

Make more than fifty percent of your meals raw salads, combined with nuts, seeds and fruits. Eat lots of plant based proteins: [such as, vegetables (avocado, broccoli, spinach, kale, peas, and sweet potato), legumes (such as lentils and beans), nuts and seeds (including sesame, sunflower, almonds, walnuts, and hazelnuts), non-dairy milk (almond, coconut, and/or oat milk), gluten-free grains (quinoa, amaranth, and buckwheat [if you can tolerate them]). And take Spirulina and Chlorella for their nutrient and protein content.]. Supplement with: Vitamins B, C and E (at the very least!); plus omega-3 fatty acids (as in fish oils), Co-enzyme-Q10 (Footnote[110]), and live acidophilus and other live bacteria[111]. Use some fermented foods, like Miso and sauerkraut. Chew your food well, and use a squat-toilet (if at all possible) to optimize elimination. (And if you don't have a squat toilet, use a foot stool – sit on the toilet with your feet on the stool [of 9-12 inches in height] - to simulate that squatting position). Drink eight glasses of filter water per day. Do the reading, and find out for yourself. Monitor the effects of dietary changes on your moods, emotions and energy levels, and adjust accordingly.

The best way to do that is to keep a food diary for a few weeks, and record everything you eat and drink. And also record your exercise and sleep patterns. And check each day to see how you feel: *Is your energy up or down since yesterday? Is your mood up or down since yesterday? Do you feel physically better or worse than yesterday? Any sign of skin allergies?* And if any of those indicators is negative, that should be linked back to what you ate 24 to 30 hours earlier [approximately]. Plus what has been happening during those 24 to 30 hours: like sleep disturbance; lack of physical exercise; increased stress from any source; the emergence of a problem that you feel you cannot handle; and so on. (If you can't track it back on your own, see a professional helper to support you).

And consult a suitable nutritionist, medical expert or health coach, when and if necessary.

~~~

(b) Some general dietary guidelines

If we can generalize at all, it is advisable to eat lots of fresh vegetables and fruit: seven or eight portions per day (mainly vegetables, and much less fruit [because fruit contains fruit sugars, which can raise your blood glucose levels to problematical levels]!)

Many experts recommend the *Mediterranean diet.* Some recommend the *Okinawa diet.* Or the *Nordic* diet. And some the *Paleo diet,* though we have reservations about the Paleo/ Atkins/ Ketogenic diets, which will be discussed later.

The safest way to *begin* is probably to follow the UK National Food Guide (or the US equivalent 'food pyramid'), or our variation on that set of guidelines. (See the start of section 3(a) of Part 1, above).

Eating organic wholefoods is one way of minimizing the chemical pollutants that get into our bodies and impair our ability to function healthily in the face of the pressures and strains of daily life, according to Bart Cunningham, PhD.[112] Patrick Holford (2010) recommends that we eat (gluten-free) wholegrains, lentils, beans, nuts, seeds, fresh fruit and vegetables, and avoid refined, white and overcooked foods. (But we think he should have emphasised fish and vegetables before grains, lentils and beans. [Fish twice per week is probably optimal for most people. Some might be able to handle three times. But others need to be careful they do not provoke an allergic reaction to fish!]).

There is also recent research which suggests a link between trans-fats (including hydrogenated fats in processed foods) and aggression, irritability and impatience.[113]

But which fruits and vegetables should we eat? Patrick Holford (2010) recommends dark green, leafy and root vegetables. He lists spinach, carrots, broccoli, sweet potatoes, green beans, and Brussels sprouts. He favours eating (as much as possible) raw or lightly cooked. Salad vegetables make an energizing breakfast. Holford suggests, also, that we choose berries, apples, melon, pears, or citrus fruits. He suggests moderation in the consumption of bananas, because of the high sugar content. For this reason, we should also limit out consumption of dried fruits (to something like 6-10 raisins or sultanas, etc., per meal). Kiwis and blueberries are low GI (Glycaemic index, or sugar content). Variety is the key. Keep the sugar content low, especially if you are particularly sensitive to fruit and vegetable sugars. (See the FodMaps diet, and the Anti-Candida diet).

The Stress Management Society gives the following advice: "*If you want a strong nervous system, boost your intake of vitamins B, C and E, together with minerals magnesium and zinc. The best source of these nutrients is from food, rather than supplements. So eat a balanced diet of meat, nuts, seeds, fresh fruit and vegetables and oily fish. If you need to snack during the day, try pumpkin or sunflower seeds and fruit, particularly bananas. Fresh organic food is the best source. If you can't get fresh, frozen vegetables are a reasonable alternative as much of their nutritional content is retained.*" [114] (However, it may be that a low-meat, high vegetable, moderate carbohydrate diet is best: Greger (2016), page 67 and 201-203).

We suggest you follow most of the advice of the Stress Management Society, except for the supplementation of vitamins and minerals; and it's probably best to *keep your meat consumption low*. Unless you are on a wholly organic diet, your food will be largely denatured and devoid of much nutritional value; therefore you need to use vitamin and mineral supplements of a good, natural-source quality.

It seems to be important to keep your meat consumption low – not just for red meat, but also for white meats. Meats seem to increase the omega-6 fatty acids (including arachidonic acid) in the body (perhaps because they are mostly grain fed, instead of grass fed). Dr Michael Greger writes that: *"...Maybe the pro-inflammatory compound arachidonic acid found in animal products can 'adversely impact mental health via a cascade of neuro-inflammation'."*[115]

And Greger also states that (non-organic) chicken and eggs are also a problem because of their omega-6 (arachidonic acid) content! So perhaps you should eat those foods in moderation. (And only the organic variety, because grass-fed animals are high in omega-3 fatty acids, while grain fed animals are high in omega-6).

~~~

Some theorists believe that combining complex carbohydrates with a protein can reduce stress and provide a solid fuel for daily energy requirements (Holford, 2010). This, however, contradicts the *Hay diet*, which recommends keeping carbohydrates and proteins separate, in meals separated by at least four hours! (You could experiment with the Hay diet to see if it works for you). Others argue that too much carbohydrate could cause stress – and it is reliably established that refined carbohydrates ('junk foods' – like white bread, processed cereals, sugar, sugary drinks, etc.,) do cause stress and other problems in the body. (See the section on 'sugar' below).

On the other hand, oily fish - like salmon, mackerel and sardines - with green vegetables and complex carbohydrate (like whole grains [which are gluten free]) - are believed to be particularly beneficial.

Patrick Holford recommends five servings of fruits and vegetables per day; and four or more servings of wholegrains. (A serving, roughly, is half a cup of cooked green vegetables, or one whole apple or banana, or one slice of bread. For more precise guidelines, you can search online for a definition of a "serving").

There are scientific studies to support the claims about the impact of oily fish (which contain essential fatty acids [especially omega-3's]) on the reduction of panic attacks, for example. (Perretta, 2001, page 90)[116]. So eating oily fish at least twice each week seems to be a sensible step for good brain health.

...

Some people are fructose intolerant – including people who suffer from Candida Albicans[117], or IBS).

~~~

The Stress Management Society, in the UK, emphasizes the importance of drinking lots of water over the course of the day:

"If you want to deal with stress, drink water", they write. *"It hydrates every part of the body* and *brain and helps you to better cope with stressful situations. A good rule is to take a few sips every 15 minutes. The best source is room-temperature still water bought in glass bottles (some plastic bottles can leach chemicals into the water inside) or use a jug filter system that you fill from the tap."*

(Stress Management Society, 2012/2016)[118].

~~~

4. What kinds of foods should we avoid for the sake of our physical, mental, and emotional health and wellbeing?

"The food you eat can be either the safest, most powerful form of medicine or the slowest form of poison" Ann Wigmore[119]

We should avoid food that has been <u>processed</u>, including processed meats, trans-fats (or hydrogenated super-heated oils), fried foods, sugar and sugary refined grains, and alcohol; and we should minimise our intake of saturated fat from meat and dairy products (Holford, 2010). We also need to avoid gluten and excess caffeine. All of these food stuffs cause problems for our bodies (or body-brain-minds). Each of these foods will be described next, and the effects on the body-brain-mind will be outlined.

(a) Trans-fats:

"Trans fat is lethal". Stanfield (2008)[120]

Trans-fats are vegetable oils (which, in their original form, are healthy) but they are *industrially processed*. The industrial process adds hydrogen to vegetable oil, which causes the oil to become solid at room temperature. And the process of hydrogenating these vegetable oils results in unsaturated fatty acids, which are 'rogue' fat molecules: (Stanfield, 2008).

What happens is as follows: The industrial process consists of boiling the vegetable oils at a temperature above 260 degrees centigrade. Because of the intense heat, the atomic structure of the oil is altered, the reason being that the molecules in the oil have been vibrated so much. This means that, when they are consumed by a human, the trans-fatty acids raise serum levels of LDL-cholesterol (or "bad" cholesterol), and reduces levels of HDL-cholesterol, (or "good" cholesterol), and can promote inflammation[121] in the body. This can cause endothelial dysfunction, and influence other risk factors for cardiovascular diseases.

The motivation of 'food technologists' for damaging oil in this way is this: The partially hydrogenated oil is less likely to spoil, so foods cooked or mixed with trans-fats have a longer shelf life. Some restaurants use partially hydrogenated vegetable oil in their deep fryers, because it doesn't have to be changed as often as do other oils. So convenience is traded for health!

In bakeries, trans-fats are used as a cheaper alternative to butter, so we find these fats in bakery goods such as cakes, biscuits, snack bars (including 'healthy' energy cereal bars). It is also found in takeaway food: *"Sometimes as much as 40% of their overall fat content can be trans fats"*. (Stanfield, 2008).

The effects of trans-fats on the body-brain-mind are wide-ranging. These completely unnatural, man-made fats, cause *chaos* in your body-brain on a cellular level and stop natural biological processes taking place. Studies have linked trans-fats to cancer because they interfere with enzymes your body uses to fight cancer. And there is at least one major study linking trans-fats to angry outburst and problems with rage[122].

These fats can cause diabetes because they interfere with the insulin receptors in your cell membranes; and they cause obesity. And trans-fats can cause major clogging of your arteries. (Among women with underlying coronary heart disease, eating trans-fats increases the risk of a sudden heart attack, ***threefold***).

Maggie Stanfield stated in her book that: *"Just one doughnut a day that contains trans-fats could be increasing your risk of heart disease fivefold"*.

Trans-fats even interfere with your body's use of beneficial omega-3 fats, (which are essential for maintaining your brain!) and have been linked to an increase in asthma. (Dr Mercola, 2010)[123]. And anything that reduces the beneficial effects of omega-3 fats, also invite the development of depression and anxiety in the consumer.

Eating diets rich in omega-3 fatty acids, as in oily fish, like salmon and sardines, and taking omega-3 supplements, like cod liver oil, or krill oil, can improve physical health and emotional stability.

See the section on 'Fats and oils', in Part 3, below, for advice on how to choose and use healthy oils in the kitchen.

~~~

(b) Sugar

"Avoid any form of sugar, and foods with added sugar". Holford (2010, Page 428).

Julia Ross, a psychotherapist based in California, wrote a very useful book titled 'The Mood Cure'[124]. This was based on her research findings into natural nutritional solutions to emotional problems, implemented at her clinic. She found that sugar was a big part of the mood problems her clients encountered. She writes: *"Many of our clinic's clients have been freed from the moodiness they've endured for years, simply by dropping sugar and refined white flour starches from their menus. No supplements, no other changes, dietary or otherwise, were required"*. (Page 122, Ross, 2002)

Sugar is described as one of the most addictive substances on the planet, and it was imported into Europe in the 1100's as a prized drug. It was considered so valuable that apothecaries kept it under lock and key, and the slave trade was created in order that there could be cheaper and quicker ways of gaining access to this highly addictive substance.

Dr Daniel Amen (2012)[125] describes sugar as: *"Toxic calories"*. But why? Here are some of the reasons:

Firstly, sugar is a *refined*[126] carbohydrate. There are different types of sugars: white and brown sugar, honey, (raw and processed) molasses, cane sugar, many artificial sugars, fruit drinks and natural fruit juices without the fibre.

Sugar is *eight* times more addictive than cocaine. It creates fat around our organs, and contributes towards premature ageing.

It takes the body a long time to get rid of sugar from the immune system. For as long as 4-6 hours after eating sugar, your immune system will still be damped down and recovering, because sugar and the immune system are enemies.

Sugar doesn't just reduce immune function but is also likely to cause diabetes and lead to obesity, both of which conditions will lower your mood. It increases inflammation in the body; causes brain cells to fire erratically, and can send blood sugar levels *"on a roller-coaster ride"* (Amen, 2012).

Many scientists believe that if you have very high insulin levels, as a result of consuming sugar, then this can contribute to cancer. (Boyd, 2003)[127]. Sugar affects our digestion in negative ways, leading to bloating, cramps, sluggishness and headaches. And it destroys *collagen*[128], which is one of the most important building blocks of the human body.

All types of sugars are 'fast releasing' which means that they deliver a high glycaemic load which stimulates a rise in blood sugar levels. And high blood sugar leads to a stress response, including anger and/or anxiety.

Why is this bad for the body-brain-mind? What happens is that the body-mind responds to this sudden increase in sugar in the bloodstream by releasing insulin, which then propels the sugar into the cells. This can overload the cells, so if there is too much sugar, this is transformed into a substance called glycogen, which is stored in the liver and muscles.

When that storage capacity has been reached, the rest is stored as fat. In addition, as suggested earlier, white sugar has had about 90% of its vitamins and minerals removed. Too much sugar increases adrenaline[129] - (the stress hormone – known in the US as 'epinephrine') - to a great extent, which negatively impacts our moods and emotions.

Here is an example of what happens: Researchers at Yale University in the US gave 25 healthy children a drink which had the equivalent amount of energy that was in a popular soft drink.

The next thing that happened is called the *'Rebound blood sugar drop'*. When there is a fast increase in the amount of sugar in the blood, then insulin overcompensates for this by taking too much sugar out of circulation. This results in a compensatory increase in the children's adrenaline to over five times its normal level, for up to five hours after taking in the sugar. And if there is too much adrenaline in the bloodstream this results in irritability and anxiety, and the children also had difficulty concentrating: (Holford, 2007)[130].

Finally, sugar is very bad for our teeth, because the bacteria in our mouths are fed by sugar. And poor dental and gum health are now linked to

Alzheimer's disease and heart disease.[131] Because the brain is so close to the gums and teeth, dental health is closely linked to brain-mind health.

~~~

(c) Alcohol

"Alcohol acts just like sugar, biochemically, only more so. It contains more calories per gram and gets into your bloodstream faster". (Ross, 2002)

~~~

"As soon as you start to get drunk, you are damaging your brain". (Holford, 2010)

~~~

Alcohol is defined by the Oxford English dictionary as: '*A colourless, volatile flammable liquid which is produced by the natural fermentation of sugars and is the intoxicating constituent of wine, beer, spirits, and other drinks, and is also used as an industrial solvent and as fuel'.*

What is the effect on the body? The physical effects of alcohol are as follows: Firstly, 20% of it goes straight into our bloodstream, and what is left is taken in all over the body. It can permeate almost every biological structure of the body because cell membranes are extremely permeable to alcohol.

Alcohol dissolves (essential) fatty acids *inside* the brain. Then it replaces helpful omega-3 DHA, (which is docosahexaenoic acid, a long chain omega-3 fatty acid). This elimination of omega-3 DHA is very bad for us, because this substance provides cardiovascular health benefits, supports visual performance and enhances brain health, including memory. DHA represents up to 97% of the omega-3 fats in the brain.

Alcohol *replaces* DHA with docosapentanoic acid, which is a less valuable form of omega-3, and it also stops the process of fats being converted into DHA and prostaglandins. This is the reason why the memory is affected by alcohol.

The body's reflexes are slowed down by alcohol, there is reduced co-ordination, impaired thinking, poor judgement, depression, impaired memory and a reduced ability to control motor functions. And alcohol, because it is a disinhibitor, allows angry outbursts which would normally be controlled.

Patrick Holford (2010) describes alcohol as the brain's worst enemy, because when the liver is unable to detoxify any more alcohol, then *it attacks the brain*. As a result, the communication systems within the brain are thrown into disarray and it affects our memory – so we forget our problems.

Dr Perricone (2002) recommends drinking a small amount of wine with a meal. To drink any more is to invite a very quick increase in blood sugar in your body, resulting in a strong inflammatory response in every part of the body[132].

Pure spirits are even worse. Because the alcohol content of hard liquor is extremely high, there is considerable harm to cell plasma membrane (or the structure of our cell walls); and to the interior of the cells; as well as triggering the inflammatory response – which seems to be implicated in the causation of most major diseases, including major depression and anxiety.

Alcohol also affects our ability to get a sound night's sleep: Drinking alcohol in the evening can make us feel drowsy but then afterwards it triggers an influx of adrenaline in our body systems. Adrenaline is a hormone which is released as a reaction to excitement or stress, and it makes us wake up, hours later, usually in the early hours of the morning. And high adrenaline levels can make us feel anxious and panicked.

Alcohol extracts water from our cells, and dehydrates every cell in the body, accelerating the ageing process. It also generates huge amounts of free radicals, (which are unstable molecules that can damage the cells in the body). This increases the drinker's risk of hormonal cancers, particularly breast cancer.

It places an enormous strain on the liver, which then has a reduced ability to detoxify the body. And fatigue, dehydration, weight gain and late-onset diabetes, mood swings, and poor eyesight are also some of the consequences.

Its effects on the mind are as follows: it initially increases feelings of relaxation and happiness and sociability, but this can develop into more negative feelings and behaviours, including depression.

According to the NHS in Scotland, more than half of people who ended up in hospital because they'd deliberately injured themselves, said they'd drunk alcohol immediately before or while doing it. And 27% of men and 19% of women gave alcohol as the reason for self-harming.[133]

Finally, if you drink alcohol regularly, the level of serotonin in your brain is lowered, and (according to one dominant theory) as this controls your moods, feelings of depression are more likely to take place. (However, this theory of low serotonin being linked to high depression has never been demonstrated in practice; and there are serious counter arguments). So, it may be that drinking alcohol regularly causes depression via *some other biochemical route* altogether, such as through inflammation affecting mitochondrial functioning!

~~~

(d) Caffeine

The Oxford dictionary's definition of **caffeine** is:

*'An **alkaloid**[134] compound which is found especially in tea and coffee plants and is a stimulant of the central nervous system'.* (Waite, 2012).

Caffeine is also found in cocoa and cola drinks and in some drug preparations as a preventative for migraines.

Julia Ross, in her book titled *'The Mood Cure'*, describes caffeine as one of serotonin's number 1 enemies, along with diet pills, ephedra, ma huang[135] and cocaine (Page 29, Ross 2002). Since serotonin is widely seen as underpinning our positive moods, this is said to be not good. (However, since it now seems that the serotonin-depression link is highly contested, it may be that caffeine operates in a different way to lower mood)[136].

Research findings indicate that the people who drink the most coffee suffer chronic depression as well.[137] But caffeine also depletes potassium, calcium, and zinc, vitamin C, and the B vitamins. It also weakens and overstimulates the kidneys, pancreas, liver, stomach, intestines, heart, nervous system and adrenal glands and over-acidifies the 'ph' (the balance of acidity and alkalinity levels in the stomach and body generally), causing premature ageing, and compromising health and well-being. (And we do not currently know *how* it might cause or worsen depressive symptoms).

Also, caffeine has a negative effect on the quantity and the quality of our sleep, and can make us tired and irritable; and anxiety can be increased by the use of caffeine.

Caffeine can also affect academic skills: A study published in the *American Journal of Psychiatry* studied 1,500 psychology students and divided them into four categories, depending on their coffee intake: Abstainers; Low consumers (one cup or equivalent a day); Moderate (1-5 cups a day); and High (5 or more cups a day).

The Moderate and High consumers were found to have higher levels of anxiety and depression than the Abstainers; and the High consumers had the greatest incidence of stress-related medical problems, as well as a lower academic performance. (Gilliland and Andress, 1981, pp. 512-4).[138]

Holford (2010) has explained that, with increases in your consumption of caffeine, there is a corresponding insensitivity, within the brain, to the body's own natural stimulants of dopamine and adrenaline.

So then more stimulants are needed to feel normal, and these push the body to produce more adrenaline and dopamine. These result in adrenal exhaustion, and so the result is less motivation and less energy in the body. Indifference and apathy can follow. For some people, the effects of caffeine can result in them being diagnosed with schizophrenia or mania.

Patrick Holford stated that: *"As a nutritionist, I have seen many people cleared of minor health problems such as tiredness and headaches just from cutting out their two or three coffees a day".* (Holford, 2010: page 93).

~~~

(e) Processed food (or 'Junk food')[139]

"Junk moods come from junk foods. Junk foods are addictive and lead to overeating. Overeating leads to overweight". (Ross 2002)

Processed or 'junk food' is food that has been transformed from its raw, natural state by chemical or physical means. The food has been altered from its natural state so that it can be packaged in cans, boxes or bags. Or it has been pre-cooked in a fast-food take-away restaurant, using high calorie, low nutrient constituents; or with high trans-fat and sugar ingredients.

And it can come from a variety of sources. Felicity Lawrence, in her book titled *'Not on the Label'* (2004)[140] explains how a ready-made lasagne: *"...can have about 20 different ingredients which could have originated from all over the world, according to Tara Garnett of the Sustainable Transport Trust, Transport 2000."*

This type of food can cause real problems for your body, for the following reasons:

Firstly, the food can be high in bad fat and/or sugar and can have very few nutrients, and lots of calories (or simple sugars). In fact, the food company, Mars Food, which makes Dolmio and Uncle Ben sauces, has recently announced that it will put a health warning on these and other products, to say that *they shouldn't be eaten more than once a week.* This is because their food sauces are so high in salt, sugar and fat. (*Daily Mail*, 2016)[141].

Secondly, with processed food there can be a health risk from excessive sodium (which is salt). Bearing in mind the welfare of our hearts, Melodie Ann Coffman at the 'Healthy Eating' website, in an article entitled, 'The Disadvantages of Junk Food'[142], considers that we should not eat more than 1,500 milligrams of sodium each day (which is three quarters of a teaspoon). (A single take away meal can contain more salt than a whole day's allowance). Too much sodium in our diets can increase blood pressure, so steering clear of processed food can help us to avoid getting high blood pressure.

The processed foods that contain the most sodium include delicatessen meats, hot dog sausages, and microwave dinners. The sodium comes from salt and other sodium compounds which are used to give the food more flavour and make it last. But too much sodium can disrupt the potassium-sodium balance.

It may be that a high sodium-potassium ratio results in stress and anxiety; while a too-low ratio results in depression and fatigue. But the kind of salt you need to avoid depression is iodized salt (enriched with iodine), and this is not normally the kind of salt used in junk foods and processed foods in general. (You can get your iodine needs met by taking a kelp supplement).

Also related to the sodium levels, there is the risk of stroke. The more chips, French fries and pepperoni pizzas which are eaten, the higher the risk of stroke becomes.

There is very little fibre in processed junk food, and fibre is essential to keep our bowels moving.

Otherwise, we can become constipated, and it can become painful for us when we eventually pass faeces; and regular bowel movements reduce toxicity in the body.

And anything which improves bowel function tends to support optimum emotional functioning

~~~

(f) Gluten

Cereal flours (mainly wheat flours, but also rye and barley) contain proteins called gliadins and glutenins, which become glutinous when the cereal flours are mixed with water.

These substances (gliadins plus glutenins) are called, (when combined), gluten; and they can inflame and cause breaks in the lining of the digestive tract. This can lead to food particles escaping through the gut wall into the bloodstream, causing inflammation.

(In the case of oats, this grain contains *avenin*, which could cause inflammation in some individuals. And oats also tend to be contaminated by other grains during the growing or processing or packing processes).

Sensitivity to gluten is called gluten intolerance, and the main form is called coeliac disease. However, we also are now aware of non-celiac gluten sensitivity (NCGS); and to non-gut-based neurological disturbances caused by gluten. (Sources: Perlmutter, 2014 [who cites twenty sources, including eight from academic journals, with two from *The Lancet*]; Ross, 2003 [who cites six sources, including four from academic journals, like the *New England Journal of Medicine*]; Hadjivassiliou, 1996 [who discovered the 'gluten syndrome']; plus 16 other sources from academic journals)[143].

The latest thinking in the world of neurological medicine is that gluten affects the gut, *and* it affects the brain. It is no longer "...*regarded as principally a disease of the small bowel*". (Hadjivassiliou, in Perlmutter, 2014: page 53). Sometimes it affects the brain *because* it has affected the gut; and sometimes it affects the brain, *without* showing any obvious evidence of a negative impact on the gut! This is known as 'the gluten syndrome': Ford (2009). And there are blood markers (antibodies) of its presence in the body-brain, even in the absence of intestinal damage. See Footnote 143.

According to Hadjivassiliou (1996): "*Our data suggest that gluten sensitivity is common in patients with neurological disease of unknown cause and may have aetiological* (or causative – Eds) *significance*".[144]

How does gluten affect the gut? Gliadin, within gluten, pulls apart the *tight junctions* that exist between the cells in our guts. The space between the cells start to widen, and the *result* is that toxins and larger molecules of food (that normally pass through the intestine and are eliminated in bowel movements), begin to leak into the blood circulation system of our bodies. This is called 'leaky gut syndrome'.

As a result, you get increased inflammation in your body when your intestinal barrier is compromised. This means that you are susceptible to health challenges such as rheumatoid arthritis, food allergies, asthma, eczema, coeliac disease, inflammatory bowel disease, HIV, cystic fibrosis, diabetes, autism, Alzheimer's and Parkinson's.

What happens is that the blood-brain barrier (which has been thought of as a "highly protective, fortified portal keeping bad things out of the brain") is weakened if the gut is leaky, and this lets in molecules that are really bad for the brain, including bacteria, viruses and proteins that would normally have been prevented from crossing the blood/brain barrier[145].

According to Julia Ross (2003), thousands of people are affected by gluten, and there are many studies which validate the theory that depression can be caused by gluten intolerance. She describes the symptom of depression disappearing when wheat and other grains are removed from the diet.

Here is Julie Ross (2002) describing her experience of the effects of gluten:

"People with gluten intolerance have low levels of the antidepressant, anti-anxiety brain chemical serotonin, and gluten has been implicated in mental illness since at least 1979". (Page 126).

The fact that gluten is implicated in mental illness, or emotional disturbances, like anxiety and depression, does not prove that the link is via serotonin. This proposed link is heavily contested. (See later). But there is undoubtedly a link *of some kind* – see Footnote 145 – and gluten therefore has to be taken seriously as a risk factor in the causation of neurological and emotional problems of unknown origin. Dr Michael Greger has argued against such a stance, but we have dismantled his argument in a footnote, below).

~~~

Some people have a formal diagnosis of Celiac disease, and those individuals should stay well clear of gluten-containing foods, to avoid damaging their intestinal tracts further.

Some people have a formal diagnosis of Non-Celiac Gluten Sensitivity (NCGS), linked to a neurological problems or disorders, with biomarkers for gluten antibodies in the blood. And those individuals have to remain gluten-free for life.

And, it seems, some people *self-report* that they have all the symptoms of gluten sensitivity, and their symptoms do improve when they *exclude* gluten-containing foods.

However, that third category of non-diagnosed, self-reporting gluten sensitivity individuals *may be misdiagnosing* the source of their own problem. According to a recent study, involving 59 individuals on a self-instituted gluten-free diet, for whom celiac disease had been excluded, the real source of their problems was Fructans (which are a form of sugar found in vegetables and grains). (Source: Skodje, G.I. et al., 2017, in press).

As a precautionary approach, nobody should assume that they are Fructan sensitive rather than gluten sensitive, unless and until they get themselves tested - not just for Celiac disease, but also for Non-Celiac Gluten Sensitivity (with biomarkers for gluten antibodies).

~~~

Apparently, in the US, according to Kelly Brogan, the wheat crop is composed of varieties of grains which have been modified so that more gluten is produced, because food technologists believe this will improve the composition of baked goods, creating more "puff" in them. (Michael Greger, 2016, argues against this point. However, a blog by the Agricultural Marketing Resource Centre seems to support Kelly Brogan's argument rather than Michael Greger's)[146].

Brogan also states that gluten is one of the most notable food items that is known to make a dramatic difference to the brain, as it raises the production of endorphins.

"The gluten in these grains affects the brain like an opiate......that's why you may love or feel comforted by your bread or pasta – your brain gets a drug-like rush every time you eat those foods." (Page 126)

Some other ailments that have been linked to gluten include: bowel problems, headaches, diabetes, chronic exhaustion, bad moods, depression and severe anxiety.

~~~

5. What kinds of regular supplements (of vitamins, minerals, etc.) should we take to support our physical health and emotional wellbeing?

Do we need to take supplements? Here are several different views on the type of daily supplements that we need to take. In this process, I will summarise some of the main views of a variety of specialists in the field of nutrition, and other health researchers:

(a) The British National Health Service (NHS) view

The NHS Choices website[147] considers that *"most people can get all the vitamins and minerals they need by getting a healthy, balanced diet"*. However, they accept that people do take vitamin and mineral supplements, and they warn that they need to make sure that they are not taking higher amounts than they need.

They quote the guidelines of the National Institute for Health and Care excellence (NICE) which considers that some members of the population could be at risk of getting insufficient nutrients. They refer to pregnant women, as well as those contemplating having a baby, as being in need of a folic acid supplement to prevent neural tube defects. (However, they seem to overlook the fact that most people – who cannot afford high quality foods, including organic foods – are eating denatured foods which have few if any nutrients [e.g. junk foods]. That some people are skipping meals to make ends meet. That many people skip breakfast because of poor time management. And they also overlook the fact that most people do not know which foods deliver which vitamins, so that it is often more convenient, and optimizing of health, to simply take a strong multivitamin and mineral supplement every day, plus a B complex preparation; plus a couple of grams of vitamin C, as a minimum!)

NHS Choices also mention that vitamin D supplements should be taken by all pregnant and breastfeeding women. Also children between the ages of 6 months and 5 years should take them, and people who are 65 or over. (They fail to mention that there is a definite link between vitamin D deficiency and depression. Dr Mercola emphasizes that we should get our daily need for vitamin D from direct sunlight, for which purpose we would have to stop using sunscreen creams, or use very weak barriers![148] And neither NHS choices nor Dr Mercola take account of the fact that many of us live in parts of the world where it is difficult to get adequate amounts of vitamin D from sunlight all year round!)

NHS Choices acknowledge that children between the ages of 6 months and 5 years old need to take supplements containing vitamins A, C and D because there may be a lack of variety in their diets.

A medical doctor (GP) might recommend vitamin supplements, the NHS Direct website states, if you had a medical condition; and they cite the example of iron supplements being recommended when someone has iron deficiency anaemia.

~~~

(b) A Nutritional Therapist's perspective

Julia Ross (2003), who is the Executive Director of the Nutritional Therapy Institute Clinic in Mill Valley, California has a different approach towards the use of supplements. She is a psychotherapist and, since 1986, she has been using a combination of nutritional therapy and holistic medical care, with conventional counselling, at the Nutritional Therapy centre which is in the San Francisco Bay area in America.

She has created a 'Master Supplement Plan' which is a basic list of supplements that she recommends for everyone, for the long term, regardless of any conditions such as anxiety or depression that they may have.

She recommends elements that occur naturally in foods and that have a consensus of opinion on their wholesomeness. The nutrients she includes are intended to rebalance and restore the level of nutrients in the body.

She has pointed out to the readers of her book - 'The Mood Cure', (2003) - that there are certain factors that stop us achieving a full level of nutrition from food alone and she mentions the following: the amount of light and/or heat to which foods are exposed; the age of the food; inadequate soil used; and the effect that processing has on the food.

Because modern methods of agriculture have resulted in reduced levels of nutrition in our foods, and many of these foods are further denatured by the food processing industry, you are strongly advised to take a good quality multivitamin and mineral supplement, plus a full spectrum B-complex, including B9 (folate); plus magnesium and calcium. You will also benefit from extra vitamin C (at least one gram per day, and perhaps more). Perretta (2001) recommends the following foods in particular: avocado; mushrooms; spring greens and spinach; liver; millet; guava and papaya. Green vegetables are recommended by many nutritionists. And don't forget the oily fish (which contain lots of essential fatty acids [especially omega-3's])! It aids all brain functions, including managing stress. (Best oily fish: Wild Alaskan salmon, which is available fresh or in tins at Marks and Spencer [UK]; tinned sardines, which can be with tomato sauce for taste purposes; grilled fresh mackerel; or trout).

Ross (2003) also points out that that nutritional needs can vary from person to person, and describes factors which can cause an increased demand for nutrients in the body, such as: levels of stress; undetected illnesses which could have affected someone's level of health; genetic factors; and their level of physical exercise.

Furthermore, the National Diet and Nutrition Survey, by the Food Standards Agency (2004) found that only 14 percent of respondents are eating the recommended five portions of fruit and vegetables every day; and the majority are not getting their full recommended daily allowance (or Reference Nutrient Intake [RNI]) of essential nutrients[149]. This points to a clear need to promote nutritional supplementation alongside a better diet.

(c) A dissenting voice

However, in contrast, a professor at the Yale School of Public Health's Division of Chronic Disease Epidemiology, Susan Taylor-Maine, is of the opinion that supplements are not appropriate, because they *"deliver vitamins out of context."* (Ballantyne, 2007).[150] There are thousands of phytochemicals, which are protective against chronic ailments such as Alzheimer's disease, cancer, cardio-vascular disease, which are available in vegetables and fruit and other foods, according to Taylor-Maine. She cites the example of isothiocyanates in cabbage and broccoli, carotenoids in carrots and tomatoes, and flavonoids in red wine, soy and cocoa.

She considers that this fusion of the phytochemicals and vitamins has much more impact on the body than if a nutrient was taken on its own. The example cited is lypocene, which is the carotenoid responsible for the red colour of tomatoes.

Because it has been associated with a lower risk for prostate cancer, there has been a lot of supplement manufacturers who have created supplements of lypocene.

However, in Taylor-Maine's opinion, the research suggests that the chemical composition of the food is more beneficial, so that eating tomatoes or tomato products like pasta sauce and ketchup would contain all the varied nutrients inherent in the food. (What she ignores is that this is not an either/or problem. Most people who take vitamin and mineral supplements also try to eat a balanced diet, so that, in addition to getting a reliable source of nutrients [from the supplements], they may also get the range of phytonutrients that she mentions, [assuming those phytonutrients are not also depleted by modern methods of food production!] And you will see, below, when we come to look at research on the provision of vitamin and mineral and omega-3 supplementation of the diets of violent prisoners, in the UK, that *the supplements alone* helped to reduce anger and violence, without any change to the *actual foods* consumed! So, quite clearly, *supplementation works* to help with mood management! This is empirical proof, as against Taylor-Maine's non-empirical theorizing.)

(d) In favour of supplements

In contrast with Taylor-Maine, Patrick Holford states - in his book titled *'Optimum Nutrition for the Mind' (2010)* - that he considers supplements to be essential. He considers that nutrition holds the key to optimising mental health, and reducing mental health problems.

He cites evidence of the effectiveness of supplements in a research project conducted by Gwillym Roberts and David Benton in 1988[151]. They ran a randomised, double-blind, placebo–controlled trial. Sixty children were involved in the research study. Thirty of them were put on a special multivitamin and mineral supplement which was created to make sure they had an ideal intake of key nutrients.

The other thirty children were on an identical looking placebo. The children's IQ scores were measured at the start of the trial, and again after 8 months.

After the 8 months of taking the supplements, there was an increase of over 10 points in the non-verbal IQ of the children. Also some children were getting more than a 20 point improvement in their IQ.

No changes were observed in those on the placebos, or a control group of students who hadn't taken any supplements or placebos.

Holford stated: *"The study was published in the Lancet medical journal and was the subject of a BBC Horizon TV documentary, the day after which every single children's multivitamin in Britain sold out."*(Page 121)

He also recommends essential fat supplements, because they promote brain function and health; as well as supplementing with amino acids[152], in particular for people suffering with depression or neurotransmitter deficiencies.

(e) A critique of Holford´s position

Ben Goldacre has criticised Patrick Holford's views on the need for supplements in our diet, and considers that, as Holford sells supplements with his own brand name on them, then by implication there are commercial interests at work in his promotion of the need for supplements.[153] However, this would only be a valid criticism if there was *no evidence* – from reliable research sources – for claims of efficacy by vitamin pill manufacturers. But that evidence does exist!

Ben Goldacre describes Patrick Holford as a *"man who sells pills"*. Goldacre ("a man who sells books castigating others") also describes himself as being very critical of the *"whole phenomenon of pill dependence"*, and thinks that commercial interests are trying to persuade people that all our problems of lack of sleep, headaches, lack of sexual appetite, and heart disease *can be cured by biological means*. He considers that these afflictions are as a result of our lifestyle and social behaviour, and are not easily cured. (It is quite wrong to imply that Patrick Holford believes that all health problems can be cured by vitamin supplements, and supplements alone!)

We totally agree with Goldacre's claim that it is impossible to solve *a lifestyle imbalance* by working on any **one** aspect of that imbalance (such as supplementing vitamins and minerals). But Goldacre is *disingenuous* in presenting his argument in this way. *Almost nobody in the field of lifestyle medicine* is suggesting that people should "**just** take supplements"! This, apparently, includes Patrick Holford. See for example the three video testimonials on Holford's website - here: https://www.patrickholford.com/health-club. These video testimonials are not "all about Holford's supplements". These three individuals, who have recovered from various diseases or health conditions with the help of Patrick Holford's 'lifestyle management' approach, mention: **Diet** (including the glycaemic load diet) … **supplements** … **mental attitude** … and **physical exercise**. So it is not all about supplements by any means.

The fact that Goldacre focuses on the 'commercial interest' that Holford has in promoting supplements is a sign of how *shallow* his critique is. He does not mention any *weakness* in the idea that supplements can be *helpful* (alongside diet and exercise approaches) for people who want to take responsibility for managing their own health and wellbeing. People in glasshouses should not throw stones. Ben Goldacre has a 'commercial interest' in "debunking" Holford and others. Ben Goldacre, it seems, is a 'professional debunker of apparently *scientific efforts* (as well as *pseudoscience*)'. He gains money from *selling books that castigate other people's efforts.*

In Goldacre (2012), he makes the following opening statement, with which we heartily agree:

"Medicine is broken. And I genuinely believe that if patients and the public ever fully understand what has been done to them – what doctors, academics and regulators have permitted – they will be angry". (Goldacre, 2012. Page ix)[154].

This statement, logically, should put Goldacre in the same camp as Holford and others who are leading a movement towards 'lifestyle medicine', where individuals *take personal responsibility* for their own health, through diet, exercise, mind management, stress management, vitamin and mineral supplementation, and so on.

This author (Renata Taylor-Byrne) has used multivitamin and mineral supplementation for years – alongside organic food, balanced diet, adequate water consumption (which means at least six glasses per day), elimination of sugar, alcohol, tobacco, (most) grains, and other sources of inflammation – to maintain her own physical health and emotional well-being.

My co-author of this book (Jim Byrne) has used a similar strategy of balanced and healthy diet, supplementation, exercise, meditation, relaxation, and so on, to manage his own health and well-being.

We do, of course, accept that any particular brand of vitamin pill, or any type of pill, could have negative side effects, and consumers should monitor how they feel 24 to 36 hours after taking a new vitamin pill, to see how ti affects their energy, mood and skin response (if any). And if problems build up over time, not only should they experiment with the elimination of particular foods, but also particular vitamin pills, to see what might be causing the problem.

But to advocate the elimination of all vitamin supplements because the 'Little Pharma' industry promotes its own products is not a sensible response. There is, as yet, no evidence (that we know of) that 'Little Pharma' engages in the kind of dirty tricks that characterizes Big Pharma!

(f) Additional forms of dietary supplementation

Dr David Perlmutter (2015)[155] recommends, for optimum brain health, that people supplement with probiotics[156]. This is to ensure that there are more good gut bacteria in the body than bad, and that there is enough to strengthen the lining of the intestines, reduce gut permeability, and any inflammatory molecules, and increase BDNF[157], which is the brain's growth hormone.

In his book titled *'Brain Maker' (2015)*, he describes the views of the biologist and Nobel laureate Elie Mechnikov who observed that for humans to live a long life, a healthy balance of bacteria in the gut was essential. He considered that the good bacteria must outnumber the bad, and Dr Perlmutter states that since Mechnikov put forward this thesis, more and more scientific research is confirming the idea that… *"Up to 90% of all known human illness can be traced back to an unhealthy gut"*. (Page 7).

That deserves to be repeated. It seems, from scientific studies, that: *Up to 90% of all known human illness can be traced back to an unhealthy gut. And this, by implication, may also refer to all emotional disturbances which are not based on social-psychological sources that can be identified – such as external stressors, loss, failure, frustration, or interpersonal conflict.*

This idea is certainly supported by scientific evidence cited by Enders (2015, pages 114-133).

Perlmutter approves of supplementation with live bacteria and considers that five core probiotic species are the best ones for supporting brain health. These are: *Lactobacillus plantarum, Lactobacillus Acidophilus, Lactobacillus brevis, Bifidobacterium lactis,* and *Bifido-bacterium longum.*

He also recommends five supplements that will encourage and preserve an equilibrium of healthy bacteria in the gut: DHA, turmeric, coconut oil, alpha-lipoic acid and vitamin D.

~~~

Of course, if you cannot afford to buy probiotic supplements, you can try to consume pre-biotic foods, which manufacture probiotics in your gut. As a general rule, high fibre foods promote the growth of friendly bacteria. One of us (Jim) supplements with psyllium husk for this purpose – though we both eat high fibre diets.

A local life coach in Hebden Bridge – Max Kohanzad - has written about prebiotics:

"There is a way to fix the gut and replenish your gut with good powerful healthy gut bacteria. Firstly stop eating wheat, alcohol, cheese, milk and sugar. If you can, don't eat any grains or pulses for about two weeks (think Atkins diet with organic meats and wild fish) so that your gut wall has a chance to heal.

"You can eat most vegetables, but do aim to mainly feed your good bacteria by eating lots of asparagus, green bananas, parsnips, leeks, onions, garlic, endives, cold potato and or cold rice.

Secondly invest in the best pre- and probiotics you can afford.

...

"This small article is not intended to replace medical advice".[158].

~~~

Much of this advice will be helpful to many people. There are, as always, exceptions to be considered:

Caveat 1: If you are suffering from IBS, you would be advised not to eat the pre-biotic foods listed above, since many of them may be high in FodMaps (fructans, oligosaccharides, disaccharides, and polyols). Indeed, when one of us (Jim Byrne) changed to a largely low-FodMaps diet, his symptoms of Candida Albicans (including physical tiredness and itchiness, plus lowered mood) quickly improved!

Caveat 2: To resolve any outstanding questions you might have regarding whether or not to supplement with multivitamins and minerals, friendly bacteria, or other nutrients, please talk to a good, personally recommended, lifestyle health professional, or a nutritional therapist. (If you are over the age of forty years, they might also recommend that you supplement with digestive enzymes).

And when you make dietary changes, keep a food diary or journal, and monitor the effects of those changes on your mood, energy level, and skin condition.

~~~

6. How good is the evidence that anxiety, anger and depression can be created by the wrong kind of food and drink?

CBT and REBT theorists take the view that most human disturbance is caused by the *beliefs* and *attitudes* of the client; their 'negative automatic thoughts'; or 'irrational beliefs'. In E-CENT counselling and therapy, we take the view that emotions are innate (as 'affects'), including a capacity for anger/rage, grief/sadness/depression, and anxiety/fear/concern. But it often takes particular kinds of environmental triggers to precipitate strong feelings of anger, anxiety or depression – such as losses, failures, threats, dangers, and so on. But the list of factors that can contribute to emotional problems is very long indeed. (See Byrne, 2016)[159].

On the other hand, we also emphasize that the state of the human organism, in terms of stress, relaxation, health, nourishment, and so on, has a lot to do with how environmental stressors are experienced.

For example, in our experience, a *substantial minority* of clients present with emotional disturbances which cannot be linked – or *entirely* linked, or satisfactorily linked – to their beliefs, attitudes, or even their life challenges. Amongst these cases are:

(a) People who have symptoms of **depression** because of their sugary diets, which sugars cause an overgrowth of 'unfriendly bacteria' in their guts (especially Candida Albicans. See Part 3 for more on this subject). And they are too physically drained to do any exercise.

(b) People who are wrecking their relationships, at home and in work, because of **angry** and **rageful** outbursts, which seem to be largely (or significantly) caused by their overconsumption of junk food (containing lots of trans-fats and sugars). And:

(c) People who are **anxious** and **panicked** because of over-consumption of caffeine, sugar, alcohol, recreational drugs and other stimulants; and who are failing to exercise.

There are many different views on how effective changes in diet can mitigate the problems which are created by harmful diets and I will give you a summary of these views, firstly in relation to the experience of anxiety.

(a) Anxiety and nutrition

Before we look at the role of diet in causing and curing anxiety, we had better define what we mean by anxiety.

(i) What is anxiety?

The *Oxford English Dictionary* (Waite, 2012) defines anxiety as a *"feeling or state of unease or concern"*. And Nicky Hayes (1994)[160] describes it as a state of emotional arousal which persists.

She gives the example of being anxious about paying bills. This can be a **constant worry**, and not just a passing concern. She describes it as **an unpleasant emotion**, and it is a state of physical arousal, and is also described as stress.

Anxiety (in the present moment) is built upon our innate sense of fear of threats and dangers (which seem to be just up ahead, in the immediate future). Of course, our *innate* sense of fear, with which we are born, is socialized by our family of origin, and our schooling, so that it takes forms which are historically dictated.

Back to Nicky Hayes' example: Worrying about paying bills, for example, if prolonged, can interfere with our physical health. This can result in our immune system lacking sufficient strength to fight off colds, infections and serious illnesses. So anxiety can lead to physical illness, and not taking care of our physical body can also lead to anxiety.

Many people who experience regular feelings of anxiety either "self-medicate" or go to the doctor, who then prescribes tranquilisers (or, even worse, antidepressants). Here is an interesting statistic quoted by Patrick Holford (2010).

"In one week in Britain, we pop 10 million tranquilisers, puff 10 million cannabis joints and drink 120 million alcoholic drinks" (page 174). And much of this seems to be directed at reducing our feelings of anxiety.

Dale Pinnock (2015)[161] describes anxiety as one of the most common mental health disorders in the UK, and affecting more women than men; and mainly people in the 35-59 age group.

He considers anxiety to be a valuable constituent of our survival skills, and *only* becomes a problem for people when there is a build-up of anxiety. It is very practical to be apprehensive about a challenge to our skills or self-concept, and it makes us want to take measures to improve the stressful situation we are in. But if nothing is done about it, it can develop into a general anxiety disorder. This means that people suffer from anxiety continually, and even when the obvious anxiety-arousing situations are eliminated, the anxiety doesn't go away. It simply moves onto another problem. It has become a generalized state of arousal, looking for things to worry about.

(ii) Nutrition for anxiety

So how can nutrition help in relation to these high levels of anxiety? There are certain substances which the body needs which will reduce anxiety levels. And one such substance which has a powerful effect on the nervous system is omega-3 fatty acid, which is present in fish oils, plus plant and nut oils. (Common sources of omega-3 fatty acids include cod liver oil, and krill oil).

Pinnock (2015) cites evidence of the benefits that were derived by 68 students who took part in a 2011 double-blind, crossover trial or research experiment. (Kiecolt-Glaser, and colleagues, 2011)[162]. This research was considered to be the first double-blind trial to conclude that there could be anxiety-reducing benefits in omega-3 fatty acids. And there are earlier scientific studies to support the claim that oily fish can be helpful in the reduction of panic attacks (which are a result of anxiety about anxiety about anxiety). (See Perretta, 2001, page 90)[163].

However, as there were no participants in the Kiecolt-Glaser (2011) study who were diagnosed (officially) as having a specific anxiety disorder, at the time of the research, this fact has to be taken into account.

But this is balanced out by the fact that *"...there are literally hundreds of anecdotal reports of omega-3 offering benefits to patients with anxiety issues. Reports abound from practitioners, on patient forums, and so on".* (Pinnock, 2015).

Pinnock (2015) also considers that magnesium, glutamine, and blood sugar management play key roles in the reduction and management of anxiety.

Magnesium is very important for the body in terms of ensuring relaxation in the muscles, reducing nervous tension, and helping the mind to slow down. It is involved in over 1,000 biochemical reactions in the body, and is described by Pinnock as *"one of the most deficient minerals in the modern diet".* So he encourages people to consume seeds and nuts, dark green leafy vegetable like spinach and kale, and fruit: e.g. bananas.

Magnesium is also recommended for anxiety by Linda Lazarides, who "...has worked as a pioneering alternative health professional in a GP practice", in the UK, "treating hundreds of people referred to her by a doctor"[164]. She mentions the following food sources of magnesium: "Bitter chocolate, leafy green vegetables, nuts, sunflower and sesame seeds, soya beans, whole grains (particularly [gluten free] oats." (Page 281).

She also recommends "standardized extracts" of the "power mushroom", Reishi. (Page 290).

Glutamine is a constituent of the neurotransmitter, GABA (gamma-amino-butyric acid). GABA has a calming effect on adrenaline and noradrenaline, and serotonin. If there is a low level of GABA in our brains we can experience tension and anxiety (and depression and insomnia).

Glutamine isn't available in the UK as it has been classified by the European Union as a medicine. It isn't found in food but its constituents are, and one of these is the amino acid glucosamine. The food sources of this nutrient are obtained from spinach, walnuts, broccoli, brown rice, almonds and bananas.

Another important factor in the management of anxiety involves regulating our blood sugar levels[165]. Dale Pinnock considers this to be a simple skill to master, *"...but the impact it can have on your mind **and** mood is quite staggering."* (Page 36)

Why can it make such a difference? The reason is because the sugar that we get in our bodies from processed foods such as white bread, white rice, white pasta, chocolates and fizzy drinks (to name a few junk foods) is immediately available, and immediately affects us. The body doesn't have to work hard to digest the food and extract the nutrients.

As a result, blood sugar rises rapidly and we can feel full of energy as a consequence. But this reaction is very bad for our body, which handles this sudden influx of sugar by releasing the hormone *insulin*. This informs our cells to mop up excess sugar very quickly.

As a result of this activity by our insulin secretions, our blood sugar then drops, but it goes *too low*. Because of this drop, the hormone adrenaline is released. This is to initiate the unleashing of *stored* glucose, and then the experience of adrenaline is felt by the body. And *"...adrenaline is to anxiety what petrol is to a bonfire"*: (Pinnock). You will then experience a change in your breathing rate; your heartbeat gets faster and faster; and your mind starts to race. These symptoms can be very unpleasant if you are already prone to experiencing anxiety.

Pinnock (2015) recommends always combining protein in a meal with unrefined carbohydrates[166], so that the digestion of a meal takes longer and releases energy for the body in small increments, rather than as a sudden onslaught with the corresponding release of adrenaline. This is said to be a good mood and energy level stabiliser. (However, this contradicts the Hay diet, which suggests not combining protein and carbohydrates, because a sluggish digestion can promote a toxic gut and promote inflammation and disease!)

A better strategy, and one that many theorists advocate, is to avoid refined carbohydrate[167] and simple sugars; to mostly eat vegetables, to reduce meat[168]; to eat lots of oily fish, like salmon and sardines; and to eat seeds, nuts and fruits (to the degree that you can tolerate them).

Dale Pinnock thinks that our diet can be a very useful tool for improving our health, because like a drug, food affects the internal environment of the body. In his view: *"To dismiss nutrition within the healthcare picture is at best irresponsible, at worst insane"*.

~~~

(iii) Gut bacteria and anxiety

Dr Perlmutter (2015), who is a neurologist, describes anxiety disorders as affecting more than 40 million Americans, and he considers, on the basis of the research he has been doing, *that anxiety is strongly related to a state of disturbance in the gut bacteria.* When people experience unrelenting anxiety, then this means that they may be experiencing what is described by some theorists as an anxiety disorder. This includes panic disorder, obsessive-compulsive disorder, and social phobia and generalised anxiety disorder.

Perlmutter considers that anxiety disorders are caused by a combination of factors which include the condition and processing ability of the gut, and the bacteria which inhabits it. Dr Perlmutter states: *"When the balance of gut bacteria isn't right, other biological pathways – be they hormonal, immunological or neuronal, aren't right either. And the brain's processing centres, such as those that handle emotions, aren't right either.....I've found that patients report never feeling anxious or depressed until they start having problems with their guts. Coincidence? I think not"* (Page 87).

He quotes two significant experiments to substantiate his argument: In a 2011 study published in the Proceedings of the National Academy of Sciences, mice fed probiotics had significantly lower levels of the stress hormone corticosterone, than mice fed plain broth. (J.A. Bravo *and colleagues*, 2011).[169]

The second study he describes was conducted at Oxford University. Neurobiologists found that giving people prebiotics (which is food for the promotion of good bacteria in the gut), resulted in positive psychological effects. It was conducted by K Schmidt *et al.*, (2014)[170]

Forty-five adults between the ages of eighteen and forty-five took either a prebiotic or a placebo every day for three weeks. The participants were then tested so that their ability to process emotional information could be ascertained.

The underlying theory was that if the participants had a high level of anxiety to start with, then they would be more sensitive to and react more quickly to evidence of negativity. The types of negativity shown were negative words and images.

What was observed by the Oxford researchers was that, compared to the placebo group, the individuals who had taken the prebiotics paid more attention to positive information, and less attention to the negative information.

This effect, which has been noticed with individuals on antidepressants or anti-anxiety medication, indicated that the prebiotic group experienced less anxiety when faced with the negative stimuli.

Also, the researchers discovered that the people who took the prebiotics had lower levels of cortisol, when measured via their saliva samples, which were taken in the morning, when cortisol levels are at their highest.

Dr Perlmutter considers that these examples are relevant to the growing evidence of research studies that show a connection between mental health and gut bacteria, in particular in relation to anxiety.

On page 88 of *Brain Maker*, Perlmutter describes a client called Martina, 56, who came to him because she was suffering from anxiety and depression. She had been taking anti-depressants and non-steroid inflammatory drugs (NSAIDs) for 10 years. He immediately ordered laboratory tests which revealed that she was particularly sensitive to gluten and had low levels of vitamin D.

She also had a very high level of LPS. LPS stands for "lipopolysaccharide". This is an endotoxin, which means it's a toxin which comes from within the bacteria in the intestines. When this toxin gets into the bloodstream it triggers an intense inflammatory response in the body. (Normally this endotoxin is blocked from getting into the bloodstream by the *tight junctions* that are present between the cells lining the intestines, which are loosened by gluten and NSAIDs [See footnote 171]).

But when there is damage to the junctions (as can happen with gluten and NSAIDs) then the lining becomes leaky and permeable[171]. Then LPS goes into the blood circulation and can inflict damage on the body. So the level of LPS in the blood indicates that there is leakiness in the gut and of the presence of inflammation in the body in general.

Dr Perlmutter explained to the client that he needed to return her gut to full health. He recommended a gluten-free diet, an oral probiotic program, with probiotic foods and vitamin supplementation.

He also recommended other changes in her lifestyle, such as aerobic exercise and more hours of sleep. Then he asked to see the client again in six weeks.

He describes her as being *"transformed...she looked radiant"*. He and his colleagues at his clinic in Florida always take a picture of their clients at their first session and at the end of the treatment, and he has posted the "before" and "after" pictures of Martina here: www.DrPerlmutter.com.

Her chronic anxiety had vanished and she was now off all medications (although Dr Perlmutter points out that he did not recommend that she stopped her medication. Apparently she had stopped taking her antidepressant four weeks prior to the first appointment with him).

"I feel like the fog has finally lifted", she said to the doctor, and reported that she was sleeping well, enjoying her exercise and for the first time in decades was having regular bowel movements.

Dr Perlmutter has found reports by researchers whose experiments have been printed in the Journal of Applied Microbiology, who have described the potential of specific types of *lactobacillus* and *bifidobacterium*, in probiotic form, to reduce anxiety, and restore the gut to normal functioning and intestinal health.

Jenny Sansouci, who wrote a research paper on 'Nutritional approaches to anxiety' in 2002[172], summarised some of the key points of her nutritional research in her internet blog. She described the fact that millions of Americans take anti-anxiety medication, with the side effects of "...*slurred speech, tiredness, mental confusion, memory loss and delirium*".

She has found that people's diets play a very big role in reducing anxiety, and that medicinal drugs are unnecessary as a form of treatment. She considers the top offenders for the creation of anxiety in the human body are as follows: caffeine, sugar, artificial sweeteners and alcohol. She cites an example of the Starbucks "Grande–sized" coffee, which contains 330 mg of caffeine. And if a dose of caffeine is 300 mg or above, then this causes a very strong, sudden increase in tension and anxiety. This response has been corroborated in one research study.

She states that when we consume sugar, it has the effect of causing our blood sugar to drop, resulting in an increase in anxiety, light-headedness, irritability and feelings of weakness. She also mentions artificial sweeteners, which are composed of chemical elements which reduce the level of serotonin in the brain, with the result that stress, anxiety and depression are experienced. (Again, the link is most likely not via serotonin, but some other, as yet undiscovered, route).

The bottom line seems to be this: Avoid caffeine, or keep your consumption low, because caffeine can simulate anxious arousal in the guts and chest, causing the mind to panic. Keep blood glucose levels even, by consuming slow-burning foods, and avoiding sugary and starchy foods, process foods, junk foods of all kinds. Keep your magnesium and GABA levels high, by eating dark green leafy vegetables (like spinach and kale); nuts (walnuts and almonds); and seeds; fruit (e.g. bananas); and gluten-free oats (if you can tolerate them), and others. Take probiotics for gut health, and eat lots of fibre (including supplementing with psyllium husk) to serve as prebiotics, which encourage the growth friendly bacteria. Avoid gluten, sugar and artificial sweeteners and alcohol. Consume calming foods: Drink camomile tea and eat lots of salads with lettuce, which has a calming effect. Finally, eat lots of oily fish, and take omega-3 fatty acid supplements, like cod liver oil and/or krill oil.

~~~

... End of extracts...

~~~

Appendix C: Meditation as anti-anxiety practice

The content of the appendix recently appeared in our book, *The Bamboo Paradox*, (Byrne, 2020)[173].

~~~

What is meditation, and how can you do it?

Copyright (c) By Renata Taylor-Byrne and Jim Byrne – November 2019/ April 2020

~~~

Meditation involves sitting quietly, 'doing nothing'. It is a simple process of *paying attention to your breathing*, and letting your thoughts settle down and *letting your mind become peaceful.* It's about *'being in the present moment'*, relaxed, and with *bare awareness* to your immediately present environment. And that is why it is so helpful in reducing and controlling your anxiety level. To feel anxious, your attention has to be on a future threat or danger (all other things – including diet, exercise, sleep, etc. – being equal). But when you are deliberately meditating, your attention is concentrated in the present moment, and you are also focussed on 'brushing away' and thoughts that enter your mind: thoughts of the past or future! (However, meditation is just one strand of our recommended approach to anxiety management. If you fail to exercise, sleep well, and eat the right kinds of foods, and avoid the wrong kinds of foods, mediation, in and of itself, will not eliminate your anxiety problems!)

Meditation is best performed each morning for 10 to 15 minutes. (Twenty or thirty minutes would be even better; but you can build up to that over time).

You don't have to have a special meditation posture (but it can help to get you into the right frame of mind).

Therapeutic, non-religious meditation, involves focusing the mind on some external thing: (an external object, or an internal sensation, like the movement of your own breathing). This causes your thoughts to slow down, and your attention to remain in the present moment.

~~~

Imagine you and I have a pond in our minds, with lots of silt and debris at the bottom. Our normal daily routines churn up the silt and debris, and this clouds our mind and our vision, and produces stress and strain, and unhappiness, and poor perspectives on life. We often become humourless and constantly worried. Meditation is a process for allowing all the silt and debris (from the remembered past and the imagined future) to settle down to the bottom of our mind-pond, to restore clarity of vision/ perspective, to prevent depressive rumination or anxious anticipation; to restore a sense of ease and contentment, and to allow our natural happiness to return.

Simply sitting in one place, quietly counting your breaths, in and out, as they happen, is an amazingly beneficial exercise. This helps your brain, your blood pressure level, your nervous system, your level of physical and mental energy; and it strengthens your immune system, and improves your sense of composure. But for our present purposes, the most important consideration is that, by keeping your mind in the present moment, you cannot feel any anxiety about future threats and dangers.

Scientific Verification

There is substantial evidence that meditation has a positive effect on anxiety, though it's probably less dramatic than the effect of physical exercise.

In an article in the *Journal of the American Medical Association* (JAMA), in 2014, it was concluded that meditation reduces anxiety, depression and pain, according to the meta-analysis of 47 studies; (but it does not appear to help with other problems, including substance abuse, sleep and obesity).

The findings of the review of the evidence in the literature included this: "...we included 47 trials with 3,515 participants". (The participants did about 2.5 hours of meditation each week, for eight to 12 weeks). "Mindfulness meditation programs had moderate evidence of improved anxiety ... (and)... depression..." And: "...We include(d) only RCTs

(Randomized Control Trials) that used 1 or more control groups in which the amount of time and attention provided by the control intervention was comparable to that of the meditation program". So only respectable scientific studies were used. The lead author Dr Goyal, works at the Johns Hopkins School of Medicine[174].

Science Daily reported in 2011 that: "Mindfulness Meditation Training (which is what meditation consists of) Changes Brain Structure in Eight Weeks".

The *ScienceDaily* report, (Jan. 21, 2011), says: — "Participating in an 8-week mindfulness meditation program appears to make measurable changes in brain regions associated with memory, sense of self, empathy and stress. In a study that will appear in the January 30 issue of *Psychiatry Research: Neuroimaging*, a team led by Massachusetts General Hospital (MGH) researchers report the results of their study, the first to document meditation-produced changes over time in the brain's grey matter". (See the Britta K. Hölzel et al reference, above).

There are also lots of other reports on the internet on the efficacy of meditation, but this is the first to be able to scientifically link those changes to brain structure changes. (See the recommended reading at the end of this appendix). We can now definitively say that meditation is not just a palliative, not just a cognitive distraction. It changes the brain-mind for the better!

What does meditation do for you?

Why is meditation so good? It reconnects you to the *real world* – grounds you in reality – and enables you to slowly separate your wishes, thoughts and fantasies from what is actually going on around you. Regular practice also produces "long-term changes in sympathetic nervous system activity", and "quiets down the nervous system". This is a great aid to our resilience when we meet stressful events in our lives.

You reconnect with yourself as a physical and emotional being. You learn to *calmly* watch your mind and its endless activities, and not get pulled into 'working on the past', or emotional fortune-telling and worrying about future events (which haven't happened yet). And if you do not worry about the future, you cannot become anxious!

If you are very tense and stressed, and cannot imagine what a wonderful state of relaxation would feel like, then try watching a relaxation video on YouTube. It operates differently than meditation, except that they both focus on getting you to reduce and eliminate unnecessary thought.

Our brains are bombarded with information all the time from our social environment and the media. We need time to absorb, digest and sift through all this information in order to sort out the **food** from the **toxic garbage**. And all that is done effortlessly by our brain if we give it the time and space to do its job.

There are very many physical and psychological benefits to the daily practice of meditation. This has now been confirmed in a small but growing number of scientific research studies in the East and the West. And western science has become more and more interested in the benefits of meditation, and of Buddhist philosophy, as potential new aspects of the psychology of wellbeing. You can find this evidence on the internet by conducting your own searches. Try searching these key words: "research on meditation"; "science and meditation"; "meditation and stress". Or take a look at the sources listed in the references below as your starting point.

When we don't take the time to relax, and provide the mental space for information processing (which is maximized by the process of meditation) we experience a build-up of stress. We toss and turn in our beds, trying to deal with problems, creating others, never giving our brain a break, and sleeping fitfully and lightly.

Did you know that when we meditate, it is the only time our brains truly rest? They don't rest when we are sleeping – but we need to sleep for various housekeeping purposes, so do not skip sleep and substitute meditation. That won't work. But a short meditation session can help to top up your sleep. It also reduces the production of cortisol (which is one of the major stress hormones).

The Buddha taught the technique of focusing your awareness on your breathing, while sitting in an alert posture. You can count your breaths in and out – counting 'One' on the inbreath; 'Two' on the outbreath; 'Three' on the inbreath; and, finally, 'Four' on the outbreath.

Then repeat this process, over and over again.

Let your breathing slow down, and allow your bellow to expand on the inbreath, and to go flat again on the outbreath.

Try to feel the inbreath moving upwards through your nostrils. And expand your belly when you breathe in, instead of lifting your rib cage. Always breathe from your belly, like a baby does, and if it helps you, put the palm of one hand flat on top of your belly, and feel it move up and down as you breathe.

Meditation is very simple, but also very effective.

First: the location/setup. You can either sit on a cushion on the floor, with your legs crossed; or you can sit in an armchair, with your back straight. Try resting one hand on the other, in your lap, and allow your thumbs to lightly touch each other. Make sure there are no distracting, avoidable noises, in your environment, such as radio, TV, etc. (Normal 'noises off' can help the meditation, if you just let them come and go). Let your eyelids droop and focus your eyes downwards and straight ahead.

Second: the process. One approach is to count '*One*' on the first in breath, and '*And*' on the out breath. Then count '*Two*' on the second in breath, and '*And*' on the out breath. (Count silently in your mind). Then '*Three*' on the next in breath... All the way up to '*Four*'... '*And*'. Then back to 'One' again. Try to sit quietly for about fifteen or twenty minutes, preferably every morning. Don't try to *forcefully* stop yourself thinking – just *gently return your attention to your breathing, and counting your breaths again, if you lose track*. Try to focus all your attention on your breathing, your expanding and contracting belly, and the counting of the breaths.

The point is that your mind will wander – that is in the nature of 'monkey mind'. And so your job is to keep bringing it back to a point of concentration, and to keep reminding yourself to breathe, and to pay attention to your counting. As time goes by, you will get better and better at concentrating, but in the beginning you mind is bound to wander.

Once you have the knack of counting your breaths, focus your attention on something simple and still, in front of you, like I use my bedroom slippers.

If you find this hard to do, try Glenn Harrold's 'Meditation for Relaxation' audio program.

Or, try attending a meditation class for a while, until you know how to do it on your own. Then do it at home for the rest of your life. It will keep you happy, relaxed, de-stressed and un-anxious. It will also help to keep you looking and feeling youthful.

Don't be too influenced by the views of others on meditation. It is a practice that is easy for other people to make fun of. That is their loss! The Buddha suggested that the best way to experience the value of meditation (and everything else in life) was to: "Find out for yourself".

In our (Renata's and Jim's) own personal experience, regular daily meditation will not only improve your physical and mental well-being, it will also improve your efficiency and effectiveness, including your concentration ability. You will find problems much easier to handle and resolve. This is well summed up in the following words by Eckhart Tolle: "Obstacles come all the time. If you get upset, that means the ego is back. When obstacles come, if you're not upset, and you're still present, you will look at whatever the obstacle is with a penetrating gaze of presence, which is stillness also. You look at whatever obstacle arises, you bring this penetrating stillness to it, and that is like a light that shines on it and dissolves the obstacle or shows you a way around it. That's the power of consciousness."

Remember that to feel the full benefits of meditation, you need to develop the habit of doing it every day.

As you build up a daily habit of meditation, you will find that the stillness that existed during your meditation will tend to stay with you throughout the day, and help to calm you in stressful situations.

If you find it hard to get started, begin with just five minutes per day, and gradually build up to 10, 15, 20 minutes.

~~~

Recommended reading:

Hölzel, BK, Carmody, J., Vangel, M., et al. (2011). Mindfulness practice leads to increases in regional brain gray matter density. *Psychiatry Research: Neuroimaging, 2011*; 191 (1): 36 DOI: 10.1016/j.pscychresns.2010.08.006

Brain Longevity, by Dr Dharma Singh Khalsa, (1997), London: Century. (Pages 301-319).

Zen Made Easy, by Timothy Freke, Godsfield Press, 1999. (Pages 62-70).

Watts, A. (1962/1990) *The Way of Zen.* London: Arkana/Penguin. (Pages 174-179).

Zen Mind, Beginners Mind, by Shunryo Suzuki. Random House, 2006.

Everyday Zen, by Charlotte Joko Beck, London: Thorsons, 1999.

Science Daily, (2011) Mindfulness meditation training changes brain structures in eight weeks. Available online at: http://www.sciencedaily .com /releases/ 2011/ 01/110121144007.htm. Accessed: 8th February 2011.

~~~

Appendix D: Three strategies to control anxiety and worry

The material in this appendix recently appeared in our book, *The Bamboo Paradox*, (Byrne 2020).

~~~

Zen Tigers and Strawberry Moments

Buddhism teaches us to live in the present moment. And if you strive to keep your mind focused on the present moment, you cannot go off into the future to worry about threats and dangers; thus avoiding problems of extreme or inappropriate anxiety.

But living in the moment is easier said than done. Here's a practical process to support that important aim.

Copyright (c) Jim Byrne and Renata Taylor-Byrne, 2010/2011/2019/2020

~~~

Let me tell you a story about the philosophy of life of a Zen master. The gender of the Zen master (mistress?) in this story is irrelevant. So you can choose to read the story as if it was about a man or a woman, to suit your preference.

One day, a Zen master/mistress went into the jungle. S/He was enjoying the scenery: trees, vines, flowers; and listening to the sounds of the birds chirping, and various animals moving around and calling to each other. Suddenly s/he saw a tiger. Unfortunately, the tiger also saw the Zen master. S/He ran for his/her life; but s/he ran so fast that s/he ran off the edge of a cliff. Falling, s/he grasped for a tree root which projected from the face of the cliff, and ended up hanging from this root with his/her left hand. The tiger reached the top of the cliff, and stared down hungrily at him/her, but could not reach him/her.

The Zen master looked down to the foot of the cliff, and saw another tiger, looking up hungrily. Then, a couple of feet above his/her left hand, s/he noticed two little mice gnawing through the tree root, and s/he realised that before long s/he would (theoretically) go crashing down to the foot of the cliff, when the root broke. Then s/he noticed, to his/her right, a small strawberry bush, with a large, ripe, wild strawberry. S/He reached out and plucked the strawberry with his/her right hand, and popped it into his/her mouth. It tasted delicious.

~~~

Explanation: A Zen master does not concern themselves with the **past** (the tiger up above); nor with the **future** (the tiger down below). S/He is supremely centred in **the present moment** (the 'strawberry tasting' present moment). The strawberry flavour is intended to communicate the *blissfulness* of being in the present moment, with no distractions from the past or the future.

Clarification: Zen Masters do not ignore things that need to be done. If there is something that can be done (or controlled) about probable future threats or dangers, then s/he does that. If something can be done to clean up a past loss or failure, then she does that. But once controllable actions have been taken, the Zen master returns to the present moment. Why?

Because: "Only in a hut *built for the moment* can you be free from fear!"

Or, as the Buddha is said to have said: "One hair's breadth difference between what you want and what you've got and heaven and earth are set apart".

So, we have to focus our mind on the present moment, and accept the things we cannot change, and only try to change the things we can!

~~~

Back to the illustration of the tiger as the threat in the future, and the upset in the past.

The past	The present moment	The future
The past no longer exists, and therefore cannot harm you. (However, it does still influence you from non-conscious levels of mind!) The 'tiger' is up above, and cannot reach you. (The tiger in the past cannot come into the present and harm you, but your habits from the past come into the present and control your current behaviours!)	The present moment is a razor-sharp moment of blissful being. (We never experience it. We make up our 'individual moments' from the previous ten seconds or so, and extrapolate from there into the [imagined] near future). There are (normally, or most often!) no 'tigers' in the present moment. So if you can centre yourself in the present moment (as in meditation) then there is nothing to worry about (for the duration of that bout of meditation!)	The future is difficult and hard to know. It has not arrived yet, and its shape is unknown. (It's good to try to take account of the 'probable future; to plan to protect yourself; and then let your expectations and projections go!) The 'tiger' is down below, and cannot reach you. (No amount of worrying will get rid of all potential tigers from the future. Life is difficult, now, and [most likely] in the future; but it can [normally, and most often] be coped with!)

Table 1: The tigers in the past and in the future

~~~

In his book entitled 'How to Stop Worrying and Start Living', Dale Carnegie, also deals with the past, present and future. I have extracted just three of his strategies, and related them to the Zen Tiger story, as follows. They are listed as quotations at the top of each of the three columns in Table 2:

The past	The present	The future
"No use crying (endlessly) over spilled milk". (See clarification about 'Human Tears', below). ~~~ It would be a mistake to say, "I **should not** have gone into the jungle, then I would not be in this mess, hanging from this tree root, with two tigers to worry about!" Why would it be a mistake? Because you cannot change that reality now. You cannot choose your options retrospectively!	*"Live your life in day-tight compartments"*. ~~~ The only time that really exists is now. The past is dead and gone. The future is just a dream. So enjoy the present moment. If you can get your mind out of the past and the future, you will find that the present moment is blissful. Practice daily meditation to get your mind into the present moment.	*"I'll cross that bridge when I come to it"*. (But I'll also do whatever realistic forward planning that I can!) ~~~ If the tiger is there when you fall, it *must* be there when you fall, but you have no way of knowing that it *will* be there, since all kinds of things may have changed by the time the 'future arrives'.

...table continued...

The past	The present	The future
There is no point lamenting *this kind* of reality (and especially endlessly!). Some realities need to be lamented – such as the death of a significant other person; or the loss of a job; or some such highly significant loss or failure). Whatever happened actually did happen, because of all the little steps that had already been taken, by you, other people and the world.	Write about your current problems – your old losses and failures from the past; your current worries; and your worries about the future – in your 'Daily pages' – which you should write every morning (or evening. Morning is best!)	The tiger may have gone home for lunch, or a missionary might have happened along the lower trail, and the tiger might be busy eating the missionary when you fall. Or you might fall on the tiger, and accidentally break its back – putting it out of action!

Table 2: Tears, bulkheads and bridges in the future

~~~

Clarification about Human Tears

By Jim Byrne and Renata Taylor-Byrne, October 2018

The more we try to simplify our philosophy of life, the more we are in danger of over-simplifying it! And an over-simplified philosophy of life – like the extreme Stoicism of Rational Emotive Behaviour Therapy (REBT); or the emotion-denying theory of CBT – will just lead us into misleading others.

Once upon a time, I (Jim) subscribed to the over-simple statement: "There's no use crying over spilled milk!" It came with the territory of having parents who lacked empathy for the suffering of children. And that is where Dale Carnegie and Albert Ellis got it; although it was already there in Greek and Roman philosophy – from a time when you could be taken in slavery to clean the homes of the Athenian ruling class – or thrown to the lions to entertain the bored populace of Rome. Spilled milk seemed supremely unimportant in the context of slavery or death by being savaged by a lion. But in the modern world, we have more sense of entitlement than people had in ancient Greece or Rome. (Though we often are no more secure than they were – in a neoliberal world of immoral bankers!)

Anyway, back to human tears:

Extensive research by Dr William Frey (a psychiatric biochemist), in 1949, demonstrated that crying is an essential way of eliminating stress hormones under conditions of sadness and grief. Here's the most relevant point: "Human tears, unlike the tears of any other animal, contain a substance called ACTH, the hormone that actually sets off the stress response and is literally washed away by a good cry".[175]

So there is a very good point to 'crying over spilled milk', or any significant loss or failure, such as the death of a close relative or love object; or the loss of a job, career, or part of your own body, or a valued asset!

Therefore, the quotation should now be amended to this: *"There is no point crying __endlessly__ over spilled milk – though you should do whatever __grieving__ is necessary to __complete your experience__ of losses and failures, including symbolic losses and failures".*

~~~

More on living in the present

Dale Carnegie teaches many ways to get yourself into the present moment, including this quote from Sir William Osler:

"Our main business is not to see what lies dimly at a distance, but to do what lies clearly at hand".

He is clear that 'living in the past', is a waste of emotional energy. This is his advice:

"Shut off the past! Let the dead past bury its dead ..."

He is also clear that 'living in the future' is an unnecessary burden:

"...the load of tomorrow, added to that of yesterday, carried today, makes the strongest (person) falter. Shut off the future as tightly as the past... The future is today. There is no tomorrow. The day of our salvation is now. ... Prepare to cultivate the habit of a life of (living in) 'day-tight compartments'. ..."

If you think of something that needs to be done tomorrow, write it down in your diary, or on an action list, and then return your attention to this moment now. This is the only moment that exists.

If you think of something from that past that worries you, write it out (in your Daily pages); learn what you can from that experience, and then move on.

Once you have trained yourself to live your life in day-tight compartments, then what? Then you are faced with how to live well in the now:

"Think of your life as an hourglass". If you don't know what an hourglass is, it is like a giant egg timer, made of two glass compartments, connected by a narrow tube. Sand flows from one compartment down into the other, and measures the passage of time: three minutes for an egg-timer; one hour for an hourglass.

Dale Carnegie writes: "You know there are thousands of grains of sand in the top of the hourglass; and they all pass slowly and evenly through the narrow neck in the middle. Nothing you or I could do would make more than one grain of sand pass through this narrow neck without impairing the hourglass".

"You and I and everyone else are like this hourglass. When we start in the morning, there are hundreds of tasks which we feel that we must accomplish that day, but if we do not take them one at a time, and let them pass through the day slowly and evenly, as do the grains of sand passing through the narrow neck of the hourglass, then we are bound to break our own physical and mental structure".

Therefore, Dale Carnegie's advice to us all is this:

"One grain of sand at a time... one task at a time". Pace yourself. (If anybody uses the concept of 'multi-tasking' in your presence, call the local mad house and have them dragged away. Multi-tasking is a Big Lie! We must do One Thing at a Time!)

One thing at a time! If we tackle our work life in this way, then we can go on and on, healthily and productively. And if we deal with our personal problems, our worries, in this way, one at a time (in written form – in your journal or notebook – so we can see them clearly, and think about them clearly) – then we can worry constructively (and much more briefly!) To illustrate this point, Dale Carnegie presents this quotation:

'Anyone can carry his/her burden, however, hard, until nightfall. Anyone can do his/her work, however hard, for one day. Anyone can live sweetly, patiently, lovingly, purely, till the sun goes down. And this is all that life really means'. Robert Louis Stevenson.

Don't try to live your life a week or a month at a time:

"Each day is a new life to a wise person".

Don't waste your life dreaming of tomorrow. Live your life today:

"One of the most tragic things I know about human nature is that all of us tend to put off living. We are all dreaming of some magical rose garden over the horizon – instead of enjoying the roses that are blooming outside our windows today". (Dale Carnegie).

Or we are worrying about some dreaded nightmare up ahead, which, despite never arising, drains us of our vitality today, and spoils the only life we have: *this precious moment, Now!*

Live your life in day-tight compartments, and enjoy the moment:

"Most of us are...stewing about yesterday's jam and worrying about tomorrow's jam instead of spreading today's jam thick on our bread right now". Dale Carnegie.

At this point the two stories merge. The Zen master's life was supremely centred in the present moment, and therefore s/he could reach out and pluck the wild strawberry of the present moment. And Dale Carnegie equates this present moment with the sweet taste of jam. If you do not know why the beautiful taste of the strawberry, or the sweetness of jam, is used to describe the present moment, you have never *meditated*. Try it and see. (See Appendix C, above).

When you come into the present moment, life is beautifully sweet. There is no possibility of sustained anxiety!

Copyright (c) 2020: Jim Byrne and Renata Taylor-Byrne

April 2020 – Hebden Bridge

~~~

Appendix E: Journal writing exercises to calm your body and mind

In this appendix I want to present two extracts from my book on how to heal your childhood trauma, using writing therapy. (Byrne, 2020, in press).

~~~

Here is the first extract:

Quick, introductory tutorial on therapeutic writing

1. The Pennebaker approach:

Dr James Pennebaker's approach goes like this:

(a) For the next three days, sit somewhere quiet, and write for 15 to 20 minutes about the main emotional disturbance that you currently want to work on.

(b) Write the whole story out, as quickly as possible. Do not worry about grammar or public presentation. Just tell the story.

(c) Count the number of negative words and positive words. If the negative words exceed the positive words, rewrite the story until there are more positive than negative words. Do not aim to remove all negative words, since you need some negative words to express something that is causing you emotional pain.

(d) On Days 2 and 3, ask yourself:

- What do I know about this problem today, that I did not know yesterday?

What have I learned about what caused this bit of the problem, or that bit of the problem?

How can I make this story more coherent today than it was yesterday?

And then rewrite the story to take your answers into account.

~~~

Hopefully, that process will help to surface some key issues for you to work through.

~~~

2. Philippa Perry's approach:

"To begin self-observing, ask yourself these questions:

What am I feeling now?

What am I thinking now?

What am I doing at this moment?

How am I breathing?" (Page 16, Perry, 2012

The idea is to write these questions in your diary, or journal, and then write out your response to them, based upon self-observation. You could also add a question or two about how tense you feel; how good/bad is your posture; the nature of your environment; etc.

Of course, you don't have to follow Perry's questions religiously. You could equally ask yourself:

What is working in my life? (A gratitude searching question!)

What is causing problems in my life? (Problem identification)

What would a solution look like? (Identification of a goal or goals)

How might I get from where I am now (the problem) to where I want to be (the goal)?

And finally: *What actions do I need to take to get there?*

Philippa Perry continues: "These simple questions are important because when we have answered them, we are in a better position to proceed to the next question:

What do I want for myself in this new moment?"

(This is the question I have already identified above).

Sometimes just asking these kinds of questions results in an immediate decision to change something. This applies to any kind of problem in your life. With regard to the specific question of breath-holding, which can indicate an anxiety problem, Philippa Perry continues:

"For example, when we bring our attention to our breathing we become aware of how we are inhibiting it, and while we remain aware of it we tend to breathe more slowly. Change happens, if it needs to, when we become aware of what we are, not when we try to become what we are not". (Page 17).

The purpose of Phillipa Perry's questions is to get you to 'ground' yourself. To get you in touch with your body-mind, and to get your feet back on the ground. This may then improve your capacity to self-observe, and to identify your problems, which can be addressed with some of the questions I listed above (e.g. the problem identification and goal setting questions).

~~~

3. Julia Cameron and other approaches:

Julia Cameron wrote a book, called 'The Artist's Way' (1992)[176], in which she recommends that you sit down every morning and write out three pages of stream of consciousness. (To begin with, three pages may seem impossible; so just write as much as you can manage! And then increase your productivity over time).

If you get stuck, just keep on writing: "I am stuck. I am stuck. I don't know what to write…!" Etc. And after a little while some new ideas will come into your mind, and you continue again.

You can combine Julia Cameron's approach with some other systems, such as the *Skilled Helper* model, in which you ask and answer the following questions:

1. Where am I now (in terms of needing help or healing)?

2. Where would I like to get to (in terms of a new feeling state; or resolving a specific problem)?

3. What actions could I take to move me towards that goal?

Or you could use the WDEP model, as follows:

W = *What do I **want** (in terms of healing or problem solving)?*

D = *What am I currently **doing** (to achieve that goal)?*

E = ***Evaluation** of progress? (How well is this going?)*

P = *Improve your* **plan** (or change your **plan** in some way, if necessary)

~~~

You could also try writing poetry which expresses your stuck emotional pain, as this can help you to get in touch with the feelings, and to process and digest them, so they can disappear!

Or you could begin to write a short story (one or two pages to begin with), about some toy; or some little animals. Fictional stories work best to get at the tensions in your non-conscious mind. If you try to write pure autobiography, that may cause your mind to close down; to repress painful memories; and so on. But writing simple fiction stories, and/or poems, allows you to get close to your undigested pain, without panicking or closing down.

Finally, you could take some of your writing to a counsellor or psychotherapist, and ask for guidance.

~~~

...

And the second extract is a substantial portion of Chapter 2 of my book, 'How to Write a New Life for Yourself', (Byrne, 2018[177]).

~~~

Prelude

"In my experience of many decades, writing accelerates the time it takes to get someone unstuck by about fifty percent. Writing author-izes (counselling and therapy) clients: it introduces them to themselves, while also teaching a self-regulating and self-understanding skill".

(Noppe-Brandon, 2018).

~~~

Keeping a diary, or a journal, or writing on a regular basis, has been shown in scientific studies to be good for your physical health and your emotional well-being: (Esterling, L'Abate, Murray, and Pennebaker, 1999[178]; and Pennebaker, 2002[179]). It is also important for creative thinking (Cameron, 1992); and for reflective thinking in business and professional self-management (Tracy, 2004)[180].

As Pollard (2002) writes:

"Although there is a gulf of difference between the two, therapeutic writing can also unlock creative writing. Whitbread and Orange prize-shortlisted novelist Jill Dawson has kept a journal since she was nine. 'It has helped me personally and also made me a better writer,' she says, 'because going over and over something eventually makes it clearer. A dream you don't understand may make sense two years later. Obviously, it undergoes radical transformation before it becomes writing that you would want published, but it is a part of the process. You can find feelings by writing in this raw way that you can then explore using different events in a story.'"[181]

~~~

In this chapter, we will take a look at some practical strategies for managing stress, processing emotional experiences and solving problems, using writing therapy (Pennebaker and Evans, 2014); and 'thinking on paper' (Tracy, 2004: 157). My intention is to get you experimenting with writing therapy, or reflective writing, sooner rather than later; to help get your anxiety under control.

If you are suffering from anger, anxiety or panic, or a general feeling of being pressured beyond endurance, then this section should be helpful for you (...). You might also have practical problems, at home, at work, or in education or training, which are seriously concerning you; and you need to find a solution. ....

....

1. Introduction

...

Whether you are struggling with problems of anger, anxiety or panic, depression, stress, or difficult practical problems, you could benefit from writing out your difficulties, so you can see them on paper.

This is different from the normal approach of seeing a counsellor, psychologist or psychotherapist. However, if your problems are severe, it might be better to see a professional helper face-to-face at first, and later to add in the process of writing about your feelings and your practical problems. And if you are *seriously depressed* it might not be a good idea to use writing therapy, as it *might* make your symptoms worse. (This is *not inevitable*, and some depressed individuals have used writing therapy to cure themselves [for example, Schiffman, 1972[182]]; but there is a risk, especially if you only focus on writing *negative* words and ideas).

On the other hand, it would be a mistake to think that writing therapy (as in journal writing, for example) can only be used in mild to moderate disturbances. There is a famous case of an American war veteran (a returnee from Vietnam War), who was extremely 'shell-shocked' – or suffering from post-traumatic stress disorder – to such a degree that he could not fit back into society. He wandered the streets of San Francisco, with his possessions in a shopping trolley, until one day he accidentally found himself outside of a building in which a writing therapy course was going on. He went in, learned a simple system for keeping a therapeutic journal, and from that day onwards he kept a journal, in which he exorcized all his 'war demons' – and found his way back into a normal life! And to a career as a novelist. (Mulligan, 1997)[183].

So, obviously, writing therapy can be as potent as face-to-face therapy, and some theorists have claimed that it is even more potent! (Wiseman, 2009). But please note the points I made in the Preface. Certain things that we gain from having our emotional pain witnessed cannot be replicated in writing therapy; and it is easier to be re-parented by a therapist than it is to learn over time how to re-parent ourselves.

~~~

So what does writing therapy consist of? The quick answer could be expressed in any of the following three ways:

(1) *Thinking on paper*: as recommended by Brian Tracy (2004: 157).

The reason this can be so therapeutic is this:

You cannot actually 'think' separately and apart from your *feelings* and *perceptions*. When you engage your mind in the task of writing, it is inevitable and unavoidable that your thoughts, feelings, attention, perception, memories, and so on, *are all working together, just below the level of conscious awareness*, and in the process of writing a revised narrative of your problems, you also 'iron out' your negative feelings and tangled emotions! You make new meanings by seeing past experiences in a new light).

~~~

(2) *Writing about two or three pages each day*: as recommended by Julia Cameron (1992).

This is a 'stream-of-consciousness' process, in which you give expression, in writing, to whatever thoughts, feelings, attitudes, concerns, worries, or whatever, that happen to float up into conscious awareness.

This gives you access to creative thoughts, problem solutions, and useful insights.

~~~

(3) **Writing for about 15 minutes per day**, over a period of three or four days, as advised by James Pennebaker (2002). This is normally a more focussed task, which involves writing about a specific problem, pulling it apart, trying to make sense of it; and *gradually* gaining greater understanding of how to master it).

~~~

2(a) Initial guidelines

Notwithstanding the points made above about the unique advantages of seeing a counsellor or therapist for face-to-face help, it is nevertheless true that writing about yourself and your experience could transform your life into a hugely exciting adventure; a more productive, creative experience of happiness and fulfilment. But you have to actually do it (!) to get the benefit. And there can be problems with the process of getting yourself to do it!

Are you willing to *make a commitment* to write about yourself and your life? Yes or No?

If Yes:

Option 1: Are you willing to commit to writing for five to ten minutes every morning and evening, from Monday to Friday of each week?

If Yes, then good. If No, then:

Option 2: Are you willing to commit to writing about yourself and your life every Monday, Wednesday and Friday of each week? Yes or No?

If you are willing to agree to Option 1 or 2 above, then: Please write that decision down: "I am now committed to…" Fill in the blank.

Post your written commitment somewhere prominent, so you will see it at least a couple of times per day.

Next: Can I recommend that you commence acting on your commitment tomorrow morning, soon after getting out of bed?

If you agree, then let us begin with some small, easy steps.

Firstly, the Kaizen approach to change says we should always make small, easy steps towards larger goals, to avoid panicking the part of our brain-mind that keeps us on track as creatures of habit. To bypass those habit-patterns we need to communicate to our brain-mind that this (new practice) is just a minor deviation from the norm.

Secondly, you need to have some reward and penalty in mind to help to keep your commitment on track, and to stop the old habit-pattern (of Not writing in the morning) reasserting itself. This will be discussed below.

So let us begin with two, general self-management strategies:

Strategy No.1: Starting the day

In order not to overload yourself, begin with an A5 page (148 x 210 mm). If you use a Filofax, or a Junior Desk Day-Timer, then that is the perfect size. Or use a ruled, A5 notebook. *First thing every morning* – or at least three mornings per week to begin with - sit in a comfortable space, and write whatever is on your mind. If your mind is blank, write this: "My mind is blank. My mind is blank. My mind is blank".

This will help to free your thinking-feeling-perceiving, and the words will begin to flow. Write down whatever comes up. It could be worries, concerns, anger; or a sense of grief about some loss. Or some practical problem that you failed resolve in the past, or one that you want to resolve today. Whatever comes up, write it down.

Fill the A5 page, and possibly a second page, and then read back over it and make any changes that occur to you. If it's all too negative, change some of the words, and make them more hopeful, encouraging, and try to see the light at the end of the tunnel.

Try to have more positive words than negative words, but do not delete all negative words, since the world is actually a difficult place to be.

End with an action plan: *What action could I take today to change any of those things that seem to me to need changing?*

When you have completed this process, you can have your breakfast as a reward.

If you fail to complete the process, then you should *still have your breakfast*, but only AFTER you have done *30 minutes of house-cleaning*.

This combination of rewards (breakfast) and penalties (house-cleaning) should help you to do the task of writing your 'starting the day' activity.

(Over a period of weeks or months, you can move up from an A5 pad to an A4 pad; and increase your pages from 1 to 2; and later to 3. There's no rush!)

Strategy No.2A: Ending the day

At the end of your working day, either before you leave your workplace, or soon after returning home, sit down with your A5 notebook, and, on the front of the page, write answers to these questions:

1. What went well today?

2. What went badly?

3. What did I learn today?

4. What can I be grateful for today?

5. Which of my goals or action items did I complete; and which are still incomplete?

Then turn the page over, or start a new page, and write down six goals, or action items, for tomorrow which, if achieved, will take your life in the direction that you desire.

When you have completed this 'ending the day' process, you can have your evening meal as a reward. And even if you fail to do this process, *you still have your evening meal*, but only AFTER you have done *30 minutes of vigorous house-cleaning.*

These rewards and penalties will most likely keep you on track doing your end of the day writing process.

(Over a period of weeks or months, you can move up from an A5 pad to an A4 pad; and increase your pages from 1 to 2; and later to 3. There's no rush!)

~~~

Strategy No.2B: Daily Pages, or Morning Pages

I think of this process as writing my Daily Pages, because I write them at all kinds of different points in the day. Julia Cameron (1992), from whom I learned this process, calls them *Morning Pages*, because she recommends that they be done at the start of each day, to clear the mind for the day ahead. This is how she describes this process:

"Morning Pages are three pages of longhand, stream of consciousness writing, done first thing in the morning. There is no wrong way to do Morning Pages – they are not high art. They are not even 'writing'. They are about anything and everything that crosses your mind – and they are for your eyes only. Morning Pages provoke, clarify, comfort, cajole, prioritize and synchronize the day at hand. Do not over-think Morning Pages: just put three pages of anything on the page...and then do three more pages tomorrow."

Julia Cameron sees this process in various ways:

As building a bridge into a better future;

As a form of windshield wipers, which clean the screen through which you see your life and your road ahead;

As a small feather duster, which can get into all the nooks and crannies of your problems, and clean them up.

In our experience, they are a form of daily meditation upon the salient features of your life; out of which more constructive action arises; and our thinking and emotions improve.

If you want to experiment with this process, just begin to write. Just whatever comes up in your mind.

If you are blocked, write this: "I am blocked. I am blocked. I am blocked".

If you don't know what to write, write this: "I don't know what to write. I don't know what to write. I don't know what to write."

Just keep going – writing whatever comes up - until you have filled three pages of A4 writing pad, and then stop!

Many individuals have written to Julia Cameron to tell her what they gained from writing their Morning Pages.

Those gains include:

- greater creativity: (people begin to live their artistic dreams);

- better problem solving;

- healing of emotional wounds;

- giving up drugs and alcohol (which is what Julia Cameron did for herself using this process);

- creating hope of a better future;

- developing a healthier lifestyle, in terms of diet, exercise, sleep;

- and so on.

And this approach can be used to get your anxiety under control, especially combined with the Nine Windows Model from Chapter 3, above.

~~~

2(b) Overcoming your resistance to writing

Humans are creatures of habit, and you are (presumably) a human being who is in the habit of *Not Writing* in the mornings. For these reasons, you may find it *difficult* to begin to write when you get up in the mornings.

You may experience strong emotional resistance to any such change in your morning routine. I want to make sure I help you to get over any resistance you might feel to writing in the mornings.

If you have found, in practice, that you have been able to implement the strategies outlined above, then you do not need any coaching on overcoming resistance, and you can skip to section 2.3 below.

On the other hand, if you said you would try Strategies 1 and 2A, or Strategy 2B, above, but could not make yourself do it, then please read this section:

Because you have been struggling to establish a writing habit, I want to coach you through this resistance. Therefore, tonight, please set up an A5 page where you normally eat your breakfast at home. (If you normally skip breakfast, you need to know that this practice is a major cause of stress and anxiety. [See Taylor-Byrne and Byrne, 2017; and Byrne, 2018]. You need to eat a slow-burning breakfast[11] to provide fuel[12] to carry your body-brain-mind calmly, efficiently and happily through to mid-morning).

So, please put an A5 page of ruled paper in your 'breakfast location' at home. (Next to it, place a note saying this: 'I am now committed to writing for five to ten minutes...'; adding the frequency of this practice: (five mornings, or three mornings, or whatever you have decided).

Sit down as soon as you see this page, and begin to write about how you feel this morning; or what you are thinking this morning; or how well or how badly your slept; or what you dreamed about; or your plans for the day; or whatever comes up in your consciousness.

If your mind is totally blank, write this: "My mind is blank".

---

[11] Slow-burning foods include protein, such as eggs, cheese, bacon, fish; and complex carbohydrates, like vegetables, fruits, etc., and are distinguished from *quick-burning* foods, like processed cereals, highly processed breads, and so on.

[12] The 'fuel' that you need is glucose, but not from refined sugars or sugary foods. Highly processed carbohydrates produce a rush of sugar, which results in a heightened stress response. (See Taylor-Byrne and Byrne, 2017; and Byrne, 2018).

And if it is still blank after writing that statement, then write it again: "My mind is blank". Over and over again, until the mental 'log jam' clears!

If you feel stuck, write this: "I feel stuck!" Over and over again, until the log jam clears.

If you feel angry about this exercise, write this: "I feel angry about this exercise". Over and over again.

If you do not know what to write about yourself or your experience, write this: "I do not know what to write!" Over and over again. Until something worth writing comes into your mind.

This activity of keeping on writing when you do not know what to write is highly effective in getting you past 'writer's block'; or emotional log jams!

Write for five minutes. Then have your breakfast.

If you do not write on this fateful day, drastic action is called for! Why? Because this is the day on which you must either *overcome your* **resistance** *to writing*, or get stuck in the role of a non-writer for the foreseeable future! And this is the drastic action that I recommend to you:

If you do not write for five to ten minutes, then, on this crunch occasion, you cannot have your favourite breakfast; but must eat something that you dislike eating. You also have to stay at home – not go to work, school, college, shopping, etc. – unless and until you do your five minutes of writing.

And if you stay home all day, you cannot have your preferred lunch, nor your preferred evening meal (but have to eat things you dislike), unless and until you have done your five to ten minutes of writing about yourself and your life.

And you cannot go to bed that night, unless you have done your five to ten minutes of writing about yourself and your life. Instead you must stay up for an hour and do some heavy household cleaning tasks.

At some point, the 'habit-controller' in your brain-mind will surrender, and let you begin this new habit of writing every morning for five to ten minutes.

(This approach is called 'living your commitments', and is very different from saying you will do something, and then letting it slide!)

~~~

3. Dealing with emotional difficulties

Of course, the processes described above will only help with general self-management needs. They will not be sufficient if you are wrestling with serious emotional problems, or particularly stressful events.

Strategy No.3: Emotional processing

Get a large (A4) notebook to use as your self-therapy journal, or stress diary. A spiral-bound, hard covered notebook would be best.

Set some quiet time aside, just for you to work on your journal. (Since this activity will inevitably improve your productivity, it is legitimate to take this time out of your working day!)

Write down the answers to these questions:

*1. What is **the actual problem** in my life which is making me unhappy at this time?*

*2. What are the **feelings** that are bothering me at the moment?*

*3. What are the **difficult thoughts** that I am wrestling with?*

*4. Is there a problem with the ways in which I am **behaving** at this time?*

Reflect upon what you are writing, as you go along:

*Name the **feelings*** that are troubling you. If you don't have ready names or labels for those feelings or emotions, then please read Appendix B, which explains how to understand and manage your emotions.

Look for patterns in *what you are writing*: Try to **make sense** of your problems:

- look for **cause and effect**;

- pros and cons;

- options and possibilities.

Try to identify *possibilities for change* or improvement.

Try to 're-frame' your problem, so it looks and feels better, even if you cannot as yet get rid of it. (See Chapter 3 for the Nine Windows Model, with brief questions. Answer those questions before returning to your journal).

Try to produce an improved understanding of your problem, in the form of "an *empowering* narrative", rather than a "*de-powering* story".

But what exactly is an *empowering* narrative?

An example of an empowering narrative is one in which things are bad like our anxiety about a future threat or danger), but it could get better:

- "if I can do X";

- or "if I can escape from Y";

- or "if I can get help from Z"; etc.

Or, you might consider that some things are bad, but there are also things for which you can be grateful. So that you experience a sense of balance.

An example of a *depowering narrative* would be one in which you list all the bad things in your life; or all the obstacles in your way; and you overlook the fact that "Life is BOTH difficult and non-difficult"! (See Chapter 3 above). So add back in the non-difficult bits; or the possibilities of improvement; or the potential routes out of your situation; and then you have a more empowering narrative!

If you are struggling to create an empowering narrative, then please work through Chapter 3, which is the Nine Windows Model, which will help you to think-feel-perceive more flexibly about your life's problems.

And, if that still does not facilitate your being able to generate an empowering narrative about your current problem(s), you could go to see a counsellor, coach or psychotherapist and get some face-to-face help. Then, armed with some new ideas, return to your journal writing!

Strategy No.4: Tracking sources of stress

Stress is a major problem in the modern world. The speed of life is too much for our stone-age bodies. And insecurity abounds, in work, in relationships, in the very sustainability of the world economy.

As a general summary, we can say that stress – including anxiety - is a body-brain-mind experience of distress, which occurs when the pressures bearing down upon us – or apparently bearing down upon us – exceed our coping resources.

Develop your awareness: If you are ever going to manage your stress level, then you have to become aware of the *external sources* of your stress, and your contribution to it. One of the best ways to develop your awareness of the sources of stress in your life is to keep a *stress diary*. The purpose of the stress diary is to track down the specific stress problem(s) you are confronting.

Try to identify your problems in this order:

1. What happened, or what happens? What did I feel, and how did I behave?

2. Draw a picture or diagram of your life, including the stressful elements; and label each element so you can begin to see how they each relate to the others.

3. Focus on a specific incident or experience of stress. Ask yourself:

About this incident, what can I control and what is beyond my control? (See Window No.1 of the Nine Windows Model, in Chapter 3, below).

Are my expectations in line with reality? (Are they realistic?)

Am I exaggerating the degree of badness of the situation? (See Window No.4 in Chapter 3).

Have I reminded myself that life if difficult for all human beings? (Since it is difficult for all human beings, at least some of the time, why must it not be difficult for me? [See Window No.5 in Chapter 3]).

Since life contains difficult bits and non-difficult bits, am I reminding myself of the non-difficult bits of my life? Am I aware of the bits I should feel grateful for? Or do I focus only, or mainly, on the negative aspects of my life? (See Window No.4 in Chapter 3).

Write out those questions (above) and attempt to answer them.

4. Look closer at the control issue: *About this problem, what can I control today? Can I change the situation? Can I change my self-talk?* (Then commit yourself to control what you can control, and to give up trying to control what seems to be beyond your control. [See Window No.1 in Chapter 3, for a deep insight into this area.])

5. *Who could help me with this problem? To whom could I talk about it?* (Make any appointments that are necessary).

6. *How can I relax and unwind, to let go of my tension and stress?* (You might need to learn about the importance of exercise and relaxation, including some systems or techniques for you to explore. Or you might need to focus on improving your sleep pattern – all of which are covered in chapters above).

For more guidelines on writing therapy or journal writing, please see my book, *How to Write a New Life for Yourself*. (Byrne, 2018a).

Re-reading this appendix is strongly recommended. Dale Carnegie used to recommend that readers of his books should read each chapter three times before moving on to the next one. We would strongly recommend that approach here. It takes a lot of effort to embed any new habit or to master any new skill.

First reading ❐

Second reading ❐

Third reading ❐

~~~

Appendix F: How to change habits related to anxiety

The content of this appendix first appeared as Part 6 of our book on diet and exercise: (Taylor-Byrne and Byrne, 2017).

How to change for good

By Jim Byrne and Renata Taylor-Byrne

Copyright © Jim Byrne and Renata Taylor-Byrne, 2017/2020

~~~

Section 1: Introduction to habit change

By Jim Byrne

In this section, and the next, we intend to give you all the tools you need to implement the behaviour changes which have been recommended in the main body of this book.

1. General theory

In our system of coaching, counselling and therapy (known as the E-CENT[184] perspective), humans are seen as creatures of habit, rather than rational thinkers. (Or, rather, we are *both*; but the emotional past most often proves to be *more powerful* than our present, surface-level thinking; which is how and why we have survived for so long. We don't have to sit around thinking about how to respond to potential threats. We just automatically do what has kept us safe in the past!) Whatever we did before, you can bet most humans will tend, normally, to repeat in the present – except sometimes. Sometimes we may step outside of our past performances, but *not normally*.

In this sense – the sense of being creatures of habit – humans are clearly *products of the past*; *shaped* by the past; *driven* by past experiences; and *acting out* scripts and stories which they *constructed (with the help of their parents and teachers) in the past.* In response to 'present time' stimuli

- which are experienced *as if they were a **repetition** of the past* – we most often do what we are in the habit of doing.

Because we humans are **dominated** *by the past* – all our knowledge and skill and habitual behaviour comes to us from our past, which is stored in our body-brain-mind in the present moment. We cannot 'dump the past'; cannot step away from the past; or behave as if we do not have a specific, personal, historical past.

We learned to eat from our mothers; and we often copy our parents' attitudes towards exercise, sleep, alcohol, smoking, and so on. And we also pick up their emotional patterns, like inappropriate anxiety or a tendency to panic under pressure.

So change has to be *gradual*, because it involves the *breaking* of powerful habits. And it requires *self-discipline*, and some kind of *support system*.

~~~

2. The benefits of exercise and dietary self-management skills

Diet is not about weight loss, in the main, but about eating healthily; and not just for physical health, but also for emotional wellbeing. Our guts and our brains communicate constantly, and when we eat the wrong foods, we tend to disrupt our normal gut flora and friendly bacteria, which then produces negative effects upon our brain-mind, and thus upon our moods and emotions, and our ability to think straight. Excess sugar causes stress and anxiety; gluten damages our guts and disrupts our brains. Caffeine speeds up our nervous systems, by secreting stress hormones, and this makes us anxious and jumpy. And sedentary lifestyle allows the build-up of stress hormones, and slows down the lymphatic drainage of toxic substances from our bodies.

Exercise is important because it affects the electro-chemical functioning of the whole body-brain-mind, reducing stress hormones, releasing happiness chemicals, and promoting oxygenation of every cell, plus the movement of lymphatic fluid; and thus promoting physical *detoxification* and improving physical health and emotional wellbeing through *stress reduction*.

~~~

3. Our approach to behaviour change

We believe in *gradual* change!

We do not want to encourage you to *overload yourself* with self-change action lists! Or, to put it better: We do not want you to believe that you *have to change everything* on your self-change list *today, right now, immediately* and totally!

You cannot do it anyway. Because we are creatures of habit, if we try to change too much too quickly, the deeply emotional, habit-based part of us will panic, and rebel; and not allow it to happen. It's too scary.

So, therefore, change takes time.

Change take effort.

Change takes commitment.

And the best way to proceed is slowly, incrementally, and self-supportingly!

4. A personal example

To make this point well, I (Jim) would like to present an example from my own life:

About fifteen years ago, I found I had lost all my self-discipline in relation to daily physical exercise. I had gone from being a regular exerciser to a regular procrastinator! I could not bring myself to do any exercise whatsoever. So, for a long time I was stuck in this 'pre-contemplation' stage. I was not planning to change anything!

Then, as the weeks and months drifted past, I became more and more annoyed with myself, because I knew I was risking serious damage to my physical health and my emotional wellbeing. At this point I became a 'contemplator'. I was contemplating, or thinking about, change, but I could not quite bring myself to do anything about it. I kept 'planning' to change; or 'trying' to change; but I did not change!

Then one morning I felt so bad about my procrastination, that I became 'determined' to do something about it. This is, obviously, called the 'Determination Stage' of behaviour change. (Prochaska, Norcross and DiClemente, 1998)[185]. That was when I remembered the *Kaizen* method of 'gradual improvement'[186]. This system, introduced to Japan by some American teachers, including W. Edwards Deming, at the end of the Second World War, teaches a process of gradual refinement and progress, instead of huge jumps and big goals.

So I decided on the smallest goal I could come up with, which would be acceptable to me. I felt I could run on the spot, right by my armchair, for thirty seconds, and then sit down. I stood up – (this is the Action step) - feeling hopeless, and I did it. I ran on the spot to the count of thirty. That is to say, when my left foot hit the floor, I counted '1'. Then, when my right foot hit the floor, I counted 'And'. When my left foot fell again, I counted '2'. And so on, up to thirty foot falls; like gentle jogging, but on the same spot. Then I sat down. *I felt great!*

I felt such a sense of self-efficacy – of self-esteem – that I was amazed. Such a small step forward, and such a big reward in terms of how good I felt about myself.

So, the next day, I decided to run on the spot for the count of sixty (foot lifts and falls). When I sat down, I felt even better.

The third morning, I could not stop when I reached 60, or 120, or 240. I was hooked.

I had persuaded the resistant, emotional, non-conscious part of myself that I would not die, or fall apart, if I did my physical exercises; so I went back to doing my old Judo club calisthenics, my Chi Kung, and my press-ups and sit-backs.

And this is the key point: This is how we want you to tackle whatever personal-change goals you come up with, as a result of reading Part 1 and Part 2 of this book.

We do not want you to demoralize yourself, by *aiming too high*, too soon, only to fail; and then to abandon all attempt at personal change. We want you to be *realistic*, and we want you to give yourself the best chance of *succeeding* in making those changes you choose for yourself!

~~~

5. A second example: Using rewards and penalties

The second story I want to tell you follows on from the first.

So, I did my exercises four or five mornings each week, for quite some time, but then I began to skip them, if I was 'too busy'; or if I was 'running late'. So, I remembered another very important principle of behaviour change: rewards and penalties!

So I made this commitment to myself:

"Every morning that I do my exercises, I will give myself permission to read six pages of a novel that I like, as a reward. And if I fail to do my exercises, I will immediately take *two £1 coins* (which totals close to $3 US) from my bookcase shelf, and go out into the street, and drop them both down the nearest drain, so they become irretrievably lost!"

Needless to say, I did not skip any exercise sessions from that point onwards!

~~~

In Section 2 …, below, Renata presents an even more powerful system of behaviour change, which you can use to make those changes you want to make to your diet and exercise regimes.

~~~

6. The stages of change

So now, we hope, you have an understanding that change has to be *gradual*.

Change begins at the **Precontemplation** stage, when you are not planning any change at all. Then it proceeds through **Contemplation**, when you are *thinking about* changing something. Then on to becoming **Determined** to change something. Then you take **Action**. And even after that, you can slip back. So you have to work at **Maintenance** of the new habit. When you feel yourself slip back, you have to repeat whatever process you used to make the change. And you have to be vigilant, to make sure you don't slip back too easily.

The important point is this: You cannot make any changes until you reach the *'determination'* stage; and it's best to have a system of *rewards* and *penalties* in place.

One of the best rewards, of course, is the realization that – when you manage your lifestyle well - you are getting control of your anxiety level; and improving your physical and mental health. (And you will also look more attractive, and be more creative, and be more successful in your relationships, at home and in work!)

~~~

Next we will present Section 2: How to change your negative habits, below.

~~~

Section 2: How to change your negative habits

By Renata Taylor Byrne - Copyright © Renata Taylor-Byrne 2016-17/2020

~~~

1. The nature of habits

What are habits? Here are two definitions from the Merriam-Webster dictionary:

(1) Habit is "… (a) *behaviour pattern acquired by frequent repetition or physiologic exposure that shows itself in regularity or increased facility of performance"* and/or:

(2) It's "*…An acquired mode of behaviour that has become nearly or completely involuntary.*"

~~~

And here is the viewpoint of one of the fathers of American psychology:

> "*All our life, so far as it has definite form, is a mass of habits".*

> *William James, 1892*

~~~

We are habit-based human beings, and the more we know about how we form habits, the *easier* it will be for us to change old ones that aren't working for us, and to create new ones.

A researcher at Duke University in 2006 discovered that more than 40% of the activities people engaged in every day were habits, and not decisions they had made.

And some theorists would say that our habit-based functioning is as high as 95% (Bargh and Chartrand, 1999)[187].

Throughout the animal world, habit based behaviour is the norm. This has served survival well, which is why it is ubiquitous.

Humans have the greatest capacity of all animals to change our habits, but we will never become habit-less.

Our brains have developed the ability to create habits because they allow our brains to save effort, and to function more efficiently without having our minds cluttered with the mechanics of the many basic behaviours we have to follow each day.

~~~

2. The structure of a habit

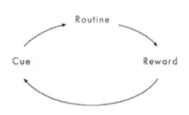

In his book, *The Power of Habit,* Charles Duhigg[188] looked very closely at the specific features of what makes up a habit. In his view, a habit is like a loop that has three parts: the cue; the routine; and the reward. Here is a picture of that loop:

Firstly, there is a *cue* (a trigger that starts off a *routine*: e.g. the sound of the alarm clock in the morning is a cue, which triggers the routine of getting up).

Here's *an example of a cue* that I recently found in the *Sunday Times Magazine*, in an article by Viv Groscop (who performed her one-woman show at Edinburgh in August this year [2017]). Viv stated that, to make her exercise routine strong, she started keeping her workout clothes and trainers next to her bed, so they were *the first things she saw- the cue!* – *in the early morning*, as soon as she woke up. (She lost 3 stone [or 42 pounds in weight] in one year through changes in her exercise and nutrition habits).

2. Secondly, this cue is followed by *a routine.*

A routine is here defined as *any* pattern of behaviour. Examples include: eating, going to the pub, watching a TV programme, going to the gym, doing homework, buying clothes, smoking, placing a bet, etc.

3. Finally, there is a *reward* – the most important part of the loop.

All habits have a *reward* at the end of them. Here are some examples of rewards:

(1) The feeling of comradeship when drinking at the pub;

(2) the rush of pleasure after you have just done a bout of exercise;

(3) giving yourself a cup of (decaffeinated!) coffee when you've done your daily exercise. And:

(4) seeing the *good, pleasurable results* of any difficult task.

~~~

3. The importance of craving!

*For habit change to work you have to **crave** the reward.*

This is an important alert: You have to *really crave* the reward, or you *won't* have the incentive to change your behaviour. Charles Duhigg describes a research project undertaken by the National Weight Control Agency. The agency examined the *routines* for eating food that had been created by people who were successful dieters. They investigated more than 6,000 people's routines.

What was discovered was that *all* the successful dieters eat a breakfast (which was cued by the *time* of day). But they also had very real, *very desirable rewards* in place for themselves if they stuck to their diet plans – and it was the reward that they craved. (For example, being able to fit into new clothes in a smaller size; or having a flatter belly, etc.)

And if they felt themselves *weakening* in their commitment, they *changed their focus onto the rewards* that they would get if they *kept* to their plans. This visualisation, of the very real rewards they would get, kept them strong in the face of temptation.

Apparently people who started new exercise routines showed that they were more likely to follow an exercise routine if they chose a *specific cue* (first thing in the morning, or as soon as they get in from work, or before bedtime).

So having a cue in place is **crucial** *to initiating the new behaviour (or routine).*

The new behaviour (or **routine**) follows from the cue.

Let me give you a personal example: Jim and I get up in the morning, and the first thing we do is to have breakfast, because we *crave* the pleasure of raw salad with seeds and nuts, and minor embellishments.

The *end of breakfast* **cues** us to meditate, and we crave the rewards of meditation, (a lot of which have to do with stress management, health and happiness, plus creativity).

Then, *the end of meditation* **cues** us to begin our physical exercise (Chi Kung [or Qigong], the Plank, some press-ups and sit-backs, and so on]) which we **crave** because of the physical and mental health benefits that we gain.

So, the **reward** is what people crave at the end of their routines. Some of the *rewards* mentioned in Duhigg's research were having a (small amount of) beer, or an evening of watching the TV without guilt.

As my own experiment, I (Renata) wanted to establish a daily habit of exercising my arm muscles, to firm them up. Therefore, I set up a **cue** which is the start of the BBC TV programme **'Pointless'**, at 5.15pm every day.

When I hear the theme music for *Pointless*, I get out our "Powerspin" device – which simulates weight training - and do a pre-planned (recommended) set of exercises.

This exercise **routine** is designed to strengthen my arms and back muscles, and core (stomach); and it is very simple, but involves some physical exertion.

And the **reward** for me (which I *crave* strongly – otherwise it won't work) is the knowledge that my arms and back and core muscles are getting stronger and fitter, and that this will keep me fit and able to carry heavy objects into old age! And so far, so good – I've only missed a few times!

~~~

4. Duhigg's own experiment

Charles Duhigg did a really interesting personal experiment to see if he could change one of his own habits. He was eating too many cookies (or biscuits) and he was starting to put on weight. He did an explanation and a description of his experiment which you can see on YouTube. He broke the habit, by working out what the reward was (and it had nothing to do with cookies/biscuits). Once he knew what the reward was, he found it very easy to substitute a new routine which did not involve eating junk foods! Here is the address of his video clip at YouTube: https://youtu.be/W1eYrhGeffc

~~~

5. The importance of substitution

What if we have a habit that we want to change? Can we get rid of it?

How do we go about it? Charles Duhigg states that we **can't** get rid of old habits – but what we can do is *substitute* new routines for the old ones, and get the same rewards.

He explains that a golden rule of habit change, which has been validated by repeated studies for a long time, is as follows:

"To change a habit, we must keep the old <u>cue</u>, which delivers the old <u>reward</u>, but change <u>the routine</u>.

"That's the rule: if you use the same cue, and provide the same reward, you can shift the routine and change the habit. Almost any behaviour can be transformed if the cue and reward stay the same". (Page 62)

He gives the example of someone who wants to give up cigarettes. If the person wanting to quit smoking fails to find something else to do (a new routine), when they start to crave nicotine, then they will be unable to stop! It will be *too hard* for them. That's why, in Section 1 of Part 6 above, Jim emphasizes substituting stevia for sugar, before giving up the sugar. The reward is the sweetness. The cue may be thirst. But the routine does not have to involve sugar, so long as it involves some sweetness; and stevia is a safer form of sweetness.

6. Stopping addictions

Charles Duhigg states that the organisation called *'Alcoholics Anonymous'* (**AA**) is effective in helping people reduce their drinking habits because it examines and shines a very clear light on the **cues** which trigger drinking in people; and the **AA** program deliberately encourages people to **identify** the **cues** and **rewards** that encourages their alcoholic habits, and then *assists them* as they try to find new behaviours (or routines).

So the implied question that **AA** asks an alcoholic is: *"What rewards do you get from alcohol?"*

"In order for alcoholics to get the same rewards that they get in a bar, AA has built a system of meetings and **companionship** *– (the individual 'Sponsor' that each person works with) – that strives to offer as much escape, distraction and catharsis as a Friday night bender."* (Page 71)

If someone wants to get support from another person, they can receive this by talking to their *sponsor* or by going to a *group meeting*, rather than "toasting a drinking buddy".

A researcher called J. Scott Tonigan has been looking at the work of *AA* for more than ten years, and he states that if you look at Step 4 of the 12 step program, (which is to make a *'searching and fearless inventory of ourselves and to admit to God, to ourselves* and *another human being the exact nature of our wrongs'*), you will see that something crucial is taking place, which he sums up like this:

"It's not obvious from the way they are written, but to complete those steps, someone has to create a list of **triggers** *for all their alcoholic urges. When you make a self-inventory, you're figuring out all the* **things** *that make you drink..."* The **cues!**

7. The rewards of drinking

The *AA* organisation then asks alcoholics (or alcohol dependent individuals) to look really hard for the **rewards** they get from alcohol, and the **cravings** that are behind the behaviour. And what is discovered?

*"Alcoholics crave a drink because it offers escape, relaxation, companionship, the blunting of anxieties and an opportunity for emotional release....the **physical effects** of alcohol are one of the least rewarding parts of drinking for addicts."* (Page 71)

So what *AA* does is gets you to create *new routines* for your spare time *instead of going out drinking*. You can relax and talk through any worries or concerns you might have at the meetings.

*"The triggers (cues) are the same, and the payoffs (rewards) are the same, it's just the **behaviour** that changes,"* states Tonigan.

~~~

8. The result of one experiment

To summarise the value of one particular experiment, Duhigg showed that the former alcoholics in the study only succeeded in eliminating their drinking behaviour because they developed new routines which followed the old *triggers* (or *cues*), and gave them their comforting *rewards*.

Apparently the techniques that were developed by the *AA* for changing habits have also been successfully applied to children's temper tantrums, sex addictions and other types of behaviour.

The **AA** is described in Duhigg's book as an organisation which creates techniques to change the habits associated with the use of alcohol:

"AA is in essence a giant machine for changing habit loops and though the habits associated with alcohol consumption are extreme, the lessons AA provides demonstrates how almost any habit – even the most obstinate – can be changed." Charles Duhigg

He makes it clear in his book that overeating, alcoholism, or smoking, are ingrained habits that take real commitment to change. But if you know how your habits are working, this makes it easier to experiment with new behaviours.

~~~

9. Analysing your own habits

If you look very carefully at the **cues** that cause you to avoid physical exercise, or to eat foods that you now know to be bad for your physical and emotional health, and you work out the rewards that you currently get from the *avoidance routine*, or the *consumption routine*, then you can easily identify a new **healthy routine** to substitute for the old unhealthy routine.

It might be best to begin with exercise, because this may help you to find the commitment to change other habits, including some eating habits.

Why is this?

~~~

10. Creating 'keystone habits'

Exercise seems to be a 'keystone habit' that has a beneficial, 'knock-on' effect. When people begin exercising, and it can be as little as once a week, they begin to change other, unconnected habits in their lives. It has been discovered that they reduce their smoking, spend money less, and have more understanding for their family and the people they work with.

"Exercise spills over", stated James Prochaska (a University of Rhode Island researcher). *"There's something about it that makes good habits easier."*

Other studies have revealed that families who are in the habit of having their meals together regularly – which is another 'keystone habit' - raise children with higher school grades, more emotional control, better homework skills and increased confidence.

Apparently making your bed every morning is also a keystone habit, which has a spill over effect. It is correlated with a higher level of happiness, stronger skills at sticking to a budget and a higher level of productivity.

So, by beginning to use the kaizen approach (described in Jim's section above), to get in the habit of doing a few minutes exercise each day, you will be starting a cascade of potential change. Over time, you can learn how to exclude all of the toxic foods; to get on to an exciting, healthy and enlivening diet; and to be happier, healthier and more creative. (But do it slowly, gradually, incrementally. And reward yourself at every step)

~~~

11. Habit reversal

Here is a quote by Nathan Azrin, who was one of the people who developed habit reversal training:

*"It seems ridiculously simple, but once you are aware of how your habit works, once you recognise the **cues** and the **rewards**, you're half-way to changing it."*

Today, habit reversal is used to treat gambling, depression, smoking, anxiety, procrastination, and sex and alcohol addiction etc. And you can now use it to change your exercise and dietary habits too.

Charles Duhigg makes the point that although the habit process can be simply described, it doesn't mean that it's **easily** changed. As Mark Twain argued, a habit cannot be flung out of the window by any person, but has to be coaxed downstairs a step at a time! You cannot eliminate habits that no longer serve, you can only **replace them** with new habits that support your goals. You have to be aware of what you want (the implicit reward – the thing that you crave), and work to create new habits (or routines) that will get you what you want.

Charles Duhigg states:

"It's facile to imply that smoking, alcoholism, over-eating or other ingrained patterns can be upended without real effort. Genuine change requires real work and self-understanding of the cravings driving the behaviours. No one will quit smoking because they can sketch a habit loop.

"However, by understanding habits' mechanisms, we gain insights that make new behaviours easier to grasp. Anyone struggling with addiction or destructive behaviours can benefit from help from many quarters, including trained therapists, physicians, social workers and clergy.

"Much of those changes are accomplished because people examine the cues, cravings and rewards that drive their behaviours and then find ways

*to **replace** their self-destructive **routines** with healthier alternatives, even if they aren't aware of what they are doing at the time. Understanding the cues and cravings driving your habits won't make them suddenly disappear – but it will give you a way to change the pattern."* (Page 77)

It may also help to get you from the 'contemplation stage' of behaviour change to the 'determination stage'.

Once you are determined, you are halfway there. And if you know what the reward will be – and you put secondary rewards and penalties in place – then you are on the home run!

~~~

12. Conclusion

In this appendix, we have given you all you need to change any of your habits related to diet and/or exercise; or any other area of your lifestyle: like sleep, relaxation, etc. All you need now is the *determination* to use this information to bring about the changes that you want to see.

Do you crave release anxiety? If so, which of your unhelpful dietary routines, or lack of activity routines, or sleep routines, do you want to change first? What can you substitute for that routine which you would find rewarding? Once you know the cue, the routine and the reward, all you have to do is make the substitution.

If you want 'belt and braces' support, then set up an additional reward and penalty (as described above) to make sure you stick to the new routine! And try to get social support for your changes.

Good luck!

Renata Taylor-Byrne

~~~

Appendix G: How to understand and manage your emotions: specifically anxiety

The content of this appendix is extracted from Chapter 7 of our book on Lifestyle Counselling (Byrne, 2018)[189].

~~~

Extract 1:

Evolutionary psychology

While Buddhism and Stoicism mainly apply *the negative theory of emotion –* which assumes that *all* emotions are problematical - evolutionary psychology promotes the idea that our emotions arose, and were selected by nature, because *they served to keep our ancestors alive*. This is a *positive* theory of emotion.

Evolutionary psychology is an attempt to build a science of psychology, based on inferences - (many from anthropological studies; and many which appear to be little more than applied logic, or philosophical thought experiments) - about the ways in which our ancestors adapted to their environments, and how and why some psychological adaptations were most likely selected by nature for their survival value. For examples:

Without your innate tendency towards anger, there would be nothing to stop selfish individuals taking advantage of you, even to the extent of threatening your survival (by stealing all the available food, for example).

Without anxiety, you might sit and watch with curiosity while a lion approached you and then ate you.

Without distress (or sadness) you might be unable to attract social support when you are weakened by illness, or when you are otherwise disadvantaged and in need of extra support.

Without feelings of lust and romantic love, you might fail to attract a mate; fail to reproduce yourself; and the quality of your life might seem so poor (relative to social norms) that you could easily abandon the attempt to stay alive.

So feelings - even apparently destructive or painful emotions - can be seen to serve useful survival functions, *except when they are taken **too far**, and then they cause more harm than good.*

And, paradoxically, as pointed out by Siegel (2015), emotions are both *regulated* and *regulatory*. They are regulated (or controlled) by both internal and external factors; and we also tend to internalize those external, social factors over time. (This external factor often takes the form of verbal or non-verbal feedback from significant others [mother, father, others] about their experience of our emotional expression [or expression of affects]).

Some of our emotive-cognitive experiences (including that feedback from significant others) help us to regulate other of our emotive-cognitive urges.

Another way to say this is as follows: We have our innate affects, or emotions, *socialized* by mother/father; and this shapes *our **subsequent** capacity* to *perfink* (or perceive-feel-think). Then, when some new event impinges upon our consciousness, we use our historical capacity to perfink to regulate our current perfinking response to this new experience. (Of course, this is *an exaggerated statement of 'agency'*. In fact, it is not *"us"* that does anything! It is not so much that "we use" our historical capacity to perfink; but rather that "we are used by" our historical capacity to perfink. It is rather more that *our historical **capacity** to perfink* – which is electro-chemical, body-brain-mind, culturally shaped memories - *automatically regulates our subsequent perfinking* about new and novel incoming stimuli).

While cognitive therapists elevate 'thinking' to the driving seat of human behaviour; and affect regulation theorists elevate 'feeling' to this role; we in emotive-cognitive (E-CENT) theory, attribute overall control of the body-brain-mind to *perfinking* – which is *integrated, interwoven, perceiving-feeling-thinking;* which is so hopelessly intertwined that *it is not possible to **separate** out the strands* from each other.

The *modelling* (or *demonstration*) of emotional self-regulation by our parents – as they engage in *their own **perfinking** performances* - is another of the major internalized sources of self-regulation that we have (which begins outside of us, but ends up encoded in our neurological, higher cognitive emotions, probably largely in the right orbitofrontal cortex [OFC]).

An example of the excessive use of negative emotions would be the driver who is so angry about being frustrated by other drivers that he (or she) gets out of their car and assaults somebody – killing or maiming them; resulting in great harm to both parties.

Or the person who is so anxious they cannot go out of their own home, and thus they miss out on all kinds of social pleasures (and the possibility of earning a living!)

...End of extract.

~~~

Second extract:

The proximal cause of emotional disturbance

According to Dr Gordon Coates, all emotions can be understood as a result of our *wanting* something to happen (hope), and/ or *wanting* something else *not* to *happen* (fear)[190]. (This is very similar to the Buddha's view that all our emotional distress, or human disturbance, results from our desires. And it also reminds us of Freud's conclusion that humans are innately programmed to seek pleasure and to avoid unpleasure [or pain]).

But these conclusions by Coates could be a lightly concealed circular argument. What they seem to suggest is this: I experience **hope** because I **want** something to happen; and/ or I **want** something to happen and **therefore** I feel hopeful. Not only is this argument circular, but it also does not account for **wanting** as the 'prime mover'.

Why do I want **anything**? *And why do I want* **the specific things** *that I seem to want?*

If **wanting** is the *prime mover* of our actions/ thoughts, resulting in a cascade of emotions, *what accounts for the state of wanting itself?*

We will return to this problem, but first let us complete Coates' model. This little model, called *the Wanter-fall chart*, has two branches which flow downwards:

THE WANTERFALL CHART

Branch 1. When I **want** something to happen, I experience **hope**. When the desired outcome **occurs**, I experience **happiness** (plus something called 'propathy', which is the opposite of antipathy). But since I am now happy, and I **want** *that state to continue*, I now experience **fear**.

Branch 2. The second branch runs like this: I **want** to **avoid** a particular outcome, so I experience **fear**. When the feared outcome occurs, I experience **sadness** and antipathy.

Figure 1: The Wanterfall Chart

This little model is too circular, and cannot account for the *origins* of emotion as such. And neither can it account for the *determinants* of human wants.

The evolutionary view

The perspectives of *evolutionary psychology* and *affective neuroscience* are better sources of explanation of human emotions. According to Panksepp and Biven (2012) our evolutionary adaptations (as mammals) laid down certain subcortical structures in the limbic areas of the brain. These neurological structures underpin seven emotional systems as follows:

1. **Seeking**: This emotional system is about how the brain generates a euphoric and expectant response. (I am wired up by nature to seek: human faces; comfort; food; and as I grow, to seek novelty, stimulation. (I 'want' what I am *programmed* by nature to 'want'!) So when I am 'wanting' many experiences, I am expressing an innate, biochemical urge laid down by

natural selection. Of course, my list of wants can be, and is, expanded by my cultural conditioning and experience).

2. **Fear**: This system is about how the brain responds to the threat of physical danger and death. (I am wired up by nature [natural selection] to fear threats and dangers, because my ancestors who survived long enough to reproduce were kept alive by their fear of predators; and they passed that fear down the line, biochemically. This is my innate 'flight response'. I 'want' to survive, because I am programmed by nature of 'want' to survive! [Again, of course, I can learn to fear things that are not real threats or dangers]).

...

... End of extract.

~~~

Extract 3:

Finally, that brings us neatly to the *social model* of the individual, which I also developed in 2009.

The social individual

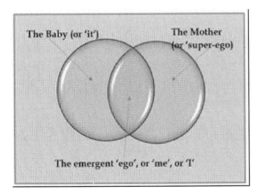

After reviewing the complex ABC model, I went on to lay down the basic E-CENT model of the mother-baby dyad, in Figure 5 of Byrne (2009b)[191], as shown in Figure 7 below.

Figure 7: The most basic model of E-CENT counselling theory

This model helped us to explore the ways in which the mother of a new-born baby has to colonize the baby; take it over; and run its life, for the sake of its survival. The first couple of years of each of our lives is spent in close proximity to mother (or a substitute carer), who is more or less sensitive to our needs; more or less responsive, attuned, and timely in responding; more or less gentle and caring; and so on.

The personality of the mother dictates the kind of care we get; and the kind of care that we got is internalized as the foundations of our first *Internal Working Model* of relationship. If she can provide us with a 'secure base', then we will grow up with a secure sense of attachment to subsequent love objects, including the individual(s) we marry[192].

It may be that the OK-Corral from Transactional Analysis (TA) captures the core decision of significance which is at the centre of the *Internal Working Model*. This is how the OK-corral model looks:

		Your Decision About Others	
		OK	Not-OK
Your Decision About Yourself	OK	1. I'm OK - You're OK	2. I'm OK - You're Not-OK
	Not-OK	3. I'm Not-OK - You're OK	4. I'm Not-OK - You're Not-OK

Figure 8: The OK Corral from TA

Thus my basic decision about my relationship with mother might be this: "I'm okay, and so is she!" But it could equally be that "I'm not okay, but she is!" And so on. That early decision, about who I am and how I feel valued or devalued, marks me for life!

This model can be translated (theoretically; propositionally) into a *Working Model equivalent*, in the form of **adult attachment styles**, as shown in Figure 9, below.

This is not a perfect fit with attachment theory, but it has some useful features, and some caveats. For example, the **preoccupied** mind-set of the anxious-ambivalent individual is based on a negative view of the self (or at least a view of the self as *not self-sufficient*, and of *desperately* needing the other person to stick around). And this causes their tendency to cling. On the other hand, they may not see their partner as 'positive' as such (and they may even cling angrily!) but they view their partner as a *positive asset* to which they must hold on!

		Thoughts-feelings about self	
		Positive	Negative
Thoughts-feelings about partner	Positive	**Secure:** (comfortable with intimacy and autonomy)	**Preoccupied:** (Anxious-ambivalent about relationship: Clingy)
	Negative	**Dismissing:** (Avoidant attachment, cool and remote)	**Disorganized:** (Confused, dissociating, blanking out: Approach-avoidance)

Figure 9: Adult attachment styles and appraisals of self and others

We can also infer, in the average case, that if the mother's (and father's [or main carer's]) way of relating to the baby results in a positive self-appraisal (which is emotive-cognitive), and in a positive appraisal of the care provided by the main carer, then the baby (and later adult) will form a **secure** attachment style, in which they are comfortable with intimacy and autonomy.

On the other hand, in the absence of good-enough parenting, the individual is likely to develop an avoidant, or anxious-ambivalent, or disorganized attachment style.

Of course, there is more to attachment styles than is suggested here.

In particular, each individual builds up a non-linguistic, non-conscious picture of *"How 'they' related to me; who that 'makes me'; and how I had to relate to 'them'; and how I must relate to any new (significant) person in front of (adult) me today."*

We do not have to think about any of this. It's all automatic and non-conscious; a set of pre-patterned ways of relating, based on foundational experiences.

~~~

It takes five or six months for us to distinguish ourselves from our mothers, and we rely upon her, not just for food and comfort and taking care of our colic, and changing our soiled clothing, and so on; but also, and perhaps much more importantly, for her ability *to sooth our* **uncontrollable** *emotions.*

Young babies cannot soothe themselves, and need external assistance with this challenge. As we grow up, we take back some of those controls, but we never completely outgrow the need for external assistance with 'affect regulation'. (Lewis, Amini, and Lannon, (2001))[193].

We need our mothers to love us if our socialized brains are to grow and provide us with an adequate measure of social and emotional intelligence (Gerhardt, 2010)[194].

As mother interacts with her baby, the baby internalizes representations of the experience of those encounters – at least those which seem emotionally significant. (Siegel, 2015)[195].

And out of those encounters, the baby constructs its *ego*, or *personality* (as illustrated in Figure 7 above).

As I wrote at that time:

"Thus the mother wires up the brain of her baby, initially by handling and managing its body; and later by introducing the baby to her language, her linguistic culture, her rules, and her language-based world." (Byrne, 2009b).

But today I would also want to add this: It is not all about language and culture. It is also about the mother's behaviours, and the child's interpretation of those behaviours; which show up as both *narrativized* and *non-narrativized experiences*!

Of course, the baby brings something to the party – his or her innate wiring in the brain stem and the limbic system; and its enteric brain (in its guts).

All of which is instinctive and emotional.

There are no 'innate beliefs', since 'beliefs' are *linguistic constructions*.

So, it is more useful to see the ABC/SOR/EFR models differently.

The *major mediating variable(s)* between:

(1) A new Activating Stimuli – coming into the senses of the child –

And:

(2) An outgoing emotional and behavioural response,

Can now be seen to be:

(3) **Experiences**, and **not** Beliefs!

~~~

That is to say, we are wired up for today by our **Previous Experiences**, from the past; *some of which have been **narrativized*** (or can be articulated in language today); and *some of which were **never narrativized***, and cannot be accessed today - because they are totally non-conscious, and beyond retrieval. But they nevertheless play a role in *guiding* our *reactions* to new events today!

~~~

I have argued above that there are seven innate emotional control systems, and there is an evaluation capacity – 'good' – 'bad' – which guides the baby's reactions to incoming stimuli. A felt experience seems either negative or positive to the new-born baby and young infant; and this triggers one of the emotional control systems: (e.g. anger or fear, or joy, etc.)

The baby, as it develops, shows signs of having pro- and anti-social tendencies, but these are shaped overwhelmingly by the mother's level of skill. A skilful mother can soothe a truculent baby; while an unskilful mother can aggravate and irritate a calm baby and render it truculent.

As the baby grows and encounters mother and father and perhaps a sibling or two, and perhaps *granny*, and *babysitters*, and then perhaps *nursery teachers*, and so on, s/he increasingly internalizes their ways of being: their Parental tendencies; their Adult tendencies; their Child-like tendencies.

And the child can also link those states to its own child-like tendencies, and, from age two years onwards, increasingly to act like a Little Professor, asking questions and exploring its environment.

But s/he (the child) mainly learns from instruction and modelling, and trial and error, and eventually can organize all those Parent, Adult and Child experiences –

with good and bad aspects –

into coherent wholes,

below the level of conscious awareness,

until his or her personality … emerges (through the interaction of A [mother] and B [baby])…

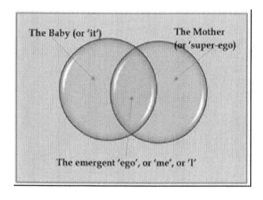

…End of final extract.

~~~

Books by the Institute for E-CENT Publications

Distributed by ABC Bookstore Online UK

~~~

The Bamboo Paradox: The limits of human flexibility in a cruel world – and how to protect, defend and strengthen yourself

Finding the Golden Mean that leads to strength and viable flexibility, in order to be happy, healthy and realistically successful

By Dr Jim Byrne; with contributed chapters by Renata Taylor-Byrne

~~~

Are human beings like bamboo? Are we designed to withstand unlimited pressure, stress and strain? Is our destiny to be sacrificed on the altar of other-directed 'flexible working arrangements'?

We live in a world in which there are dark forces that wish us to forget that we are fleshy bodies, with physical and mental needs; and physical and mental limitations; and to be willing to function like mere cogs in the wheels of somebody else's financial or technological empire.

In this book, I review the research that we have done on the limits of human endurance, and the determinants of that endurance – as well as identifying a viable philosophy of life – which will help you to optimize your strength and flexibility, while at the same time taking care of your health and happiness.

If you want to take good care of yourself in the modern mad-market, you could benefit from studying this book. It will provide you with both a compass and a suit of armour which will support you with the challenges and battles you will inevitably face.

~~~

Paperback copy: £14.99 GBP

~~~

Kindle eBook: £5.99 GBP.

~~~

How to Resolve Conflict and Unhappiness: Especially during Festive Celebrations:

Coping with and resolving frustrations, disappointments and interpersonal clashes at family celebrations like Christmas, Yuletide, Hanukkah, Eid, and Thanksgiving

Dr Jim Byrne (With Renata Taylor-Byrne)

Conflict can happen in families at any time of year. It just so happens that the first Monday after the Christmas & New Year annual holidays is called 'Divorce Day', because that is when the highest number of divorce petitions is issued. And it seems most likely that the other major family holiday times are the runners up in the divorce stakes. However, what is hidden under these divorce statistics is the mountain of personal and social misery that precedes such drastic 'solutions' to repeated conflict, disappointments and interpersonal clashes.

But there is a better way to deal with these problems. Rather than letting the misery build up over time, you can take control of both your own mind, and the way you communicate within your family and society. You can insulate your social relationships from constant or repeated misery and unhappiness; and learn to have a wonderful life with your family and friends.

The solutions have been assembled by Dr Jim Byrne in this book about how to re-think/re-feel/re-frame your encounters with your significant others; how to communicate so they will listen; how to listen so they can communicate with you; and how to manage your lifestyle for optimum peace, happiness and success in all your relationships.

PAPERBACK (£14.99 GBP) AND eBOOK (£3.99 GBP) ON CONFLICT RESOLUTION...

Don't let your relationships deteriorate. Get the solution today:

How to Resolve Conflict and Unhappiness

~~~

Anger, resentment and forgiveness:

How to get your inappropriate anger under reasonable control

By Dr Jim Byrne

This book is based on twenty years' experience by the author of providing anger management counselling and coaching to hundreds of individuals.

It includes a unique chapter on the processes required to achieve forgiveness, and a rationale for doing so. And it contains lots of insights into the philosophy and biology of anger management.

Price: £14.75 from Amazon.

~~~

Safeguard Your Sleep and Reap the Rewards:

Better health, happiness and resilience

By Renata Taylor-Byrne

A detailed review of the science of sleep, and what this tells us about the importance of sleep for a happy, successful life.

Now you can begin to understand why you need sleep; how much you need; how to optimize your chances of getting a good night's sleep; and what to do if you experience sleep disturbance. You will also learn how to defend your sleep against modern sleep-distractions.

Price: £14.99 (GBP)

How to Quickly Fix your Couple Relationship:

A brief DIY handbook for serious lovers

By Dr Jim Byrne

This book has been specially designed to provide some quick relief up front. That means that, right at the start of the book, I share with you some of the most powerful insights into how to have a happy relationships. I then help you to complete a couple of exercises that take five minutes per day, and which will begin to change your relationship situation almost at once.

Kindle: £5.02

Paperback: £12.10

How to Write a New Life for Yourself:

Narrative therapy and the writing solution.

By Dr Jim Byrne, with Renata Taylor-Byrne

Prices: from £4.22 GBP (Kindle) to £13.27 (paperback)

This book contains more than twenty exercises to help you to get more of what you want from your life.

Journal writing, and various forms of writing therapy, and reflective writing are included, with specific exercises for specific purposes.

How to Have a Wonderful, Loving Relationship:

Helpful insights for couples and lovers

By Jim Byrne (with Renata Taylor-Byrne)

~~~

Originally published with the title, *Top secrets for Building a Successful Relationship*, in 2018. Reissued with a new title and minor changes in November 2019.

~~~

Do you sometimes feel that you are just reliving your parents' relationship? The unworkable, misery-inducing pattern that you witnessed in childhood? If so, you are probably right. That is most often how relationships turn out, unless you wake up and begin to change your unconscious pattern of relating.

Most human beings long to be engaged in a loving relationship with another person who they like and admire, and who likes, admires, loves and respects them in turn.

But most people have no idea how to bring this about.

A few lucky people will automatically 'know' what to do, non-consciously, because they had parents who openly demonstrated their love for each other.

Find out how to reprogram yourself for a loving, joyful, peaceful relationship that enriches your life, instead of making you miserable and disappointed.

Prices from £6.65 GBP (Kindle) to £19.48 GBP (paperback)

How to Control Your Anger, Anxiety and Depression:

Using nutrition and physical activity.

By Renata Taylor-Byrne, and Jim Byrne

Changing your philosophy of life will not control your emotions, unless you also attend to your diet and exercise needs.

It is now increasingly being argued, by cutting edge scientists, that the root cause of physical and mental health problems is inflammation in the body, especially in the guts. The concept of leaky gut giving rise to leaky brain is increasingly being verified; and very often the causes of anxiety, depression and anger are to be found in the client's diet; or their lack of physical exercise.

By Renata Taylor-Byrne and Jim Byrne - Prices: from £3.10 (Kindle) to £9.93 GBP (paperback)

Lifestyle Counselling and Coaching for the Whole Person:

Or how to integrate nutritional insights, exercise and sleep coaching into talk therapy.

By Dr Jim Byrne, with Renata Taylor-Byrne

Because diet, exercise and sleep are increasingly seen to be important determinants of mental health and emotional well-being, it is now necessary to rethink our models of counselling and therapy. This book will show counsellors how to incorporate lifestyle coaching and counselling into their system of talk therapy. It will also help self-help enthusiasts to take better care of their own mental and physical health, and emotional well-being.

Prices: from £4.26 GBP (Kindle) to £12.64 (paperback)

Facing and Defeating your Emotional Dragons:

How to process old traumas, and eliminate undigested pain from your past experience

By Jim Byrne, Doctor of Counselling

This book presents two processes that are necessary for the digestion of old, traumatic or stress inducing experiences.

The first looks at how to re-think or re-frame your traumatic memory; and the second is about how to digest it, so it can disappear.

Prices from: £6.16p (Kindle) and £13.63 GBP (Paperback)

Holistic Counselling in Practice:

An introduction to the theory and practice of Emotive-Cognitive Embodied-Narrative Therapy

By Jim Byrne DCoun FISPC

With Renata Taylor-Byrne BSc (Hons) Psychol

This book was the original introduction to Emotive-Cognitive Embodied Narrative Therapy (E-CENT), which was created by Dr Jim Byrne in the period 2009-2014, building upon earlier work from 2003. It is of historic importance, but it has been superseded by Lifestyle Counselling and Coaching for the Whole Person, above.

Prices from: £5.83p GBP (Kindle) and £15.18p (Paperback)

***

A counsellor reflects upon models of mind

Integrating the psychological models of Plato, Freud, Berne and Ellis

By Dr Jim Byrne

Prices from: £5.99 (Kindle) and £14.99 GBP (Paperback)

Every counsellor needs to think long and hard about their perceptions of their clients. Are they based on 'common sense', or have they been subjected to the discipline of considering the theories of great minds that preceded us, like Plato, Freud, Berne and Ellis. (Ellis, of course, *oversimplified* the SOR model of mind into the simple ABC model, but he is still important because of his impact on the whole CBT theory, which currently dominates the field of counselling and therapy in the US, UK and elsewhere).

***

This next book replaces our original critique of REBT – *Unfit for Therapeutic Purposes*. We have added a 22 pages Preface which summarizes the bottom line of Dr Byrne's critique of REBT; and some detail about the way in which physical and psychological pain are processed through *largely overlapping* neurology and brain areas.

A Major Critique of REBT:

Revealing the many errors in the foundations of Rational Emotive Behaviour Therapy

By Dr Jim Byrne

There was a need to clarify the bottom line of Dr Byrne's critique of REBT, and that has been done in a 22 page Preface to the reissued, 2019 edition.

Also, we have added a reference to the research which shows that emotional pain and physical pain are both mediated and processed through significantly overlapping neural networks, which contradicts Dr Ellis's claim that *nobody could **hurt you**, except with a baseball bat.*

This is a comprehensive and devastating critique of the foundations of Rational Emotive Behaviour Therapy, as developed by Dr Albert Ellis.

Price: £23.58 GBP

~~~

***

If you want to know the essence of our critique of REBT, but you don't want to have to read 500+ pages, then this 150 page summary should appeal to you:

Discounting Our Bodies:

A brief, critical review of REBT's flaws

By Dr Jim Byrne

This book is a brief, summary critique of the main errors contained in the foundations of Rational Emotive Behaviour Therapy (REBT) theory. And especially the invalidity of the ABC model, which asserts that *nothing other than* **beliefs** intervenes between a negative experience and an emotional-behavioural reaction. (The body is ignored!)

Paperback only (at the moment). Price £9.50 GBP

The Amoralism of Rational Emotive Behaviour Therapy (REBT):

The mishandling of self-acceptance and unfairness issues by Albert Ellis

By Dr Jim Byrne

This book is an extensive, detailed critique of two of the central ideas of REBT:

(1) The concept of 'unconditional self-acceptance'; and

(2) The idea that life *is fundamentally unfair*, and that it should be accepted as such, and *never complained about.*

In the process we also deal with Albert Ellis's idea that people should *never be blamed* for anything; that praise and blame are bad; that guilt and shame are to be eliminated, and never taken to be indicators that we've done something wrong. Along the way we have a debate with Dr Michael Edelstein about the role of fairness in couple relationships.

Albert Ellis and the Unhappy Golfer:

A critique of the simplistic ABC model of REBT

By Dr Jim Byrne

~~~

This is a book of reflections upon a case study, presented by Dr Ellis in his 1962 book about the theory of Rational Therapy.

The 'unhappy golfer' is in Dr Albert Ellis's office, in New York City, somewhere around the end of the 1950's. He tells Dr Ellis that he feels terribly unhappy about being rejected by his golfing peers, and Dr Ellis tells him: *This is something you are doing to yourself!*

Ellis uses the unhappy golfer to introduce his readers to his simple ABC model of Rational (REB) Therapy, which claims – in those places that matter most – that a person cannot be upset emotionally in any way other than by their own beliefs!

This book sets out to refute this simplistic idea.

Albert Ellis and the Unhappy Golfer.

Paperback: £15.71 GBP

~~~

Daniel O'Beeve's Amazing Journey: From traumatic origins to transcendent love

The memoir of Daniel O'Beeve: a strong-willed seeker after personal liberation: 1945-1985

Transcribed by Jim Byrne

It is rare that any of us gets a chance to peer inside of the life of a troubled individual, from a dysfunctional family, and to have our lives enriched by their struggles for freedom and self-understanding. And their quest for love in a cold world can motivate us to keep trying to achieve our own emotional development.

~~~

Available in Kindle eBook for £5.54 GBP

And in paperback for £27.38 GBP:

The Relentless Flow of Fate

By Kurt Llama Byron

An Inspector Glasheen Mystery

This novel introduces the enigmatic Inspector Glasheen in his forty-eighth year of life, and his twenty-first year as a detective in the Gardai, in Dublin. A series of murders awaits him at his new posting. And one in particular, the death of a sixteen year old youth, in his bed, at home, is destined to bring up Glasheen's own demons, from a very disturbed childhood.

Paperback only at the moment, for £11.95 GBP

Endnotes

---

[1] Freeman, D. and Freeman, J. (2012) Anxiety: A very short introduction. Oxford: Oxford University Press. Page 4.

[2] **Defining anxiety:** "Anxiety is a feeling of unease, like a worry or fear, which can be mild or severe. Everyone feels anxious from time to time and it usually passes once the situation is over.

"It can make our heart race, we might feel sweaty, shaky or short of breath. Anxiety can also cause changes in our behaviour, such as becoming overly careful or avoiding things that trigger anxiety.

"When anxiety becomes a problem, our worries can be out of proportion with relatively harmless situations. It can feel more intense or overwhelming, and interfere with our everyday lives and relationships." Source: https://www.nhs.uk/oneyou/every-mind-matters/anxiety. Accessed on 28th March 2020.

~~~

[3] Bond, F.W. and Dryden, W. (1996). Why Two, Central REBT Hypotheses Appear Untestable. *Journal of Rational-Emotive & Cognitive-Behaviour Therapy,* 14(1), 29-40.

[4] Byrne, J. (2019a) *A Major Critique of REBT: Revealing the many errors in the foundations of Rational Emotive Behaviour Therapy*. Hebden Bridge: The Institute for E-CENT Publications.

Byrne, J. (2019b) *Facing and Defeating your Emotional Dragons: How to process old traumas, and eliminate undigested pain from your past experience*. Hebden Bridge: The Institute for E-CENT Publications.

[5] Byrne, J. (ed) (2018b) CBT and drugs aren't working: How Effective is Cognitive Therapy and Cognitive behavioural Therapy? A brief review of five pieces of evidence. Online: https://abc-counselling.org/cbt-and-drugs-arent-working/

[6] Griffin, J. and Tyrrell, I. (2003) *Human Givens: A new approach to emotional health and clear thinking.* Chalvington, East Sussex: HG Publishing.

---

[7] Byrne, J.W. (2019) *Holistic Counselling in Practice: An introduction to the theory and practice of Emotive-Cognitive Embodied-Narrative Therapy. Updated edition (2).* Hebden Bridge: The Institute for E-CENT Publications.

[8] "According to Buddhist principles, the "monkey mind" is a term that refers to being unsettled, restless, or confused. Writer and Buddhist Natalie Goldberg, who teaches many writing workshops, suggests that the monkey mind is the inner critic." Diana Raab, Calming the Monkey Mind - Psychology Today blog; here: https://www.psychologytoday.com/gb/blog/the-empowerment-diary/201709/calming-the-monkey-mind

[9] Kashdan, T. and Biswas-Diener, R. (2015) *The Power of Negative Emotion: How anger, guilt and self-doubt are essential to success and fulfilment.* London: Oneworld Publications.

[10] Grant, D. and Joice, J. (1984) *Food Combining for Health.* Wellingborough: Thorsons.

[11] Holford, P. (2010) *Optimum Nutrition for the Mind.* London: Piatkus.

[12] Teychenne M, Costigan S, Parker K. (2015) The association between sedentary behaviour and risk of anxiety: A Systematic Review. *BMC Public Health, 2015.* Cited in *Medical Daily,* here: http://www.medicaldaily.com/constantly-sitting-down-being-sedentary-could-worsen-anxiety-and-mental-health-338952

[13] Taylor-Byrne, R.E. and Byrne, J.W. (2017) *How to control your anger, anxiety and depression, using nutrition and physical activity.* Hebden Bridge: The Institute for E-CENT Publications.

[14] Broman-Fulks, J.J, and Storey, K.M. (2008) Evaluation of a brief aerobic exercise intervention for high anxiety sensitivity. *Anxiety Stress Coping. 2008 Apr; 21(2):* Pages 117-28. doi: 10.1080/10615800701762675.

[15] Byrne, J.W. (2020/In press) *Recovery from Childhood Trauma: How I healed my heart and mind - and how you can heal yourself.* Hebden Bridge: The Institute for E-CENT Publications.

[16] The WDEP model is structured like this:

W stands for Want. *What do I want?*

D stands for Doing. *What am I doing about what I want?*

E stands for Evaluation. *Let me now evaluate how well my Doing serves my Want.*

P stands for Plan or re-Plan. *In the light of the evaluation on point E, what should my new or revised plan be?*

I have sometimes used this model with a counselling client and discovered that what the client was Doing could never, ever, ever, in a million years, by any stretch of the most vivid imagination, help the client to get what they Want. And yet they were blithely continuing to Do what could never deliver what they Wanted. How does this happen? Because the contradiction is out of conscious awareness. Once you do the WDEP on a problem, if there is a conflict or contradiction between what you want and what you are doing, it will show up. All you need then is the courage to change your behaviour - (or what you are Doing) - or to drop your goal - (which what you said you Wanted).

~~~

[17] Gerard Egan's Skilled Helper model has three major elements:

1. Where am I now?

2. Where do I want to get to? And:

3. What actions could I take to build a bridge from 1 to 2 above?

~~~

[18] **CoRT* Tools**. This range of thinking tools is described in De Bono (1995: 49-52). CoRT-1 tools are 'attention directors', and are as follows:

- **PMI**: Plus, Minus and Interesting. Direct your attention to the Plus points, then the Minus points and finally the Interesting points. The result is a quick assessment scan. Once you've reviewed the PMI's, you can decide, 'What action should I now take?' Or you can defer that question until you also looked at the remaining six CoRT tools which follow:

- **CAF**: Consider All Factors. What should we take into account when we are thinking about something? What are the factors involved here?

- **C&S:** This tool directs attention to the 'Consequences and Sequels' of the action under consideration. The request is for a forward look at what will happen later. Different time scales can be requested.

- **AGO:** What are the Aims, Goals and Objectives? What are we trying to do? What are we trying to achieve? Where are we going?

- **FIP:** First Important Priorities: Direct attention to those things which really matter. Not everything is of equal importance. What are the priorities?

- **APC:** Alternatives, Possibilities and Choices. Create new alternatives? What are the possibilities? What are the choices?

- **OPV:** Direct attention to Other People's Views. Who are the other people involved? What are their views?

"The tools are used explicitly and directly. They are a formal way of directing perceptual attention in a defined direction". (Page 51).

De Bono, E. (1995) *Teach Yourself to Think*. London: Viking/Penguin.

*CoRT = Cognitive Research Trust.

~~~

[19] Byrne, J.W. (2020) *The Bamboo Paradox: The limits of human flexibility in a cruel world*. Hebden Bridge: The Institute for E-CENT Publications.

[20] Jacobson, E. (1980) *You Must Relax*. London: Unwin Paperbacks.

[21] Jacobson, E. (1963) *Tension Control for Businessmen*. CT. USA: Martino Publishing.

[22] Jacobson, E. (1963) *Tension Control for Businessmen*. CT. USA: Martino Publishing.

[23] Jacobson, E. (1980) *You Must Relax*. London: Unwin Paperbacks.

[24] Edlund, M. (2011) *The Power of Rest: Why Sleep alone is not enough*. New York: Harper Collins.

[25] Turner, M., and Barker, J. (2014) *What Business can learn from Sport Psychology*. Oakamoor, USA: Bennion Kearny Ltd.

[26] Meracou, K., Tsoukas, K., Stavrinos, G., et.al. (2019) The effect of PMR on emotional competence, depression-anxiety-stress, and sense of coherence, health-related quality of life, and well-being of unemployed people in Greece: An Intervention study. *EXPLORE, Volume 15, Issue 1*, January–February 2019: Pages 38-46. https://Doi.org/10.1016/j.explore.2018.08.001

[27] Ismail,N.,Taha, W., and Elgzar, I. (2018) The effect of Progressive muscle relaxation on Post-caesarean section pain, quality of sleep and physical activities limitation (2018)International Journal of studies in Nursing. Vol 3, No.3 (2018)ISSN (online) DOI: https://doi.org/10.20849/ijsn.v3i3.461.

[28] Jacobson, E. (1978) *You Must Relax: Practical methods of reducing the tensions of modern living. Fifth edition, revised and enlarged*. London: McGraw-Hill Book Company.

[29] Wolpe, J. (1968) *Psychotherapy by Reciprocal Inhibition. Redwood City, Cal: Stanford University Press.*

[30] Golomb, B.A., Evans, M.A., White, H.L., and Dimsdale, J.E. (2012) Trans-fat consumption and aggression. Online: PLoS One. 2012; 7(3):e32175. doi: 10.1371/journal.pone.0032175. Epub 2012 Mar 5.

[31] "What Is Candida Albicans?" "Candida Albicans is an opportunistic fungus (or form of yeast) that is the cause of Candida Related Complex and many undesirable symptoms including fatigue, weight gain, joint pain, and gas." "The Candida Albicans yeast is a normal part of your gut flora, a group of microorganisms that live in your digestive tract."

"Most people have some level of Candida Albicans in their intestines, and usually it coexists peacefully with the other bacteria and yeasts that live there. But a combination of factors can lead to the Candida Albicans population getting out of control, establishing fast growing colonies and biofilms, and starting to dominate your gut." Source: https://www.thecandidadiet.com/what-is-candida-albicans/

[32] Atkinson, M. (2008) *The Mind Body Bible: Your personalised prescription for total health*. London: Piatkus Books.

[33] Kiecolt-Glaser, J.K., Belury M.A., Andridge, R., et.al. (2011) 'Omega 3 supplementation lowers inflammation and anxiety in medical students: A

randomised, controlled trial'. *Brain, Behaviour, Immunity, Vol.25 (8).* Pages 1725-1734

[34] **Definition** of Mediterranean diet: A diet of a type traditional in Mediterranean countries, characterized especially by a high consumption of vegetables and olive oil and moderate consumption of protein, and thought to confer health benefits.

[35] Definition of Paleo diet: A diet based on the types of foods presumed to have been eaten by early humans, consisting chiefly of meat, fish, vegetables, and fruit and excluding dairy or cereal products and processed food.

[36] Greger, M. (2015) *How not to Die: Discover the foods scientifically proven to prevent and reverse disease.* London: Macmillan.

[37] Simopoulos (2002) produced a study which argues for a low ratio of omega-6 to omega-3 fatty acids. Here is the abstract from that paper:

"Abstract:

"Several sources of information suggest that human beings evolved on a diet with a ratio of omega-6 to omega-3 essential fatty acids (EFA) of approximately 1 whereas in Western diets the ratio is 15/1-16.7/1. Western diets are deficient in omega-3 fatty acids, and have excessive amounts of omega-6 fatty acids compared with the diet on which human beings evolved and their genetic patterns were established. Excessive amounts of omega-6 polyunsaturated fatty acids (PUFA) and a very high omega-6/omega-3 ratio, as is found in today's Western diets, promote the pathogenesis of many diseases, including cardiovascular disease, cancer, and inflammatory and autoimmune diseases, whereas increased levels of omega-3 PUFA (a low omega-6/omega-3 ratio) exert suppressive effects. In the secondary prevention of cardiovascular disease, a ratio of 4/1 was associated with a 70% decrease in total mortality. A ratio of 2.5/1 reduced rectal cell proliferation in patients with colorectal cancer, whereas a ratio of 4/1 with the same amount of omega-3 PUFA had no effect. The lower omega-6/omega-3 ratio in women with breast cancer was associated with decreased risk. A ratio of 2-3/1 suppressed inflammation in patients with rheumatoid arthritis, and a ratio of 5/1 had a beneficial effect on patients with asthma, whereas a ratio of 10/1 had adverse consequences. These studies indicate that the optimal ratio may vary with the disease under consideration. This is consistent with the fact that chronic diseases are multigenic and multifactorial. Therefore, it is quite possible that the therapeutic dose of omega-3 fatty acids will depend on the degree of severity of disease resulting from the genetic predisposition. A lower ratio of omega-6/omega-3 fatty acids is more desirable in reducing the risk of many of the chronic diseases of high prevalence in Western societies, as well as in the developing countries, that are being exported to the rest of the world." Source: Simopoulos, A.P. (2002) 'The importance of the ratio of omega-6/omega-3 essential fatty acids'. *Biomedical Pharmacotherapy, Oct 2002, Vol.56 (8):* Pages 365-379.

~~~

[38] Cunningham, J. B. (2001) The Stress Management Sourcebook. Second edition. Los Angeles: Lowell House.

[39] Winnie Yu (2012) High trans-fat diet predicts aggression: People who eat more hydrogenated oils are more aggressive. *Scientific American Mind*, July 2012. Available online: http://www.scientificamerican.com/article/high-trans-fat-diet-predicts-aggresion/

[40] Stress Management Society (2012/2016) Nutritional stress and health: The "Think 'nervous'" box. Available online: http://www.stress.org.uk/Diet-and-nutrition.aspx

[41] Gangwisch, J. et al. (2015) 'High Glycaemic Index Diet as a Risk Factor for Depression: Analyses from the Women's Health Initiative'. *American Journal of Clinical Nutrition, August 2015.*

Extract from Science Daily:

"A diet high in refined carbohydrates may lead to an increased risk for new-onset depression in postmenopausal women, according to a study published in The American Journal of Clinical Nutrition.

"The study by James Gangwisch, PhD and colleagues in the department of psychiatry at Columbia University Medical Centre (CUMC) looked at the dietary glycaemic index, glycaemic load, types of carbohydrates consumed, and depression in data from more than 70,000 postmenopausal women who participated in the National Institutes of Health's Women's Health Initiative Observational Study between 1994 and 1998."

Available online: https://www.sciencedaily.com/ releases/2015/08/ 150805 110335.htm. Accessed: 3rd October 2017.

~~~

[42] Perretta, Lorraine (2001) *Brain Food: the essential guide to boosting brain power*. London: Hamlyn.

[43] Cunningham, J. B. (2001) *The Stress Management Sourcebook*. Second edition. Los Angeles: Lowell House.

[44] Woodward, N. (2006) Stress, Diet and Body Acidification. Listed in *Cellular Chemistry*, originally published in issue 130 - December 2006. http://www.positivehealth.com/article/alkaline/stress-diet- and-body-acidification

[45] The research on milk and the emotional and behavioural effects upon a group of children, in a double blind study, published in the Lancet in the UK, has been largely ignored by policy makers. Here is a flavour of the problem, from the opening of a blog by Dr H Morrow Brown MD, FRCP (Edin), FAAAAI (USA):

"The emotional aspects of milk intolerance are so variable and so bizarre that it is difficult to select the most interesting and illustrative cases seen over the years. Emotional effects along with gastro-intestinal symptoms are commonly associated with migraine. Milk intolerant children often have a short attention span, cannot sit still, and have tantrums and poor coordination. A tendency to self-injury and destructiveness sometimes occurs repeatedly after drinking milk. Their poor coordination is obvious in their writing and "art work", because meaningless squiggles become recognizable objects or people after withdrawal of the relevant foods."

We believe it is important, because of this research, to limit the amount of dairy milk that we consume, and to substitute nut or rice milk where possible.

~~~

[46] Source: Campbell, T. (2014) Are smoothies good or bad? Newsletter, Centre for Nutrition Studies. Available online: http://nutritionstudies.org/are-smoothies-good-or-bad/. Accessed: 16th October 2017.

[47] Campbell, T.C. and Campbell, T.M. (2006), *The China Study: Startling implications for diet, weight loss and long-term health*. Dallas, Tx: Benbella Books.

[48] Source: The Real Food Guide (2017) 'What is margarine and why is it bad for you?' An online blog: http://therealfoodguide.com/what-is-margarine-and-why-is-it-bad-for-you/

[49] Holford, P. (2010) *Optimum Nutrition for the Mind*. London: Piatkus.

[50] Mosley, M. (2015) 'Which oils are best to cook with?' 28th July 2015. BBC: News: Magazine, 28th July 2015. Online: http://www.bbc.co.uk/news/magazine-33675975

[51] Dr John Briffa, 'High Anxiety', *Observer Magazine,* 19th June 2005, page 61.

[52] Perretta, L. (2001) *Brain Food: the essential guide to boosting brain power.* London: Hamlyn.

[53] Cunningham, J. B. (2001) *The Stress Management Sourcebook.* Second edition. Los Angeles: Lowell House.

[54] Lettuce and anxiety are mentioned in this blog: http://www.organicfacts.net/health-benefits/vegetable/health-benefits-of-lettuce.html

[55] Chamomile tea for anxiety and insomnia; mentioned in: http://naturalsociety .com/9-amazing-health-benefits-of-chamomile-tea/

[56] Here is the url for 'Health Unblocked' post about Chamomile tea and SSRI's: https://healthunlocked.com/anxietysupport/posts/132860526/can-camomile-tea-interfere-with-anti-depressants-and-antibiotics

[57] Winter, C. (2017) *The Sleep Solution: Why your sleep is broken and how to fix it.* Melbourne: Scribe Publications.

[58] Holford, P. (2008) *How to Quit without Feeling S**t.* London: Piatkus. and:

Pearson N.J, Johnson L.L, Nahin R.L. (2006) 'Insomnia, trouble sleeping, and complementary and alternative medicine: Analysis of the 2002 national health interview survey data'. *Archives of Internal Medicine, Vol.166 (16).* Pages 1775-1782.

[59] Walker, M. (2017) *Why We Sleep.* London: Allen Lane.

[60] Nauert, R. (2018) Sleep Loss Increases Anxiety — Especially Among Worriers. PsychCentral blog post. https://psychcentral.com/news/2013/06/27/sleep-loss-increases-anxiety-especially-among-worriers/56531.html

[61] Anwar, Y. (2013) Tired and edgy? Sleep deprivation boosts anticipatory anxiety. Berkley News (University of California). Online: http://news.berkeley.edu/2013/06/25/anticipate-the-worst/. Accessed: 22nd January 2018.

[62] Weil, A., (1995) *Natural Health, Natural Medicine*, London: Warner Books.

[63] Reid, D. (2003) *The Tao of Detox: The natural way to purify your body for health and longevity*, London: Simon & Shuster.

[64] Winter, C. (2017) *The Sleep Solution: Why your sleep is broken and how to fix it.* Melbourne: Scribe Publications.

[65] X.Liu, MD, PhD, 'Sleep deprivation can lead to smoking, drinking ((Smoking & drinking can also lead to sleep deprivation – a two way street)', Research abstract conducted by the University of Pittsburgh at SLEEP, 2007, the 21st Annual meeting of the Associated Professional Sleep Societies (APSS),15th June 2007

[66] Noever, R., Cronise, J. and Relwani, R.A. (1995) Using spider web patterns to determine toxicity. *NASA Tech Briefs 19, No.4 82*. And:

Witt, P.N. and Rovner, J.S. (1982) *Spider communication: Mechanisms and ecological Significance.* New Jersey: Princeton University Press.

[67] Drake, C., Roehrs, T., Shambroom, J. and Roth, T. (2013). Caffeine Effects on Sleep Taken: 0, 3, or 6 Hours before Going to Bed. *Journal of Clinical Sleep Medicine.* November 15, 2013. *Volume 9 (11)* Pages: 1195-1200; published online November 15, 2013. Available online: https://dx.doi.org/10.5664%2Fjcsm.3170.

[68] Stevenson, S. (2016) *Sleep Smarter: 21 Essential strategies to sleep your way to a better body, better health and better success,* London: Hay House.

[69] Mercola, J. (2019) Pump up Your Performance With Artery-Loving Nitric Oxide *and* Help Fight Free Radical Damage With Molecular Hydrogen in Just Minutes With One Super fuel Drink'. Online blog: https://products.mercola.com/hydro-nitro/?

[70] Chang, A., Aeschbach, D., Duffy, J.A. and Czeisler, C. A. (2015). Evening use of light-emitting eReaders negatively affects sleep, circadian timing, and next-morning alertness. *Proceedings of the National Academy of Sciences of the United States of America.* January 27, 2015. *Volume 112 (4)* Pages: 1232-1237; published ahead of print December 22, 2014. Available online: https://doi.org/ 10.1073/ pnas.1418490112.

[71] Littlehales, N. (2016) *Sleep: The myth of 8 hours, the power of naps, and the new plan to recharge body and mind.* London: Penguin, Random House.

[72] Winter, C. (2017) *The Sleep Solution: Why your sleep is broken and how to fix it.* Melbourne: Scribe Publications.

[73] Huffington, A. (2016) *The Sleep Revolution: Transforming your life one night at a time.* London: Penguin. Random House, UK.

[74] O'Connor, A. (2011) 'Lack of Deep Sleep Tied to Hypertension.' New York Times blog post: https://well.blogs.nytimes.com/2011/08/31/lack-of-deep-sleep-tied-to-hypertension/ (date accessed: 02/12/2018)

[75] Benson, H. with Klipper, M. (1977) *The Relaxation Response,* London: William Collins Sons &Co. Ltd.

~~~

[76] Plenke, M. (2015) The Science Behind Why We Should All Be Taking Naps at Work. Online blog (Mic): https://www.mic.com/articles/126102/naps-at-work-increase-productivity. Accessed: 18th April 2020.

[77] Hellmich, N. (2013) The best preventative medicine? Exercise. Online: dailycomet.com. Accessed: 18th June 2016

[78] Ratey, J., and Hargerman, E. (2009) *Spark: The revolutionary new science of exercise and the brain.* London: Quercus.

[79] Sapolsky, R. (2010) *Why Zebras don't get Ulcers. Third Edition.* New York: St Martin's Griffin.

[80] Reid, D. (2003) The Tao of Detox: The natural way to purify your body for health and longevity. London: Simon and Schuster.

[81] Waring, A. (2018) Breathe with Ease. Gravesend, Kent: Dot Dot Dot Publishing.

[82] Owen, M.M. (2019) 'Breathtaking'. *Aeon Magazine.* Available online: https://aeon.co/essays/do-hold-your-breath-on-the-benefits-of-conscious-breathing.

[83] Baha-ud-Din Naqshband Bukhari

[84] Dr Daniel Amen (2012) *Use your brain to change your life.* London: Piatkus.

---

[85] Waite, M. (2012) *Paperback Oxford English Dictionary. Seventh edition*. Oxford: Oxford University Press.

[86] Brewer, S. (2013) *Nutrition: A beginners guide*. London: Oneworld Publications.

[87] "Protein is a macronutrient necessary for the proper growth and function of the human body. A deficiency in protein leads to muscle atrophy and impaired functioning of the human body in general.

"Athletes and those looking to build muscle might benefit from increased protein intake, but they should be aware of the risks. Excess protein is typically processed by the body, but may cause a strain on the liver and kidneys, and may also increase cancer risk (particularly from animal sources).

"The Daily Value (%DV) for protein is set at 50 grams per day, but individuals with more muscle mass may require more.

"Foods highest in protein per calorie include fish, cheese, turkey, chicken, lean beef, pork, tofu, yogurt, milk, beans, lentils, eggs, nuts, and seeds". Source: https://www.healthaliciousness.com/articles/foods-highest-in-protein.php

Protein is constructed in all plants, using nitrogen and carbon from the atmosphere and the soil. When those plants are eaten by animals, the proteins are concentrated in the animal muscle and animal products. But seeds, nuts and some vegetables are high in protein in their own right. Animal products are 'not essential', according to the China Study! But a 'low meat and other animals products' diet might be the most sensible compromise in terms of avoiding protein deficiency. But you have to find out for yourself, by experimentation, what works for your body!

~~~

[88] "Carbohydrates are found in almost all living things and play a critical role in the proper functioning of the immune system, fertilization, blood clotting, and human development. A deficiency of carbohydrates can lead to impaired functioning of all these systems, however, in the Western world, deficiency is rare. Excessive consumption of carbohydrates, especially refined carbohydrates like sugar or corn syrup, can lead to obesity, type II diabetes, and cancer. Unhealthy high carbohydrate foods include sugary cereals, crackers, cakes, flours, jams, preserves, bread products, refined potato products, and sugary drinks. Healthy high carbohydrate foods include vegetables, legumes (beans), whole grains, fruits, nuts,

and yogurt. " Source: https://www.healthaliciousness.com/articles/foods-highest-in-carbohydrates.php

~~~

[89] "Fat is a type of nutrient, and just like protein and carbohydrates, your body needs some fat for energy, to absorb vitamins, and to protect your heart and brain health. Despite what you may have been told, fat isn't always the bad guy in the health and waistline wars. "Bad" fats, such as artificial trans-fats and saturated fats, are guilty of the unhealthy things all fats have been blamed for—weight gain, clogged arteries, and so forth. But "good" fats such as unsaturated fats and omega-3s have the opposite effect. In fact, healthy fats play a huge role in helping you manage your moods, stay on top of your mental game, fight fatigue, and even control your weight". Source: https://www.helpguide.org/articles/healthy-eating/choosing-healthy-fats.htm

~~~

[90] **Definition:** "Vitamins are nutrients your body needs to function and fight off disease. Your body cannot produce vitamins itself, so you must get them through food you eat or in some cases supplements. There are 13 vitamins that are essential to your body working well. Knowledge of the different types and understanding the purpose of these vitamins are important for good health.

"There are two types of vitamins: fat-soluble and water-soluble. Fat-soluble vitamins are stored in your fat cells, consequently requiring fat in order to be absorbed. Water-soluble vitamins are not stored in your body; therefore, they need to be replenished daily. Your body takes what it needs from the food you eat and then excretes what is not needed as waste. Here is a list of some vitamin types and common food sources:

"Fat-Soluble Vitamins

"Vitamin A - comes from orange coloured fruits and vegetables; dark leafy greens, like kale

Vitamin D - can be found in fortified milk and dairy products; cereals; (and of course, sunshine!)

Vitamin E - is found in fortified cereals; leafy green vegetables; seeds; nuts

Vitamin K - can be found in dark green leafy vegetables; turnip/beet greens

"Water-Soluble Vitamins:

Vitamin B1, or Thiamin - comes from whole grains; enriched grains; liver; nuts; seeds

Vitamin B2, or Riboflavin - comes from whole grains; enriched grains; dairy products

Vitamin B3, or Niacin - comes from meat; fish; poultry; whole grains

Vitamin B5, or Pantothenic Acid - comes from meat; poultry; whole grains

Vitamin B6, or Pyridoxine - comes from fortified cereals; soy products

Vitamin B7, or Biotin - is found in fruits; meats

Vitamin B9, or Folic Acid (Folate) - comes from leafy vegetables

Vitamin B12 - comes from fish; poultry; meat; dairy products

Vitamin C - comes from citrus fruits and juices, such as oranges and grapefruits; red, yellow, and green peppers". Source: http://study.com/academy/lesson/what-are-vitamins-definition-types-purpose-examples.html. Accessed: 14th November 2017.

But because our food is largely denatured, and most people do not know what nutrients they are getting from their food, it makes sense to take a complete multivitamin, a B-complex, and extra vitamin C in supplement form, every day.

[91] "A list of minerals in foods may not necessarily include all of the minerals needed for health and wellness. There are 14 considered in the list below (which includes common minerals, like iron, copper, zinc, selenium, and so on – JWB). These 14 minerals are divided into two types: Macro minerals and trace minerals. A mineral is considered a macro mineral if your body requires over 100 mg of that particular element. Less than 100 mg and it's considered a trace element. Both types of minerals are important for health, but the body needs far greater amounts of macro minerals than trace minerals. The best source for both macro and trace minerals is whole foods containing plant digested minerals.

"The levels of all of minerals in foods vary depending on the nutrients of the soil where the food is grown. In the case of meats, the levels of minerals in the meat correspond directly to the amount of minerals contained in the plants that the animals have eaten." Source: http://www.wellness-with-natural-health-supplements.com/list-of-minerals-in-foods.html

~~~

[92] See the following research papers, amongst others:

Shepherd SJ, Parker FJ, Muir JG and Gibson, PR (2008) 'Dietary triggers of abdominal symptoms in patients with irritable bowel syndrome - Randomised placebo-controlled evidence'. *Clinical Gastroenterology and Hepatology. 2008; 6(7):* 765-771: http://www.sciencedirect.com/science/ article/ pii/ S154235 6508001511

Halmos, EP, Power, VA, Shepherd SJ, et al. (2014) 'A Diet Low in FODMAPs Reduces Symptoms of Irritable Bowel Syndrome'. *Gastroenterology, 2014; 146(1):* 67-75

Ong DK, Mitchell SB, Barrett JS, Shepherd SJ, Irving PI, Biesiekierski JR, Smith S, Gibson PR, Muir JG. (2010) 'Manipulation of dietary short chain carbohydrates alters the pattern of hydrogen and methane gas production and genesis of symptoms in patients with irritable bowel syndrome. *Journal of Gastroenterology and Hepatology. 2010 Aug; 25(8):* 1366-73

Barrett JS, Irving PM, Gearry R, Shepherd SJ, Gibson PR (2009) 'Comparison of the prevalence of fructose and lactose malabsorption across chronic intestinal disorders'. *Alimentary Pharmacology and Therapeutics, 2009; 30(2):* 165-74.

~~~

[93] King, D.S. (1981) 'Can allergic exposure provoke psychological symptoms? A double-blind test'. *Biological Psychiatry, Vol. 16(1):* pages 3-19.

[94] See Grant, D. and Joice, J. (1984) *Food Combining for Health.* Wellingborough: Thorsons.

[95] Collings, J. (1993) *The ordinary Person's Guide to Extraordinary Health.* London: Aurum Press Ltd.

[96] Alt Health (2017) 'Hay Diet'. A blog about food combining. Available online: https://www.althealth.co.uk/help-and-advice/diets/hay-diet/. Accessed: 11th October 2017.

[97] Julia Ross (2003) writes: "The rate of depression among individuals correlates precisely with the ratio of omega-3 fats to omega-6 in the brain". (Page 149).

[98] Schoenthaler, S.J. (1983) 'The Northern California diet-behaviour program: An empirical evaluation of 3,000 incarcerated juveniles in Stanislaus County Juvenile Hall'. *International Journal of Biosocial Research, Vol 5(2)*, Pages 99-106.

Schoenthaler, S.J. (1983) 'The Los Angeles probation department diet behaviour program: An empirical analysis of six institutional settings'. *International Journal of Biosocial Research, Vol 5(2)*, Pages 107-117.

Schoenthaler S., et al (1997) 'The effect of randomized vitamin-mineral supplementation on violent and non-violent antisocial behaviour among incarcerated juveniles'. *Journal of Nutritional & Environmental Medicine 7:* Pages 343–352.

Schoenthaler, S., and Bier I. D. (2002) 'Food addiction and criminal behaviour – The California randomized trial'. *Food Allergy and Intolerance. 731–746.* Saunders. Cited in Sandwell and Wheatley (2008).

[99] Gesch, C B. et al (2002) Influence of supplementary vitamins, minerals and essential fatty acids on the antisocial behaviour of young adults. *British Journal of Psychiatry 81:* Pages 22–28.

[100] Here's the Mayo Clinic blog extract (2015):

"Here are five gluten-free whole grains, how to cook them and how to add them to your diet. Remember to aim for three servings of whole grains a day.

"**Amaranth:** About the size of a poppy seed, this pseudo-grain has a light peppery taste. Use 3 to 6 parts water to 1 part amaranth. Boil water, add grain and gently boil for 15 to 20 minutes. As it cooks, amaranth softens from the inside, releases a lot of starch and thickens the cooking liquid. Rinse cooked amaranth and let it drain before using. Use amaranth to thicken soups and stews. Add milk, fruit and a bit of honey for a healthy breakfast. You can even "pop" dried amaranth and make it into a granola-type bar.

"**Millet:** About the size of a small mustard seed, this grain has a mild flavour. Use 2 to 3 parts water to 1 part millet. Boil water, add grain and gently boil for 35 to 40 minutes. You may also "toast" millet in a hot pan before boiling to get a nuttier flavour. Top with cinnamon and peaches for breakfast. Or make a salad with halved grape tomatoes, radishes and chopped basil. Millet is also a great alternative to rice in casseroles, ground-meat dishes and stuffing.

"**Teff:** This smallest of grains is nutty and earthy in flavour. Use 3 parts water to 1 part teff. Boil water, add grain and simmer for 15 to 20 minutes. Its texture is like cream of wheat. Add cooked teff to soups or use teff as the main ingredient for polenta instead of cornmeal. Teff flour can be used to make pancakes.

"**Buckwheat:** Despite its name, buckwheat is not related to wheat. This-pseudo grain is pyramid shaped and known as kasha or buckwheat groats. To bring out its earthy flavour, cook 1 cup buckwheat with one egg in a large skillet over medium heat. Stir to keep from clumping until the mixture is dry and separated. Add 2 cups water or broth and cook uncovered over low heat for about 15 minutes. Mix cooked buckwheat with lentils, herbs and a bit of goat cheese. Or stuff peppers or acorn squash with cooked buckwheat. Buckwheat flour can be used to make pancakes.

"**Quinoa:** This pseudo-grain must be rinsed well before cooking to remove bitter-tasting saponins. You can also buy it pre-rinsed. The flavour is squash-like. Quinoa cooks in just 15 minutes. Use 2 parts water to 1 part quinoa. Mix with chopped fruit and drizzle with honey for breakfast. Or use quinoa instead of bulgur to make tabbouleh. Quinoa is also a good substitute for rice in rice pudding."

"Whether you are going gluten-free or not, these whole grains are good for you..."

Source: Nelson and Zeratsky (2015).

~~~

[101] Source: http://www.goodtoknow.co.uk/wellbeing/440541/The-Nordic-Diet

[102] Source: The Woman and Home blog, available online at: http://www.womanandhome.com/galleries/diet-and-health/35358/3/0/the-nordic-diet

[103] Source: 'Preventing depression - can food rules help?' by Paula Goodyer. Online: http://www.smh.com.au/lifestyle/diet-and-fitness/preventing-depression--can-food-rules-help-20151022-gkfolu.html

[104] Korn (2016) and Eggers (2012).

[105] Source: Superfoods Scientific Research (2012) 'Phosphatidylserine Benefits and Side Effects'. Online: http://www.superfoods-scientific-research.com/natural-remedies/phosphatidylserine-benefits.html

[106] Michalak, Zhang and Jacobi, 2012, conducted a study of the link between vegetarian diet and mental disorders, because there is "...relatively little data... available on the associations between vegetarian diet and mental health". However, their study, in Germany, based on more than 4,000 participants, failed to find a positive correlation between vegetarianism and mental illness.

Here are their results and conclusions:

"Results: Vegetarians displayed elevated prevalence rates for depressive disorders, anxiety disorders and somatoform disorders. Due to the matching procedure, the findings cannot be explained by socio-demographic characteristics of vegetarians (e.g. higher rates of females, predominant residency in urban areas, and high proportion of singles). The analysis of the respective ages at adoption of a vegetarian diet and onset of a mental disorder showed that the adoption of the vegetarian diet tends to follow the onset of mental disorders.

"Conclusions: In Western cultures vegetarian diet is associated with an elevated risk of mental disorders. However, there was no evidence for a causal role of vegetarian diet in the etiology of mental disorders."

~~~

[107] Arachidonic acid (AA [or ARA]): A liquid unsaturated fatty acid that occurs in most animal fats and some vegetable oils. It's a precursor of prostaglandins, and is considered essential in animal nutrition, including human nutrition. ARA is a form of omega-6 fatty acid. And although we need ARA, getting too much "could be problematic". (Erin Coleman, 2017). It seems we need both omega-6 and omega-3 fatty acids in our diets, in roughly equal proportions; but too much omega-6 causes (too much) inflammation, which is the basis of most chronic disease, and is also linked to depression and perhaps also to anxiety and anger, etc. The biochemistry of ARA, and omega-6/omega-3 is very complex, and highly contested, and unresolved at this point (2017) in time.

[108] Watch the movie: 'All Jacked Up': The explosive junk food documentary the food companies hope you never see; by Mike Adams, 2008: https://www.naturalnews.com/022510.html

[109] And see also Morgan Spurlock's documentary - ('Super Size Me', 2004) - about trying to live on McDonald's burgers for 30 days, and the medically confirmed negative impact on his physical and mental health! Source: http://watchdocumentaries.com/super-size-me/. Accessed: 21st November 2017.

[110] Coenzyme Q10 may be important for general health. According to the Mayo Clinic: "Coenzyme Q10 (CoQ10) is an antioxidant that your body produces naturally. Your cells use CoQ10 for growth and maintenance.

"Levels of CoQ10 in your body decrease as you age. CoQ10 levels have also been found to be lower in people with certain conditions, such as heart disease.

"CoQ10 is found in meat, fish and whole grains. The amount of CoQ10 found in these dietary sources, however, isn't enough to significantly increase CoQ10 levels in your body.

"As a supplement, CoQ10 supplement is available as capsules, tablets and by IV. CoQ10 might help treat certain heart conditions, as well as migraines and Parkinson's disease." Source: https://www.mayoclinic. org/ drugs-supplements-coenzyme-q10/ art-20362602. Accessed: 30th October 2017.

~~~

[111] According to NHS choices: "Probiotics (like Acidophilus) are live bacteria and yeasts promoted as having various health benefits. They're usually added to yoghurts or taken as food supplements, and are often described as 'good' or 'friendly' bacteria.

"Probiotics are thought to help restore the natural balance of bacteria in your gut (including your stomach and intestines) when it has been disrupted by an illness or treatment." https://www.nhs.uk/Conditions/probiotics/Pages/ Introduction.aspx. Accessed: 30th October 2017.

According to Enders (2015) changing the variety of live bacteria in the guts of lab mice can change their behaviour so radically that it is thought they could change character and temperament (in human terms)." And gut bacteria have been shown to be involved in communication between the gut and the brain in humans. (Enders, 2015).

~~~

[112] Cunningham, J. B. (2001) *The Stress Management Sourcebook. Second edition.* Los Angeles: Lowell House.

[113] Yu, W. (2012) High trans-fat diet predicts aggression: People who eat more hydrogenated oils are more aggressive. *Scientific American Mind*, July 2012. Available online: http://www.scientificamerican.com/article/high-trans-fat-diet-predicts-aggresion/

[114] Stress Management Society (2012/2016) 'Nutritional stress and health': The "Think 'nervous'" box. Available online: http://www.stress.org.uk/Diet-and-nutrition.aspx

[115] Dr Michael Greger quotes the following paper in defence of his view that vegetarian diets are better for emotional health:

Beezhold, B. L., Johnston, C. S., & Daigle, D. R. (2010) 'Vegetarian diets are associated with healthy mood states: a cross-sectional study in Seventh Day Adventist adults'. *Nutrition Journal, 9*, 26. http://doi.org/10.1186/1475-2891-9-26

[116] Perretta, L. (2001) *Brain Food: the essential guide to boosting brain power.* London: Hamlyn.

[117] "What Is Candida Albicans?" "Candida Albicans is an opportunistic fungus (or form of yeast) that is the cause of Candida Related Complex and many undesirable symptoms including fatigue, weight gain, joint pain, and gas." "The Candida Albicans yeast is a normal part of your gut flora, a group of microorganisms that live in your digestive tract."

"Most people have some level of Candida Albicans in their intestines, and usually it coexists peacefully with the other bacteria and yeasts that live there. But a combination of factors can lead to the Candida Albicans population getting out of control, establishing fast growing colonies and biofilms, and starting to dominate your gut." Source: https://www.thecandidadiet.com/what-is-candida-albicans/

~~~

"When toxic Candida by-products enter the bloodstream, they can affect the brain. This yeast toxin hypersensitivity has a number of negative neurological effects.

"Some of those effects are: memory issues, anxiety and reduction in reasoning ability. In order to get relief, the Candida needs to be controlled and minimized.

"Dealing with Depression" "Since depression can be directly caused by Candida, you should start on one of the Candida elimination programs. Both programs use a multi-step program to get the Candida under control." Source: http://www.candida-albicans-cure.com/depression.html

~~~

[118] Stress Management Society (2012/2016) Nutritional stress and health: The "Think 'nervous'" box. Available online: http://www.stress.org.uk/Diet-and-nutrition.aspx

[119] Source: http://annewigmore.org

[120] Stanfield, M. (2008) *Trans Fat: The Time Bomb in your Food: The Killer in the Kitchen*. Souvenir Press: London.

[121] *Definition of inflammation*: A localized physical condition, normally inside the body, in which part of the body becomes reddened, swollen, hot, and often painful, especially as a reaction to injury or infection. Inflammation may be responsible for most serious modern diseases. And inflammation can be caused in the guts by grains, dairy, legumes, and other apparently 'harmless' foods.

[122] 'A study performed at the University of California surveyed 945 men and women about their trans-fat intake, as well as their levels of aggression. When the survey results were adjusted for outlying factors, such as age and use of alcohol and tobacco, researchers found a strong link between aggressive behaviour and the consumption of high levels of trans fats.'

'Lead author Beatrice Golumb says, "We found that greater trans fatty acids were associated with greater aggression. This adds further rationale to recommendations to avoid eating trans fats as their detrimental effects may extend beyond the person who consumes them."

'The connection between trans fats and anger is thought to have to do with their inhibition of the body's ability to metabolize omega-3 fatty acids. Past studies have linked a lack of omega-3 with antisocial behaviour and depression, so the anger connection is not too surprising.' Sources: A University of California study, cited here: http://www.thealternativedaily.com/pissed-off-all-the-time-study-says-it-could-be-trans-fats/. And here: http://www.theguardian.com/lifeandstyle/wordofmouth/2013/apr/24/can-food-make-you-angry - Accessed: 11th June 2016

~~~

[123] Mercola, J. (2010) Scientists Unlock How Trans Fats Harm Your Arteries. (Health Blog). Available online: http://articles.mercola.com/sites/articles/ archive/ 2010/ 11/16/scientists-unlock-how-trans-fats-harm-your-arteries.aspx. Accessed: 20th May 2016.

[124] Ross, J. (2002) *The Mood Cure: Take charge of your emotions in 24 hours using food and supplements.* London: Thorsons.

[125] Amen, D.G. (2013) *Use Your Brain to Change your Age: Secrets to look, feel, and think younger every day.* London: Piatkus.

[126] According to Adda Bjarnadottir, MS, an online nutritionist: "Refined carbs have been stripped of almost all fibre, vitamins and minerals. For this reason, they can be considered as "empty" calories. They are also digested quickly, and have a high glycaemic index. This means that they lead to rapid spikes in blood sugar and insulin levels after meals" which is very bad for our physical health and emotional well-being. (Source: Authority Nutrition - An Evidence-Based Approach (an online blog). Blog title: 'Why Refined Carbs Are Bad For You'. By Adda Bjarnadottir, MS | September, 2015. Available online: https://authoritynutrition.com/why-refined-carbs-are-bad/. Accessed: 10th June 2016

[127] Boyd, D.B. (2003) Insulin and Cancer. *Integrative Cancer Therapies. Dec 2003. Vol. 2 (4):* Pages 315-329.

[128] Collagen is the most abundant protein in the human body and is the substance that holds the whole body together. It is found in the bones, muscles, skin and tendons, where it forms a scaffold to provide strength and structure.

[129] **Definition of adrenaline (or 'epinephrine' in the US):** "...a substance that is released in the body of a person who is feeling a strong emotion (such as excitement, fear, or anger) and that causes the heart to beat faster and gives the person more energy". It helps to fuel the fight or flight response.

[130] Patrick Holford (2010) *Optimum Nutrition for the mind.* London: Piatkus.

[131] Natural Health 365: *The link between gum disease and Alzheimer's.* Available online at: http://www.naturalhealth365.com/alzheimers-disease-oral-health-1552.html Accessed 20th May 2016

[132] Perricone, N. (2002) *Dr Nicolas Perricone's Programme: Grow young, get slim, in days*. London: Thorsons.

[133] NHS (2007) NHS Quality Improvement Scotland, Understanding alcohol misuse in Scotland: Harmful drinking 3 – Alcohol and self-harm'. 2007. Available online at: http://bit.ly/TbBYAX. Accessed: 28th May 2016.

[134] **Definition of alkaloid:** "Any of a class of nitrogenous organic compounds of plant origin which have pronounced physiological actions on humans. They include many drugs (morphine, quinine) and poisons (atropine, strychnine)." Source: http://www.oxforddictionaries.com/definition/english/alkaloid#alkaloid__2. Accessed: 11th June 2016.

[135] Ephedra and Ma Huang are used in widely banned or restricted supplements which are used as 'diet pills' and in illegal weight training and sports training (and which are banned by the International Olympic committee). These substances mimic adrenaline in speeding up the cardiovascular system (or heart and lungs), and (potentially) creating feelings of anxiety.

[136] Van der Veen, F. M., Evers, E.A.T., Deutz, N.E.P., Schmitt, J.A.J. (2006) Effects of Acute Tryptophan Depletion on Mood and Facial Emotion Perception Related Brain Activation and Performance in Healthy Women with and without a Family History of Depression. *Neuropsychopharmacology, Vol.32, Issue 1*, Pages 216-224.

[137] Christensen, L. (1991) The roles of caffeine and sugar in depression, *The Nutrition Report 1991*: 9(5 Pt.1): Pages 691-698. Quoted by Ross (2002; page 135).

[138] Gilliland, K. and Andress, D. (1981) Ad Lib caffeine consumption, symptoms of caffeinism and academic performance. *American Journal of Psychiatry, Vol 138 (4)*, Pages. 512-514.

[139] **Definitions of junk food:** 1. "Pre-prepared or packaged food that has low nutritional value". Source: Google search for 'junk food'. Or: 2. "Food that is not good for your health because it contains high amounts of fat or sugar": (Merriam-Webster Dictionary). Or 3. "Food that is high in calories but low in nutritional content" (Merriam-Webster Dictionary). Online Merriam-Webster Dictionary: http://www.merriam-webster.com/ dictionary/ junk%20food. Accessed: 11th June 2016.

[140] Lawrence, F. (2004*) Not on the Label: What really goes into the food on your plate.* London: Penguin Books.

[141] Daily Mail (2016) Don't eat our pasta sauce more than once a week. Pages 1 and 2, Friday April 15th (2016).

[142] Coffman, M.A. (2016) The Disadvantages of Junk Food. A blog post at the 'Healthy Eating' website. Available online at this url: http://healthyeating. sfgate.com/ disadvantages-junk-food-1501.html. Accessed: 30th April 2016.

[143] Hadjivassiliou, M., & A. Gibson, & G.A.B. Davies-Jones & A.J. Lobo, et al (1996) 'Does cryptic gluten sensitivity play a part in neurological illness?' The Lancet, Volume 347, Issue 8998, 10 February 1996, Pages 369-371

Hadjivassiliou, M., & David S Sanders, Richard A. Grünewald, et al (2010) 'Gluten sensitivity: from gut to brain'. The Lancet Neurology, Volume 9, Issue 3, Pages 318 - 330.

(Extract from summary: "Although neurological manifestations in patients with established coeliac disease have been reported since 1966, it was not until 30 years later that, in some individuals, gluten sensitivity was shown to manifest solely with neurological dysfunction. Furthermore, the concept of extra-intestinal presentations without enteropathy has only recently become accepted.") This means...

This means that neurological damage can be caused by gluten, without leaving any traces in the gut! So, seeking a diagnosis of celiac disease, or freedom from this disease, does not mean you can then safely eat foods containing gluten!

~~~

One of the 20 sources cited by Dr David Perlmutter (2014) was this one:

Ford, R.P.K. (2009) 'The gluten syndrome: A neurological disease'. *Medical Hypotheses, Volume 73, Issue 3*: Pages 438 - 440.

Here is the summary of Ford's paper on the gluten syndrome:

"Summary

"Hypothesis: Gluten causes symptoms, in both celiac disease and non-celiac gluten-sensitivity, by its adverse actions on the nervous system.

"Many celiac patients experience neurological symptoms, frequently associated with malfunction of the autonomic nervous system. These neurological symptoms can present in celiac patients who are well nourished. The crucial point, however, is that gluten-sensitivity can also be associated with neurological symptoms in patients who do not have any mucosal gut damage (that is, without celiac disease).

"Gluten can cause neurological harm through a combination of cross reacting antibodies, immune complex disease and direct toxicity. These nervous system affects include: dysregulation of the autonomic nervous system, cerebella ataxia, hypotonia, developmental delay, learning disorders, depression, migraine, and headache.

"If gluten is the putative harmful agent, then there is no requirement to invoke gut damage and nutritional deficiency to explain the myriad of the symptoms experienced by sufferers of celiac disease and gluten-sensitivity. This is called "The Gluten Syndrome"."

~~~

And here are another 14 relevant sources:

Di Sabatino, A and Corazza, GR. (2009) 'Coeliac disease'. Lancet. 2009; 373: 1480–1493

Hadjivassiliou, M, Williamson, CA, and Woodroofe, N. (2004) The immunology of gluten sensitivity: beyond the gut. Trends Immunol. 2004; 25: 578–582

Hadjivassiliou, M, Sanders, DS, Grünewald, RA, Woodroofe, N, Boscolo, S, and Aeschlimann, D. (2010) 'The neurology of gluten sensitivity'. Lancet Neurol. 2010; 9: 330–342

Gobbi, G, Bouquet, F, Greco, L et al. (1992) 'Coeliac disease, epilepsy and cerebral calcifications'. Lancet. 1992; 340: 439–443

Volta, U, De Giorgio, R, Petrolini, N et al. (2002) 'Clinical findings and anti-neuronal antibodies in coeliac disease with neurological disorders'. Scand J Gastroenterol. 2002; 37: 1276–1281

Hadjivassiliou, M, Gibson, A, Davies-Jones, GAB, Lobo, A, Stephenson, TJ, and Milford-Ward, A. (1996) 'Is cryptic gluten sensitivity an important cause of neurological illness?' Lancet. 1996; 347: 369–371

Lock, RJ, Tengah, DS Pengiran, Unsworth, DJ, Ward, JJ, and Wills, AJ. (2005) 'Ataxia, peripheral neuropathy, and anti-gliadin antibody. Guilt by association?' J Neurol Neurosurg Psychiatry. 2005; 76: 1601–1603

Volta, U, Granito, A, Parisi, C et al. (2009) 'De-amidated gliadin peptide antibodies as a routine test for celiac disease: a prospective analysis'. J Clin Gastroenterol. 2009;

Hadjivassiliou, M, Aeschlimann, P, Strigun, A, Sanders, DS, Woodrofe, N, and Aeschlimann, D. (2008) 'Autoantibodies in gluten ataxia recognise a novel neuronal trans-glutaminase'. Ann Neurol. 2008; 64: 332–343

Koskinen, O, Collin, P, Lindfors, K, Laurila, K, Mäki, M, and Kaukinen, K. (2009) 'Usefulness of small-bowel mucosal transglutaminase-2 specific autoantibody deposits in the diagnosis and follow-up of celiac disease'. J Clin Gastroenterol. 2009;

Karell, K, Louka, AS, Moodie, SJ et al. (2003) 'HLA types in celiac disease patients not carrying the DQA1*05-DQB1*02 (DQ2) heterodimer: results from the European Genetics Cluster on Celiac Disease'. Hum Immunol. 2003; 64: 469–477

Volta, U, De Giorgio, R, Granito, A et al. (2006) 'Anti-ganglioside antibodies in coeliac disease with neurological disorders'. Dig Liver Dis. 2006; 38: 183–187

Cervio, E, Volta, U, Verri, M et al. (2007) 'Sera from patients with celiac disease and neurologic disorders evoke a mitochondrial-dependent apoptosis in vitro'. Gastroenterology. 2007; 133: 195–206

Hadjivassiliou, M, Mäki, M, Sanders, DS et al. (2006) Autoantibody targeting of brain and intestinal transglutaminase in gluten ataxia. Neurology. 2006; 66: 373–377

~~~

[144] Hadjivassiliou, M1, Gibson A, Davies-Jones GA, et.al. (1996) 'Does cryptic gluten sensitivity play a part in neurological illness?' The Lancet. 1996 Feb 10; 347(8998): Pages 369-71.

[145] Leaky gut allows whole molecules to pass through the gut wall and cause inflammation throughout the body. But what is the link between leaky gut and the blood/brain barrier?

"Gluten sensitivity research identifies a connection between gluten induced leaky gut, and leaky brain. The ramifications of these findings are important to understand the broad scope of the impact gluten has in many diseases.

"We were able to identify an intestinal Zot analogue, which we named **zonulin**. *It is conceivable that the zonulins participate in the physiological regulation of intercellular tj (tight junctions) not only in the small intestine, but also throughout* **a wide range of extraintestinal epithelia as well as the ubiquitous vascular endothelium, including the blood-brain barrier.** *Dysregulation of this hypothetical zonulin model may contribute to disease states that involve disordered intercellular communication, including developmental and intestinal disorders, tissue inflammation, malignant transformation, and metastasis.*

Sources: *Journal of Pediatric Gastroenterology and Nutrition.* 2010 Oct; 51(4):418-24. And:

Annals of the New York Academy of Sciences. 2000; 915: Pages 214-222.

You can read more at: https://www.glutenfreesociety.org/leaky-gut-leaky-brain-gluten-is-an-equal-opportunity-destroyer/#7gRJBhGGWIVEj6iX.99

~~~

[146] Source: https://www.agmrc.org/commodities-products/grains-oilseeds/wheat/; which seems to suggest that 60% of US wheat production is of the hard red variety, which has a higher gluten content!

[147] Online source: http://www.nhs.uk/conditions/vitamins-minerals/ Pages/vitamins-minerals.aspxx. Accessed 4th May 2016

[148] Mercola, J. (2013) Vitamin D — One of the Simplest Solutions to Wide-Ranging Health Problems. Available online: http://articles.mercola.com/sites/articles/archive/2013/12/22/dr-holick-vitamin-d-benefits.aspx. Accessed 15 June 2016.

[149] Food Standards Agency (2004) 'National Diet & Nutrition Survey: Adults aged 19 to 64'. Volume 5.

[150] Ballantyne, C. (2007) 'Fact or Fiction?: Vitamin Supplements Improve Your Health'. *Scientific American* (Online): http://www.scientificamerican.com/ article/fact-or-fiction-vitamin-supplements-improve-health/ May 17, 2007. Accessed 26th April 2016.

[151] Benton, D. and G Roberts (1988) Effects of vitamin and mineral supplementation on intelligence in schoolchildren. *The Lancet, Vol 1 (8578),* Pages 140-143.

[152] "...amino acids in food make up protein. When protein is digested it is once again broken down into specific amino acids that are then selectively put together for different uses. These new proteins formed in the body are what make up most solid matter in the body: skin, eyes, heart, intestines, bones and, of course, muscle." Source: https://www.bodybuilding.com/fun/catamino.htm

And one of those amino acids, tryptophan, is helpful in reducing depression, and indeed, tryptophan used to be used for that purpose by physicians before antidepressant drugs, (like SSRI's), were marketed into medical practices.

~~~

[233] Goldacre, B. (2007) Patrick Holford's untruthful and unsubstantiated claims about pills: Online blog: http://www.badscience.net/2007/09/patrick-holdford-unsubstantiated-untruthful/ Accessed 14th April 2016.

[154] Goldacre, B. (2012) *Bad Pharma: How drug companies mislead doctors and harm patients.* London: Fourth Estate.

[155] Perlmutter, D. (2015) *Brain Maker: The power of gut microbes to heal and protect your brain – for life.* London: Hodder and Stoughton.

[156] **Definition of probiotics**: 'Probiotics are live bacteria and yeasts that are good for your health, especially your digestive system. We usually think of bacteria as something that causes diseases. But your body is full of bacteria, both good and bad. Probiotics are often called "good" or "helpful" bacteria because they help keep your gut healthy.' (By Mary Jo DiLonardo. WebMD Feature. Available online: http://www.webmd.com/digestive-disorders/features/what-are-probiotics. Accessed 12th June 2016)

What is BDNF? "Brain-derived neurotrophic factor, also known as BDNF, is a protein that, in humans, is encoded by the BDNF gene. BDNF is a member of the neurotrophin family of growth factors, which are related to the canonical Nerve Growth Factor. Neurotrophic factors are found in the brain and the periphery." Source: https://en.wikipedia.org/wiki/Brain-derived_neurotrophic_factor).

Furthermore: "When BDNF levels are high, acquiring new knowledge is easy, memories are retained, and people feel happier. Indeed, BDNF can even be thought of as a natural anti-depressant." (Dr John Day's blog: http://drjohnday.com/10-ways-to-boost-brain-function-with-bdnf/)

~~~

[158] Written on 5 Jun 2015 by Max Kohanzad. For more by Max, please see Max's web page, here: http://max.coach/happiness-diet-hack/

[159] Byrne, J.W. (2016) *Holistic Counselling in Practice: An introduction to the theory and practice of Emotive-Cognitive Embodied-Narrative Therapy.* Hebden Bridge: The Institute for E-CENT Publications.

In particular, see the Holistic SOR model, in Byrne (2016), which lists several factors which affect the ability of the human organism to cope with environmental stressors.

~~~

[160] Hayes, N. (2003) *Applied Psychology (Teach Yourself Books).* London: Hodder and Stoughton.

[161] Pinnock, D. (2015) *Anxiety and Depression: Eat your way to better health.* London: Quadrille Publishing Ltd.

[162] Kiecolt-Glaser, J.K., Belury M.A., Andridge, R., Malarkey, W.B., Glaser, R. (2011) Omega 3 supplementation lowers inflammation and anxiety in medical students: a randomised, controlled trial. *Brain, Behaviour, Immunity, Vol.25 (8).* Pages 1725-1734

[163] Perretta, L. (2001) *Brain Food: the essential guide to boosting brain power.* London: Hamlyn.

[164] Lazarides, L. (2002) *Treat Yourself: With nutritional therapy.* London: Waterfall 2000.

[165] "The **blood glucose level** is the amount of **glucose** in the **blood. Glucose** is a **sugar** that comes from the foods we eat, and it's also formed and stored inside the body. It's the main source of energy for the cells of our body, and it's carried to each cell through the bloodstream". (Source: Google search). "Blood sugar that is too high or too low can make you very sick. Here's how to handle these emergencies." WebMD blog: http://www.webmd.com/diabetes/blood-sugar-levels).

[166] Unrefined carbohydrates: "Carbohydrates are essential nutrients that are responsible for the production of energy in the body. They form part of the three main macronutrients, which also include proteins and fats. While carbohydrates are commonly classified into simple and complex carbohydrates, they can also be categorized as unrefined and refined carbohydrates. Refined carbohydrates are ones that have been processed or altered with the addition of artificial chemicals and sugars, and their natural nutrients such as fibres, vitamins and minerals have been reduced or eliminated. Unrefined carbohydrates are in their natural state, and they contain all the naturally occurring nutrients that are beneficial to the body.

"Unrefined Carbohydrates" - "Unrefined carbohydrates are rich in fibre, vitamins and minerals, which are necessary for the production of energy in the human body. Natural food fibre is responsible for maintaining healthy blood sugar levels, and it acts as a barrier to the digestive system by controlling appetite. The recommended daily intake of natural fibre is between 20 to 45 grams. This amount of fibre can only be found in unrefined carbohydrates, especially wholegrain bread and cereals. Other examples that contain unrefined carbohydrates include brown rice, beans, oatmeal, bran cereal, millet, barley, couscous, wheat, vegetables, lentils, herbs, lamb, poultry and other wholegrain products.

"The consumption of unrefined carbohydrates is highly recommended due to their high nutritional value. When buying foods in a store or supermarket, you should choose products that have a high percentage of fibre and minerals. When selecting cereals and bread, the ingredients should include wholegrain or whole wheat." (But watch out for gluten intolerance. Source: http://www.fitday. com/fitness-articles/nutrition/carbs/the-difference-between-unrefined-and-refined-carbohydrates.html

[167] Refined carbohydrates: "Refined carbohydrates have undergone manufacturing or repackaging processes, and they are the worst form of carbs available. Moreover, some refined carbohydrates contain dangerous chemicals that may spike the blood sugar levels and trigger other health problems.

"Refined carbohydrates do not contain the necessary nutrients that are beneficial to your health. Despite the fact that they have a sweet taste and are delightful to consume, they have very low nutritional value. These products will cause more harm than good to the body. Research shows that consumption of refined products is the leading cause of diseases and disorders such as obesity, heart disease, diabetes and cardiovascular problems.

"The main problem associated with refined carbohydrates is that artificial sugar products are often added in abundance. These additives are not only addictive, but they're also detrimental to the general health of the body, and therefore, it's best that you refrain from consuming high quantities. Examples of food products that contain refined carbohydrates include packaged cereals, white bread, white rice, pasta, cakes, biscuits, sweets, candy, pastries, pies, white flour, beer, sweet white wine, sherry and many others.

"In comparison, unrefined carbohydrates take a much longer time to be absorbed by the body than refined carbohydrates. This is because refined carbs contain a lot of sugar, which makes them easier for the body to absorb. Other than containing beneficial natural nutrients, unrefined carbohydrates are also known to be the best source of sustainable energy." Refined carbs are linked to mood disorders. Source: http://www.fitday.com/fitness-articles/nutrition/carbs/the-difference-between-unrefined-and-refined-carbohydrates.html

~~~

[168] Dr Michael Greger (2015) argues against high-meat diets, in favour of high whole grains, beans, nuts and seeds. Cut down on all meats, he says, including white meats, and eat lots more plants (meaning vegetables and fruit):

Greger, M. (2015) *How not to Die: Discover the foods scientifically proven to prevent and reverse disease*. London: Macmillan.

[169] Bravo, J.A., P. Forsythe, M.V. Chew, E. Escaravage, H.M. Savignac, T.G. Dinan, J. Bienenstock, and J.F. Cryan (2011) Ingestion of Lactobacillus strain regulates emotional behaviour and central GABA receptor expression in a mouse via the vagus nerve. PNAS 2011 108 (38) 16050-16055; published ahead of print. August 29, 2011, doi:10.1073/pnas.1102999108

[170] Schmidt, K., Cowen, P.J., Harmer, C.J., Tzortzis, G., Errington, S., and Burnet, P.W. (2014) Prebiotic intake reduces the waking cortisol response and alters emotional bias in healthy volunteers. *Psychopharmacology* (Berl.) (December 3rd 2014) [Epub ahead of print]

[171] "Gluten is the number one cause of leaky gut. Other inflammatory foods like dairy, or toxic foods, such sugar and excessive alcohol, are suspected as well. The most common infectious causes are candida overgrowth, intestinal parasites, and small intestine bacterial overgrowth (SIBO)" (Source: 9 Signs you have a leaky gut, by Dr Amy Myers, Mindbodygreen Blog: http://www.mindbodygreen.com/0-10908/9-signs-you-have-a-leaky-gut.html. Accessed: 13th June 2016). And:

"NSAIDs (like Ibuprofen) can damage your gut lining, causing a condition responsible for a whole range of ailments, from allergies to autoimmune disease. It's called leaky gut." (Source: 5 Steps to Heal a Leaky Gut Caused By Ibuprofen, by Aviva Romm, Practicing Family Physician. *Huffpost Healthy Living*: Available online: http://www.huffingtonpost.com/aviva-romm/5-steps-to-heal-a-leaky-g_b_5617109.html. Accessed: 13th June 2016)

~~~

[172] Sansouci, J. (2011) Nutrition and anxiety. Healthy Crush Blog post. Available online: http://healthycrush.com/nutrition-and-anxiety/. Accessed 20th May 2016.

[173] Byrne, J.W. (2020) *The Bamboo Paradox: The limits of human flexibility in a cruel world - and how to protect, defend and strengthen yourself.* Hebden Bridge: The Institute for E-CENT Publications.

[174] Goyal, M., Singh, S., Sibinga, E.M.S., et al. (2014) Meditation Programs for Psychological Stress and Well-being: A Systematic Review and Meta-analysis. *JAMA Intern Med.* 2014; 174(3): Pages 357–368. doi:10.1001/ jama internmed.2013.13018

[175] Frey, W. H., Hoffman-Ahern, C., Johnson, R. A., et.al. (1983) 'Crying behaviour in the human adult'. *Integrative Psychiatry, 1*, 94–100.

[176] Cameron, J. (1992) *The Artist's Way: A spiritual path to higher creativity.* London: Souvenir Books.

[177] Byrne, J.W. (2018) *How to Write a New Life for Yourself: Narrative therapy and the writing solution.* Hebden Bridge: The Institute for E-CENT Publications.

[178] Esterling, B.A., L'Abate, L., Murray, E.J. and Pennebaker, J.W. (1999) Empirical foundations for writing in prevention and psychotherapy: Mental and physical health outcomes. *Clinical Psychology Review, 19(1):* 79-96.

[179] Pennebaker, J.W. (2002) Writing about emotional events: From past to future. In: S.J. Lepore and J.M. Smythe (eds) *The Writing Cure: How expressive writing promotes health and emotional well-being.* Washington, DC: American Psychological Association.

[180] Tracy B. (2004) *Goals! How to get everything you want – Faster than you ever thought possible.* San Francisco: Berrett-Koehler Publishers, Inc.

[181] Pollard, J. (2002) As easy as ABC. *Life and Style. The Observer.* Sunday 28th July 2002. Available online: https://www.theguardian.com/ lifeandstyle/2002/jul/28/ shopping. Accessed: 7th April 2018.

[182] Schiffman, M. (1972) *Self-Therapy Techniques for Personal Growth.* Merlo Park, CA: Self Therapy Press.

[183] Mulligan, J. (1997) *Shopping Cart Soldiers.* New York: Scribner/Simon & Schuster. (Paperback novel).

[184] E-CENT stands for Emotive-Cognitive Embodied Narrative therapy. The *emotive* component of the human being, and of our approach to counselling, is emphasized, by being given first place, because humans are *primarily* emotional beings. *Cognition* (which includes attention, perception, language, and thinking), is in second place, because language and thinking are products of our socialization, rather than being innate or fixed. *Embodiment* is the physical stratum which underpins and sustains our innate feelings and our socialized language/thinking. *Narrative* is next, because we create our narratives (or stories of our experience) out of our socialized language and socially shaped thinking. And *therapy* is what we do with these insights into the social individual.

[185] Prochaska, J.O., Norcross, J.C. & DiClemente, C.C. (1998). *Changing for Good.* Reprint edition. New York: Morrow.

[186] Kaizen: A philosophy of continuous improvement, often in very small steps. In E-CENT we emphasize the importance of *gradual* change through *small* steps in personal habit change, because attempts at big steps often backfire, because the habit-based part of us rebels against the challenge of dramatic change.

[187] Bargh, J.A. and Chartrand, T.L. (1999) 'The unbearable automaticity of being'. *American Psychologist, 54(7):* 462-479.

[188] Duhigg, C. (2013) *The Power of Habit: Why we do what we do and how to change.* London: Random House.

~~~

[189] Byrne, J.W. (2018) *Lifestyle Counselling and Coaching of the Whole Person: Or how to integrate nutritional insights, physical exercise and sleep coaching into talk therapy.* Hebden Bridge: The Institute for E-CENT Publications.

[190] Coates, G. (2008) *Wanterfall*: *A practical approach to the understanding and healing of the emotions of everyday life.* An online e-book. Available at this website: http://www.wanterfall.com/Downloads/Wanterfall.pdf. Section 1: The origins of emotions.

[191] Byrne, J. (2009b) The 'Individual' and his/her Social Relationships - The E-CENT Perspective. E-CENT Paper No.9. Hebden Bridge: The Institute for E-CENT. Available online: https://ecent-institute.org/e-cent-articles-and-papers/.

[192] Bowlby, J. (1988/2005) *A Secure Base.* London: Routledge Classics.

[193] Lewis, T., Amini, F. and Lannon, R. (2001) *A General Theory of Love.* New York: Vintage Books.

[194] Gerhardt, S. (2010) *Why Love Matters: How affection shapes a baby's brain.* London: Routledge.

[195] Siegel, D.J. (2015) *The Developing Mind: How relationships and the brain interact to shape who we are.* London: The Guilford Press.

Made in the USA
Columbia, SC
15 October 2024